phase 2
low-carb recipes

Meredith® Books

Phase 2 Low-Carb Recipes

Editor: Tricia Laning
Contributing Editor: Ellen Boeke
Assistant Art Director: Erin Burns
Copy Chief: Terri Fredrickson
Publishing Operations Manager: Karen Schirm
Edit and Design Production Coordinator: Mary Lee Gavin
Editorial Assistants: Cheryl Eckert, Kairee Windsor
Marketing Product Manager: Aparna Pande, Isaac Peterson, Gina Rickert,
   Stephen Rogers, Brent Wiersma, Tyler Woods
Book Production Manager: Pam Kvitne, Marjorie J. Schenkelberg,
   Rick von Holdt, Mark Weaver
Contributing Copy Editor: Joyce Gemperlin
Contributing Proofreaders: Gretchen Kauffman, Susan J. Kling, Daryl Lorell
Photographers: Blaine Moats, Jay Wilde
Food Stylists: Paige Boyle, Dianna Nolin
Prop Sylist: Andrea McGahuey
Indexer: Elizabeth T. Parson
Test Kitchen Director: Lynn Blanchard
Test Kitchen Product Supervisor: Laura Harms, R.D.
Test Kitchen Home Economists: Marilyn Cornelius; Juliana Hale;
Jennifer Kalinowski, R.D.; Maryellyn Krantz; Jill Moberly; Dianna Nolin;Colleen Weeden;
Lori Wilson; Charles Worthington

Meredith® Books
Executive Director, Editorial: Gregory H. Kayko
Executive Director, Design: Matt Strelecki
Senior Editor/Group Manager: Jan Miller
Senior Associate Design Director: Mick Schnepf
Publisher and Editor in Chief: James D. Blume
Editorial Director: Linda Raglan Cunningham
Executive Director, Marketing: Jeffrey Myers
Executive Director, New Business Development: Todd M. Davis
Executive Director, Sales: Ken Zagor
Director, Operations: George A. Susral
Director, Production: Douglas M. Johnston
Business Director: Jim Leonard

Vice President and General Manager: Douglas J. Guendel

Better Homes and Gardens® **Magazine**
Editor in Chief: Karol DeWulf Nickell
Deputy Editor, Food and Entertaining: Nancy Hopkins

Meredith Publishing Group
President, Publishing Group: Stephen M. Lacy
Vice President-Publishing Director: Bob Mate

Meredith Corporation
Chairman and Chief Executive Officer: William T. Kerr

In Memoriam: E.T. Meredith III (1933-2003)

All of us at Meredith® Books are dedicated to providing you with the information and ideas you need to create delicious foods. We welcome your comments and suggestions. Write to us at: Meredith Books, Cookbook Editorial Department, 1716 Locust St., Des Moines, IA 50309-3023.

If you would like to purchase any of our cooking, crafts, gardening, home improvement, or home decorating and design books, check wherever quality books are sold. Or visit us at: bhgbooks.com

Our Better Homes and Gardens® Test Kitchen seal on the back cover of this book assures you that every recipe in *Phase 2 Low-Carb Recipes* has been tested in the Better Homes and Gardens® Test Kitchen. This means that each recipe is practical and reliable, and meets our high standards of taste appeal. We guarantee your satisfaction with this book for as long as you own it.

Pictured on front cover: Mediterranean Beef Salad with Lemon Vinaigrette (see recipe, page 72)

phase 2 basics

The length of time you spend on phase 1 is up to you. Most low-carb diets suggest staying on phase 1 for at least 2 weeks. Eventually graduating to phase 2 is an important step in making low-carb eating a lifestyle change and maintaining your weight loss. You need to learn how to add limited amounts of high-nutrient carbohydrates back into your diet while still controlling your weight.

Different low-carb plans have varying opinions of which foods to first return to your diet. Some suggest starting with the addition of one serving of high-fiber fruit, such as berries, apples, and grapefruit. These fruits have low glycemic indexes, meaning that they will not cause big increases in your blood sugar levels. They should be added to lunch or dinner instead of breakfast because they have less impact on your blood sugar levels later in the day. These same diet plans also suggest adding small amounts of high-fiber, whole grain cereal to your diet during the early days of phase 2.

Other diet plans don't add fruit to your diet until you've been on phase 2 for several weeks. The addition of whole grain cereals comes even later. These diets suggest gradually increasing your intake of low-carb vegetables, followed by small amounts of fresh cheeses, nuts, seeds, and, finally, berries. Check out the diet plan you are following and use its suggestions to decide which foods you're going to add to your diet in phase 2.

Even though you are adding carbo-hydrate-containing foods back into your diet, you are still limiting your total intake of carbohydrates on phase 2. That makes it important for every newly added carbohydrate to count. Choose unrefined carbohydrates, such as whole grain products, fresh vegetables, and fresh fruits. These provide fiber, which lessens the impact of carbs on your blood sugar levels. They also add abundant amounts of essential vitamins and minerals to your diet. Avoid refined carbohydrates, such as white flour and sugar. They supply few nutrients and have a big impact on your blood sugar levels.

No matter what low-carb diet plan you're following, you need to slowly add the carbohydrates back into your diet. Your goal is to continue losing weight. If you count grams of carbohydrate on your plan, add only 5 grams of carbohydrate per day back into your diet. Consume the new level of carbohydrates for a week. If at the end of the week you're still losing weight, add 5 additional grams of carbs per day for the next week. Continue with this weekly pattern of additions until you stop losing weight. Note the number of grams of carbohydrate that causes you to stop losing weight and keep your daily carbohydrate intake below that number. (For help determining the grams of carbohydrate in foods, see the carb values of common foods starting on page 378.)

On low-carb diet plans where you do not count grams of carbohydrates, add one or two carb-containing foods back into your diet for a few days. Monitor your weight and make sure that you continue losing weight. If your weight loss stops, you need to cut back on carbohydrates or try a different combination of carbohydrate-containing foods. Be aware that some foods might increase your carbohydrate cravings. These foods are not the same for all people. You have to determine which ones affect you and avoid them.

Staying Motivated on Phase 2

Most people will spend several weeks or months in phase 2. So it's important to stay committed to your eating plan. The following suggestions provide ideas on staying motivated when the going gets tough.

• Eat a variety of foods.

Boredom is the enemy of successful dieters. To combat it, try many different recipes and as many different foods as your diet plan allows. With more than 275 recipes in this book, you're already on your way to joining the ranks of successful phase 2 dieters.

Use creative substitutions of "allowed" foods for "illegal" foods. For example, try substituting antioxidant- and fiber-rich sweet potatoes for white potatoes, use nutrient-dense 100% whole grain bread instead of white bread, make low-carb mashed cauliflower to replace high-carb mashed potatoes, or wrap sandwich fillings in healthy lettuce leaves.

• Deal with temptation.

When forbidden foods lure you, remember why you are following this diet plan and visualize your success. You want to lose weight, improve your health, and feel better—all are more important than a short-lived indulgence. Sometimes you can find an acceptable low-carb alternative that will cure your craving. You might even like the low-carb choice better.

• Distinguish between hunger and the desire to eat.

People eat to satisfy hunger as well as for emotional triggers. Some may eat because they're depressed, stressed, tired, or dissatisfied. Evaluate how your moods affect your eating patterns and work to eliminate emotional eating.

• Plan menus in advance.

You're headed home from work and don't know what to have for dinner. What can you cook in a hurry that fits into your low-carb lifestyle?

Until low-carb dining becomes a way

of life for you, you need to plan ahead to avoid the pitfalls of impulse eating. Sit down and plan weekly menus. With a blueprint in place, you'll always know what's for dinner. This allows you to limit grocery shopping to once a week and restrict impulse food purchases. Before long, low-carb shopping and dining will become a habit.

• Drink plenty of water.

Dehydration-associated fatigue is the fundamental cause of food cravings for many people. Avoid those cravings by drinking adequate water every day. Fiber-rich foods need water to do their cholesterol-lowering work. Water also helps flush out waste products formed when you eat an abundance of protein-rich foods.

• Cook in quantity.

Cook enough food for two meals instead of one, then freeze or refrigerate the extra food for later use. This gives you two meals for the energy of one. You can also freeze the planned leftovers in individual containers—they make perfect lunches for home or at work.

• Invite guests to your house for dinner.

Just because you've adopted a low-carb lifestyle doesn't mean you have to give up lingering with friends over dinner. Offer to cook at your house. You can control the menu. With a selection of great-tasting recipes from this book, your guests won't even have to know they're eating diet food.

Stocking Your Kitchen for Phase 2 of a Low-Carb Lifestyle

Set yourself up to succeed by keeping your kitchen full of low-carb ingredients and creating an environment that supports an ongoing low-carb lifestyle. Most of your grocery shopping will be around the perimeter of the store. That's where you'll find the produce, dairy, poultry, meat, and fish sections— the fresh foods that make up the basis of your phase 2 diet. Many canned fruits and vegetables contain added carbs in the form of sugar. Processed foods may contain trans fats, which

may be harmful to your heart health.

When selecting fresh produce, think color. The more intensely colored or brightly colored fruits and vegetables provide the greatest amount of phytonutrients—plant chemicals beneficial to your health. Also consider season. Fruits and vegetables taste best when they're in season. If you can, shop at a local farmer's market for produce at its height of flavor and freshness.

Fish always makes a good diet choice. Fish is naturally rich in protein and high in B vitamins. Even the fattier fish, such as salmon or mackerel, are bargains for any dieter. They provide an abundance of heart-healthy omega-3 fatty acids. Keep canned salmon, tuna, crabmeat, or shrimp on hand. They're carbohydrate free and great for hurry-up meals.

Meats and poultry fit perfectly into a low-carb lifestyle. They can be grilled, baked, broiled, or sautéed for a limitless variety of main dishes. Try adding herb and spice rubs or using sugarfree marinades for extra bursts of low-carb flavor.

Other foods that you might want to stock for your carb-friendly kitchen include:

• Stone-ground whole grains, breads, cereals, and crackers. Be sure they are 100% whole grain.

• Soy products, including tofu, frozen vegetarian burgers and sausage patties, soy milk, soy nuts, and edamame, are all great sources of phytonutrients, fiber, and protein.

• Sugar-free salsas and sauces contain minimal carbohydrates and spice up plain broiled meats, fish, or poultry.

• Sugar substitutes that fit into your diet plan. Low-carb diets vary in which sugar substitutes are allowed, so keep those on hand that fit into the diet you are following.

• Flavored oils add interest and variety to salad dressings and vegetables.

What to Do When Your Weight Loss Stops

Every dieter knows about periods of time when you follow your diet but the scale doesn't budge. Usually after a week, a weight plateau will end without any changes in your habits. However, if your weight doesn't change over several weeks and you are not losing inches, you may want to consider the following questions:

• Are you strictly following your diet plan?

Keep a food diary and review it against your diet plan. Make sure that you haven't let too many carbs creep back into your daily meals. Use the chart of carb values of common foods starting on page 378 to calculate your daily carb intake. If you're consuming too many carbs, you can use the chart to decide which foods to eliminate.

• Have you started any new medication?

Some medicines influence how your body retains water and how it uses foods. If you have not let any carbs sneak back into your diet, you might want to discuss the new medication with your physician.

• Has your exercise routine changed?

Exercise is important to any successful dieter. If you've suddenly stopped exercising or even just changed your daily habits, you may not lose weight and you need to return to your healthy exercise habits.

• Are your portion sizes reasonable?

Look at the portion sizes listed on package labels and measure to see if your portion control has gotten out of hand. Even on a low-carb diet you should not overindulge.

Free Foods for Phase 2

Meat

Beef
Pork
Lamb
Bacon
Veal
Ham
Venison
All meat except those cured with added sugar or nitrates

Fish

Tuna
Salmon
Sole
Trout
Flounder
Sardines
Herring
All fish except those cured with added sugar or nitrates

Fowl

Chicken
Turkey
Duck
Goose
Cornish Hen
Quail
Pheasant
All fowl except those cured with added sugar or nitrates

Shellfish

Oysters
Mussels
Clams
Squid
Shrimp
Lobster
Crabmeat
All shellfish

Eggs

Scrambled
Fried
Poached
Soft-Boiled
Hard-Boiled
Deviled
Omelets
Prepared any style

Cheeses

Asiago
Blue cheese
Brie
Camembert
Cheddar
Cream cheese
Feta
Fontina
Goat cheese
Gouda
Gruye´re
Havarti
Jarlsburg
Monterey Jack
Mozzarella
Muenster
Parmesan
Provolone
Swiss

Foods That Can Be Added to Phase 2

Cheese

Cottage cheese
Farmer
Mascarpone
Ricotta

Nuts, Seeds, and Their Butters

Almonds
Brazil nuts
Coconut, unsweetened
Hazelnuts
Macadamias
Pecans
Pine nuts
Pistachios
Pumpkin seeds
Sesame seeds
Sunflower seeds
Walnuts

Berries

Blackberries

Blueberries

Cranberries

Raspberries

Strawberries

5 Gram Carbohydrate Counter

During Phase 2 you will increase your daily carbohydrate intake by 5 grams a day for the first week. If your weight loss continues, each week you can increase your carbohydrate intake by another 5 grams a day each following week until you stop losing weight.

Vegetables

1 cup cooked spinach

⅔ cup red sweet peppers

1 medium tomato

1 cup cooked broccoli

12 medium asparagus spears

1 cup cooked cauliflower

½ cup chopped onions

½ cup avocado

⅔ cup summer squash

Dairy

5 ounces farmer cheese

5 ounces mozzarella cheese

¾ cup cottage cheese

¾ cup ricotta cheese

¾ cup heavy cream

Nuts and Seeds

A 1-ounce serving of the following:

Macadamia nuts (10 to12 nuts)

Walnuts (14 halves)

Almonds (14 nuts)

Pecans (14 halves)

Hulled sunflower seeds
   (3 tablespoons)

Roasted shelled peanuts (26 nuts)

A ½-ounce serving of the following:

Cashews (9 nuts)

Fruits

⅓ cup fresh blueberries

¾ cup fresh raspberries

¾ cup fresh strawberries

¼ cup cantaloupe or honeydew

Juices

¼ cup lemon juice

¼ cup lime juice

½ cup tomato juice

Extra Assistance

There are a lot of features in this book to help you succeed on your low-carb diet plan. Free Foods list (p. 8), 5 Gram Carbohydrate Counter (left), and the chart of carb values of common foods (p. 378) guide you in determining which foods you can add to your diet and which ones you should avoid. The Menu Selection (p. 12) along with the Suggested Shopping List (p. 376) help you map out daily eating strategies and stock your pantry for this low-carb journey. All of these tools can assist you in managing phase 2 of your diet and can help keep you on track.

Menu Selection

Food is one of life's greatest pleasures. But cooking delicious meals day after day challenges the best of cooks. And, for those who want to serve great-tasting, low-carb dishes, the task becomes even more difficult. With the help of *Phase 2 Low-Carb Recipes*, high-flavor, low-carb cooking is easy. These menus will take the hassle out of tracking your carb intake and the guesswork out of meal planning.

Week 1

Day 1

Breakfast

Handy Egg Wraps (p. 52)	5g
Hot herbed caffeine-free tea	0g

Lunch

Ginger-Lime Chicken Salad (p. 100)	4g
¼ cup fresh blueberries	4g
Iced caffeine-free sugar-free tea	0g

Dinner

Roasted Salmon & Tomatoes (p. 103)	5g
Zucchini with Onions (p. 165)	5g
Chilled mineral water	0g

Snack

Crabmeat-Stuffed Deviled Eggs (p. 56)	1g
Total net carbs	**24g**

Day 2

Breakfast

French Onion Omelet (p. 43)	4g
3 slices crisp-cooked bacon	0g
Hot herbed caffeine-free tea	0g

Lunch

3 ounces roasted turkey breast	0g
Tomato & Zucchini Salad (p. 87)	2g
½ cup fresh raspberries	0g

Dinner

Grilled Beef Tenderloin with Cabernet Sauvignon Sauce (p. 245)	4g
Green Beans & Fennel (p. 180)	6g
½ cup fresh raspberries	3g
Iced caffeine-free sugar-free tea	0g

Snack

1 cup broccoli florets	2g
2 tablespoons sour cream dip	2g
Total net carbs	**23g**

Day 3

Breakfast

Colorful Quiche Lorraine Bake (p. 51)	4g
Hot caffeine-free coffee	0g

Lunch

North Sea Chowder (p. 67)	5g
½ cup celery sticks	0g
Hot caffeine-free sugar-free herbed tea	0g

Dinner

White Wine & Italian Herb Marinated Chicken (p. 320)	1g
Vegetables in Spicy Sour Cream (p. 168)	3g
Decadent Peanut Butter & Chocolate Mousse (p. 372)	5g
Chilled sparkling water	0g

Snack

½ cup strawberries	4g
Total net carbs	**22g**

Day 4

Breakfast

Cheesy Vegetable Baked Eggs (p. 31)	4g
2 ounces Canadian-style bacon	1g
Hot caffeine-free coffee	0g

Lunch

Italian-Stuffed Burgers (p. 275)	4g
Tossed salad (1 cup torn romaine lettuce, ¼ cup sliced cucumber, ¼ cup sliced celery, 1 sliced green onion, ¼ cup chopped tomato, and 2 tablespoons low-carb salad dressing)	5g
Iced caffeine-free sugar-free tea	0g

Dinner

Snapper Veracruz (p. 105)	5g
Lemon-Tarragon Asparagus Salad (p. 89)	1g
Chilled mineral water	0g

Snack

½ cup red raspberries	3g
Total net carbs	**23g**

Day 5

Breakfast

Veggie-Filled Baked Omelets (p. 29)	5g
2 links sausage	1g
Hot caffeine-free sugar-free herbed tea	0g

Lunch

Mediterranean Beef Salad with Lemon Vinaigrette (p. 72)	3g
1 medium apricot	3g
Iced caffeine-free sugar-free tea	0g

Dinner

Bistro Chicken & Garlic (p. 346)	3g
1 cup steamed broccoli	4g
Chilled sparkling water	0g

Snack

Amazing Artichoke Dip (p. 47)	3g
1 cup cucumber sticks	2g
Total net carbs	**24g**

Day 6

Breakfast

Scrambled Eggs with Crab & Chives (p. 20)	2g
Hot caffeine-free coffee	0g

Lunch

Creole Chicken Soup (p. 62)	6g
½ cup celery sticks	0g
Hot caffeine-free sugar-free herbed tea	0g

Dinner

Greek-Stuffed Roasted Pork Loin (p. 273)	1g
Sautéed Broccoli Rabe (p. 169)	3g
Balsamic-Pepper Strawberries (p. 374)	4g
Iced caffeine-free sugar-free tea	0g

Snack

Mega-Mushroom Caps (p. 50)	6g
Total net carbs	**22g**

Day 7

Breakfast

Denver-Style Breakfast Burrito (p. 26)	6g
Chilled mineral water	0g

Lunch

Potpourri Chicken Salad (p. 97)	4g
½ cup blackberries	5g
Iced caffeine-free sugar-free tea	0g

Dinner

Trout with Pepper Salad (p. 107)	4g
½ cup steamed asparagus	3g
Hot caffeine-free coffee	0g

Snack

Fudge-Cinnamon Puffs (p. 368)	3g
Total net carbs	**25g**

Week 2

Day 1

Breakfast

Mushroom & Pepper Frittata (p. 19)	4g
3 slices crisp-cooked bacon	0g
Hot caffeine-free sugar-free herbed tea	0g

Lunch

Hot Italian Beef Salad (p. 94)	4g
4 ripe olives	1g
½ cup green sweet pepper slices	1g
½ cup cucumber sticks	0g
Iced caffeine-free sugar-free tea	0g

Dinner

Roasted Tomato & Wild Mushroom-Stuffed Chicken (p. 307)	6g
½ cup cubed watermelon	5g
Iced caffeine-free sugar-free tea	0g

Snack

1 ounce Swiss cheese	1g
Total net carbs	**22g**

Controlling the Size

Controlling portion size is the key to successful carb counting. To make sure that the portions you're eating are reasonable, use a food scale until you can visually judge the correct amount. Also, use measuring cups to help assure that you aren't overestimating portion size.

Day 2

Breakfast

Puffy Omelet Squares (p. 23)	5g
2 ounces Canadian-style bacon	1g
Hot caffeine-free tea	0g

Lunch

Lemongrass Chicken Soup (p. 65)	1g
1 cup broccoli florets	2g
2 tablespoons sour cream dip	2g
Iced caffeine-free sugar-free tea	0g

Dinner

Pork Medallions with Brandy Cream Sauce (p. 264)	1g
Pea Pods & Onions with Dill Butter (p. 184)	5g
½ cup cubed cantaloupe	6g
Chilled sparkling water	0g

Snack

Pesto-Stuffed Eggs (p. 27)	1g
Total net carbs	**24g**

Day 3

Breakfast

Spring Omelet (p. 18)	4g
2 links sausage	1g
Hot herbed caffeine-free tea	0g

Lunch

Chilled roasted chicken breast	0g
Plum Tomato Salad (p. 95)	3g
Iced caffeine-free sugar-free tea	0g

Dinner

Sizzling Southwest Short Ribs (p. 228)	8g
Asparagus Salad with Tarragon Vinaigrette (p. 71)	2g
½ cup raspberries	4g
Chilled sparkling water	0g

Snack

½ cup celery sticks	0g
Total net carbs	**22g**

Day 4

Breakfast

Scrambled Eggs with Feta & Dill (p. 25)	3g
Hot caffeine-free coffee	0g

Lunch

Tomato-Crab Salad (p. 90)	5g
½ cup celery sticks	0g
Chilled sparkling water	0g

Dinner

Chicken with Mushroom Sauce & Italian Cheeses (p. 338)	2g
Lemon-Almond Broccoli (p. 161)	2g
Berries with Orange Cream (p. 367)	4g
Iced caffeine-free sugar-free coffee	0g

Snack

Easy Cheesy Quesadillas with Avocado, Spinach & Peppers (p. 32)	7g
Total net carbs	**23g**

Day 5

Breakfast

Baked Breakfast Portobellos (p. 42)	5g
3 slices crisp-cooked bacon	0g
Hot caffeine-free sugar-free herbed tea	0g

Lunch

3 ounces thinly sliced roast beef	0g
1 ounce Swiss cheese	1g
Spring Asparagus Slaw (p. 83)	4g
Iced caffeine-free sugar-free tea	0g

Dinner

Spring Veggies & Scallops (p. 146)	7g
½ cup cubed watermelon	5g
Chilled sparkling water	0g

Snack

1 hard-cooked egg	1g
Total net carbs	**23g**

Day 6

Breakfast

Baked Spinach-Ham Frittata (p. 22)	4g
½ cup raspberries	3g
Hot herbed caffeine-free tea	0g

Lunch

Fresh Herb Tuna Salad (p. 85)	1g
½ cup cucumber sticks	1g
½ cup celery sticks	0g
Chilled mineral water	0g

Dinner

Tequila New York Strip (p. 242)	3g
Savory Grilled Vegetables (p. 175)	6g
Iced caffeine-free sugar-free tea	0g

Snack

Strawberry-Citrus Slush (p. 366)	5g
Total net carbs	**23g**

Day 7

Breakfast

Spinach & Feta Omelet (p. 44)	4g
2 ounces Canadian-style bacon	1g
Hot caffeine-free sugar-free herbed tea	0g

Lunch

2 ounces thinly sliced roast turkey breast and 1 ounce thinly sliced provolone cheese rolled in romaine leaves	1g
Squash & Caraway Soup (p. 59)	7g
Chilled mineral water	0g

Dinner

Pecan & Lime Crusted Pork (p. 276)	1g
Romaine & Radicchio Salad (p. 86)	1g
Mocha Panna Cotta (p. 370)	7g
Chilled sparkling water	0g

Snack

⅓ cup blackberries	3g
Total net carbs	**25g**

Have It Your Way—Strategies for Dining Out

You can eat out in restaurants when you're on a low-carb diet—just choose wisely. The overall trend in restaurants is fresh and healthy with more and more restaurants offering special dishes to accommodate the low-carb customer. First, pick a restaurant whose menu doesn't revolve around bread or pasta—a seafood restaurant is an excellent choice. Ask your waiter if there are any low-carb choices on the menu and use your low-carb knowledge to guide you. Don't be afraid to ask for salad dressings on the side and skip the croutons. Pass the basket of bread and choose vegetables over rice, pasta, or potato. Look for meat, poultry, or fish dishes. Drink water instead of milk or alcoholic beverages. If you are at a fast-food restaurant, choose the low-carb option if it is available. Otherwise, banish the bun and look for items that are grilled and not breaded. If you eat out a lot, it's a great idea to familiarize yourself with the nutrition information for your favorite spots. Most fast-food places have this information available either at the counter or on their websites. Remember, eating large portions or continuing to eat even when you feel full eventually leads to your "supersizing" yourself.

Whether at home or dining out, the strategies are the same.

- Portion size does matter! Reduce your portion sizes to lose weight and lower the occurrence of chronic disease.
- Seek variety in your meal and take your time to eat delicious food.
- Eat good fats like olive oil and butter—you'll be surprised at how they help to satiate your appetite.
- Eat 1 cup of greens and ½ to 1 cup of non-starchy vegetables at each meal.
- If you must have dessert, make sure that it isn't full of sugar or refined flour. Or do as they do in Europe and choose 1 ounce of hard cheese and a few fresh berries.

Eggs & Cheese

Whether you're looking for the perfect recipe for a lingering weekend brunch or an on-the-go weekday breakfast, this chapter contains the low-carb recipes you're seeking. Packed with flavor, these quick-cooking egg and smooth-melting cheese recipes fit the taste, texture, and nutritional value requirements of savvy phase 2 dieters.

Roasted Vegetable Frittata

Prep: 35 minutes Bake: 45 minutes Stand: 10 minutes Oven: 425°/350°F Makes: 6 servings

Nonstick cooking spray

3 medium red and/or yellow sweet

　　peppers, seeded

　　and cut into quarters

4 garlic cloves, unpeeled

2 large zucchini, cut into 3×½-inch strips

1 medium onion, cut into ½-inch slices

1 tablespoon olive oil

¼ cup snipped fresh flat-leaf parsley

1 teaspoon salt

8 eggs

¼ teaspoon cayenne pepper

⅓ cup finely shredded Parmesan cheese

1. Arrange oven racks on lowest and center positions of oven. Line the bottoms of two shallow baking pans with foil. Lightly coat with cooking spray.

2. Arrange sweet peppers and garlic on one pan and zucchini and onion on the other. Brush vegetables with oil. Roast zucchini and onion on lower rack and sweet peppers and garlic on center rack in a 425° oven for 15 minutes. Remove zucchini and onion from oven. Transfer peppers to lower rack; roast 10 minutes more or until charred. Remove vegetables from oven and let stand 5 minutes. Remove garlic from skins. Coarsely chop garlic and vegetables. Transfer to a large bowl. Stir in the parsley and ½ teaspoon salt. Reduce oven temperature to 350°.

3. Coat a 9×1½-inch round cake pan with cooking spray. In a medium mixing bowl whisk together eggs, remaining ½ teaspoon salt, and the cayenne pepper. Stir into vegetable mixture; stir in Parmesan. Pour mixture into prepared pan.

4. Bake, uncovered, in a 350° oven for 45 to 50 minutes or until center is set. Remove from oven and let stand in pan 5 minutes before serving.

See photo, page 34.

8 g
carbs

2 g
fiber

6 g
net carbs

Nutrition Facts per serving: 171 cal., 10 g total fat (3 g sat. fat),
286 mg chol., 557 mg sodium, 8 g carbo., 2 g fiber, 12 g pro.

Spinach-Feta Bake

Prep: 20 minutes   Bake: 30 minutes   Oven: 350°F   Makes: 6 servings

1. Lightly coat a 9-inch pie plate with cooking spray; set aside. In a medium saucepan heat oil over medium heat. Add onion and garlic; cook and stir onion mixture until onion is tender.

2. Stir in spinach, cottage cheese, feta cheese, egg product, oregano, and pepper. Transfer the spinach mixture to the prepared pie plate.

3. Bake, uncovered, in a 350° oven for 30 to 35 minutes or until a knife inserted near the center comes out clean. Sprinkle with Parmesan cheese. To serve, cut into wedges.

Nonstick cooking spray

1   teaspoon olive oil or cooking oil

¾   cup chopped onion (2 small)

3   cloves garlic, minced

2   10-ounce packages frozen chopped spinach, thawed and well drained

1   cup low-fat cottage cheese, drained

1   cup crumbled feta cheese

½   cup refrigerated or frozen egg product, thawed, or 2 eggs, beaten

1   tablespoon snipped fresh oregano or 1 teaspoon dried oregano, crushed

¼   teaspoon coarsely ground black pepper

¼   cup finely shredded Parmesan cheese

8g carbs   **3**g fiber   **5**g net carbs

Nutrition Facts per serving: 185 cal., 10 g total fat (5 g sat. fat), 28 mg chol., 657 mg sodium, 8 g carbo., 3 g fiber, 15 g pro.

Spring Omelet

Start to Finish: 25 minutes Makes: 2 servings

⅓ cup finely chopped red sweet pepper

1 tablespoon finely chopped onion

1 teaspoon white wine vinegar

⅛ teaspoon ground black pepper

   Nonstick cooking spray

1 8-ounce carton refrigerated or frozen
   egg product, thawed, or 4 eggs

1 tablespoon snipped fresh chives,
   flat-leaf parsley, or chervil

⅛ teaspoon salt

⅛ teaspoon cayenne pepper

¼ cup shredded sharp cheddar
   cheese (1 ounce)

1 cup fresh spinach leaves

1. In a small bowl combine sweet pepper, onion, vinegar, and black pepper; set aside.

2. Spray a cold 8-inch nonstick skillet with flared sides or a crepe pan with cooking spray. Heat skillet over medium heat.

3. In a medium mixing bowl beat together egg product, chives, salt, and cayenne pepper with a rotary beater or an electric mixer on medium speed until frothy.

4. Pour egg mixture into hot skillet. Cook, without stirring, for 4 to 5 minutes or until mixture begins to set on the bottom and around edge. Using a large spatula lift partially cooked egg mixture so that the uncooked portion flows underneath. When eggs are set but still shiny, sprinkle with cheese. Top with ¾ cup spinach and half of the sweet pepper mixture. Fold one side of omelet partially over filling. Top with remaining ¼ cup spinach and remaining half of sweet pepper mixture. Transfer omelet to warm plates.

5g carbs   **1**g fiber   **4**g net carbs

Nutrition Facts per serving: 127 cal., 5 g total fat (3 g sat. fat),
15 mg chol., 356 mg sodium, 5 g carbo., 1 g fiber, 15 g pro.

Mushroom & Pepper Frittata

Start to Finish: 30 minutes   Makes: 4 servings

1. In a large nonstick, broilerproof skillet cook and stir onion and sweet pepper in 1 of the tablespoon oil over medium heat for 3 minutes. Add mushrooms; cover and cook for 1 minute. Uncover; cook and stir for 2 minutes more. Remove from heat. Transfer vegetable mixture to a bowl.

2. Preheat broiler. In a large mixing bowl whisk together eggs, water, salt, and black pepper. Stir in 3/4 cup of the cheese and the basil. In the same skillet heat remaining 1 tablespoon oil over medium heat. Add egg mixture and cook for 1 minute. Sprinkle mushroom mixture over eggs. As mixture sets, run a spatula around edge of skillet, lifting egg mixture so uncooked portion flows underneath. Continue cooking and lifting edges until egg mixture is almost set (surface will be moist). Sprinkle with remaining cheese.

3. Place the skillet under broiler 4 to 5 inches from heat. Broil for 1 to 2 minutes or until the top is just set and cheese is melted. Let stand 5 minutes before serving.

1/3 cup onion, chopped (1 small)

1/2 cup chopped red sweet pepper
   (1 small)

2 tablespoons cooking oil

3 cups sliced fresh shiitake mushrooms

8 eggs

1/4 cup water

1/4 teaspoon salt

1/4 teaspoon black pepper

1 cup finely shredded Asiago cheese

1/4 cup snipped fresh basil

5g carbs   **1**g fiber   **4**g net carbs

Nutrition Facts per serving: 360 cal., 29 g total fat (11 g sat. fat), 453 mg chol., 598 mg sodium, 5 g carbo., 1 g fiber, 21 g pro.

Scrambled Eggs with Crab & Chives

Start to Finish: 25 minutes Makes: 6 servings

3   tablespoons butter

½   cup finely chopped red
      sweet pepper

8   ounces cooked crabmeat,
      cut into bite-size pieces
      (about 1½ cups)

2   tablespoons snipped fresh
      chives or green onion tops

9   eggs

¼   cup whipping cream

½   teaspoon salt

¼   teaspoon black pepper

1. In a large nonstick skillet melt 1 tablespoon of the butter over medium heat. Add sweet pepper; cook and stir about 2 minutes or until just tender. Add crabmeat; cook about 2 minutes or until heated through. Transfer to a medium bowl and stir in chives. Cover and keep warm.

2. In a medium mixing bowl whisk together eggs, whipping cream, salt, and black pepper. In the same large skillet melt the remaining 2 tablespoons butter over medium heat; pour in the egg mixture. Cook, without stirring, until mixture begins to set on the bottom and around edge.

3. With a spatula or a large spoon, lift and fold the partially cooked egg mixture so that the uncooked portion flows underneath. Continue cooking over medium heat for 2 to 3 minutes or until egg mixture is cooked through but is still glossy and moist. Fold in crab mixture; remove from heat. Serve immediately.

2g carbs   **0**g fiber   **2**g net carbs

Nutrition Facts per serving: 241 cal., 18 g total fat (8 g sat. fat),
385 mg chol., 452 mg sodium, 2 g carbo., 0 g fiber, 18 g pro.

Cheese & Mushroom Brunch Eggs

Prep: 30 minutes Bake: 15 minutes Stand: 10 minutes
Oven: 350°F Makes: 6 servings

1. For sauce, in a small saucepan combine the whipping cream, Swiss cheese, and Parmesan cheese. Cook, whisking constantly, over low heat until cheese melts. Remove from heat; stir in wine, if desired. Set aside.

2. In a large nonstick skillet melt butter over medium heat. Add mushrooms and green onions; cook for 3 to 4 minutes or until tender, stirring occasionally.

3. In a large mixing bowl whisk together eggs, water, salt, and pepper. Add to skillet. Cook over medium heat, without stirring, until mixture begins to set on the bottom and around the edge. With a spatula or a large spoon, lift and fold the partially cooked egg mixture so that the uncooked portion flows underneath. Continue cooking over medium heat until egg mixture is cooked through but is still glossy and moist. Remove from heat. Add cheese sauce to eggs in skillet. Fold together to coat. Transfer mixture to a 2-quart square baking dish.

4. Bake, uncovered, in a 350° oven about 15 minutes or until heated through. If desired, top with tomato. Let stand 10 minutes.

¾ cup whipping cream

½ cup shredded Swiss cheese

2 tablespoons grated

    Parmesan cheese

1 tablespoon dry white wine (optional)

1 tablespoon butter

1½ cups sliced fresh mushrooms (4 ounces)

¼ cup thinly sliced green onions (2)

12 eggs

⅓ cup water

¼ teaspoon salt

⅛ teaspoon black pepper

1 cup chopped tomato (1 medium) (optional)

3g carbs **0**g fiber **3**g net carbs

Nutrition Facts per serving: 319 cal., 27 g total fat (13 g sat. fat), 480 mg chol., 308 mg sodium, 3 g carbo., 0 g fiber, 17 g pro.

Baked Spinach-Ham Frittata

Prep: 10 minutes Bake: 15 minutes Stand: 5 minutes
Oven: 350°F Makes: 4 main-dish servings

8 eggs

⅓ cup half-and-half or light cream

¼ teaspoon dried basil, crushed

⅛ teaspoon black pepper

1 tablespoon butter

¼ cup chopped onion

1 10-ounce package frozen

chopped spinach, thawed

and well drained

4 ounces thinly sliced cooked

ham, chopped

2 tablespoons grated

Parmesan cheese

1. In a medium mixing bowl whisk together eggs, half-and-half, basil, and pepper; set aside.

2. In a 10-inch ovenproof skillet melt butter over medium heat. Add onion; cook and stir until tender. Remove from heat. Stir in spinach and ham. Add egg mixture.

3. Bake, uncovered, in a 350° oven 15 to 18 minutes or until a knife inserted near the center comes out clean.

4. Sprinkle with Parmesan cheese. Cover and let stand for 5 minutes before serving. Cut into four wedges.

6g carbs   **2**g fiber   **4**g net carbs

Nutrition Facts per serving: 278 cal., 18 g total fat (7 g sat. fat), 457 mg chol., 676 mg sodium, 6 g carbo., 2 g fiber, 21 g pro.

Puffy Omelet Squares

Prep: 20 minutes Bake: 20 minutes Oven: 350°F Makes: 4 servings

1. Coat a 2-quart square baking dish with cooking spray; set aside. In a large mixing bowl combine egg yolks, onion powder, ¼ teaspoon *salt,* and ⅛ teaspoon *black pepper.* Beat with an electric mixer on medium speed about 4 minutes or until thick and lemon colored; set aside. Thoroughly wash beaters. In a medium bowl beat egg whites on medium speed until soft peaks form (tips curl); fold into egg yolks. Fold in 1 tablespoon fresh basil.

2. Spread egg mixture evenly in prepared dish. Bake, uncovered, in a 350° oven for 20 to 25 minutes or until a knife inserted near center comes out clean.

3. Meanwhile, in a small saucepan melt butter over medium heat. Add zucchini, onion, and garlic; cook and stir about 5 minutes or until tender. Stir in tomatoes and remaining 1 tablespoon basil; cook and stir until heated through.

4. To serve, divide omelet among serving dishes. Top with tomato sauce. Sprinkle with Parmesan cheese.

Nonstick cooking spray

6 egg yolks

½ teaspoon onion powder

6 egg whites

1 tablespoon snipped fresh basil

or 1 teaspoon dried basil, crushed

1 tablespoon butter

½ of a medium zucchini, quartered

lengthwise and sliced (½ cup)

¼ cup chopped onion

2 cloves garlic, minced

¾ cup chopped plum tomatoes (2)

1 tablespoon snipped fresh basil

or 1 teaspoon dried basil, crushed

Finely shredded Parmesan cheese

6g carbs   **1**g fiber   **5**g net carbs

Nutrition Facts per serving: 186 cal., 12 g total fat (5 g sat. fat), 321 mg chol., 410 mg sodium, 6 g carbo., 1 g fiber, 13 g pro.

Italian Eggs

Prep: 25 minutes Bake: 25 minutes Stand: 5 minutes
Oven: 350°F Makes: 4 servings

½ cup chopped red onion

   (1 medium)

1 medium zucchini, halved

   lengthwise and thinly sliced

   (1¼ cups)

½ cup chopped red or green

   sweet pepper

2 cloves garlic, minced

2 teaspoons olive oil or cooking oil

5 eggs, beaten

1 cup whipping cream

½ teaspoon salt

¼ teaspoon dried Italian

   seasoning, crushed

¼ cup shredded mozzarella cheese

   (1 ounce)

1. Cook and stir onion, zucchini, sweet pepper, and garlic in hot oil in a medium skillet about 5 minutes or until onion is tender. Cool slightly. In a medium mixing bowl whisk together eggs, whipping cream, salt, and Italian seasoning. Stir in cooked vegetables. Divide mixture evenly among 4 individual quiche dishes or shallow casseroles (about 4½-inch diameter).

2. Bake, uncovered, in a 350° oven about 25 minutes or until set. Sprinkle each serving with mozzarella cheese. Let stand 5 minutes before serving.

6 g carbs   1 g fiber   5 g net carbs

Nutrition Facts per serving: 354 cal., 32 g total fat (17 g sat. fat), 351 mg chol., 448 mg sodium, 6 g carbo., 1 g fiber, 12 g pro.

Scrambled Eggs with Feta & Dill

Start to Finish: 25 minutes Makes: 4 servings

1. Heat oil in a large skillet over medium heat. Add bacon and cook for 2 to 3 minutes per side or until lightly browned. Transfer to plate; cover and keep warm.

2. In a medium mixing bowl whisk together eggs, water, feta, dill, and pepper.

3. In same skillet melt butter over medium heat; pour in egg mixture. Cook, without stirring, until mixture begins to set on the bottom and around edge. With a spatula or a large spoon, lift and fold the partially cooked egg mixture so that the uncooked portion flows underneath. Continue cooking until egg mixture is cooked through but is still glossy and moist. Remove from heat. Serve with bacon.

1   teaspoon cooking oil

8   slices Canadian-style bacon

8   eggs

¼   cup water

1   cup crumbled feta cheese

1   tablespoon snipped fresh dill or
    1 teaspoon dried dill

⅛   teaspoon black pepper

1   tablespoon butter

3g carbs **0**g fiber **3**g net carbs

Nutrition Facts per serving: 344 cal., 24 g total fat (10 g sat. fat), 483 mg chol., 1,192 mg sodium, 3 g carbo., 0 g fiber, 28 g pro.

Denver-Style Breakfast Burrito

Start to Finish: 30 minutes Makes: 6 servings

6 eggs, lightly beaten

1/3 cup water

1/8 teaspoon salt

1/8 teaspoon black pepper

2 tablespoons butter

1 cup cubed cooked ham
    (6 ounces)

1/2 cup chopped green and/or
    red sweet pepper (1 small)

1/4 cup chopped onion

6 8-inch low-carb whole wheat
    tortillas, warmed*

1/2 cup shredded cheddar cheese

    Bottled salsa (optional)

1. In a medium mixing bowl whisk together eggs, water, salt, and black pepper; set aside. In a large nonstick skillet melt butter over medium heat. Add ham, sweet pepper, and onion; cook and stir for 3 to 4 minutes or until vegetables are tender.

2. Pour egg mixture over ingredients in skillet. Cook, without stirring, until mixture begins to set on the bottom and around edge. With a spatula, lift and fold the partially cooked egg mixture so that the uncooked portion flows underneath. Continue cooking over medium heat for 2 to 3 minutes or until egg mixture is cooked through but is still glossy and moist. Remove from heat.

3. To serve, divide egg mixture among warmed tortillas. Sprinkle egg mixture with cheese. Roll up tortillas. If desired, serve with salsa.

*To warm tortillas: Wrap tortillas in foil. Heat in a 350°F oven for 10 minutes.

15g carbs   **9**g fiber   **6**g net carbs

Nutrition Facts per serving: 279 cal., 17 g total fat (6 g sat. fat), 248 mg chol., 817 mg sodium, 15 g carbo., 9 g fiber, 17 g pro.

Pesto-Stuffed Eggs

Start to Finish: 30 minutes Makes: 16 servings

1. Halve hard-cooked eggs lengthwise and remove yolks. Set whites aside. Place the egg yolks, basil, mayonnaise, butter, Parmesan, pine nuts, garlic, and salt in a blender container or food processor bowl. Cover and blend or process until smooth, stopping and scraping sides as necessary. With the blender or processor running, add the warm water. Using a pastry bag or spoon, stuff egg white halves. Garnish with additional pine nuts, Parmesan cheese, and/or basil leaves.

*Hard-cooked eggs: Place eggs in a single layer in a medium saucepan. Add enough cold water to just cover the eggs. Bring to a rapid boil over high heat (water will have large rapidly breaking bubbles). Remove from heat, cover, and let stand for 15 minutes; drain. Run cold water over the eggs or place them in ice water until cool enough to handle; drain. To peel eggs, gently tap each egg on the countertop. Roll the egg between the palms of your hands. Peel off eggshell, starting at the large end.

8 large hard-cooked eggs*

⅓ cup fresh basil leaves

¼ cup mayonnaise

2 tablespoons butter, softened

2 tablespoons finely shredded
   Parmesan cheese

2 teaspoons pine nuts, toasted
   if desired

1 small garlic clove, quartered

⅛ teaspoon salt

1 tablespoon warm water
   Toasted pine nuts, finely
   shredded Parmesan cheese,
   and/or small basil leaves,
   for garnish

1 g carbs   **0** g fiber   **1** g net carbs

Nutrition Facts per serving: 97 cal., 8 g total fat (3 g sat. fat), 116 mg chol., 152 mg sodium, 1 g carbo., 0 g fiber, 5 g pro.

Baked Eggs with Cheese & Basil Sauce

Prep: 15 minutes Cook: 10 minutes Bake: 18 minutes
Oven: 350°F Makes: 4 servings

¾ cup whipping cream

3 tablespoons snipped fresh
basil or ½ teaspoon dried
basil, crushed

6 tablespoons finely shredded
Parmesan cheese

⅛ teaspoon salt

⅛ teaspoon black pepper

Nonstick cooking spray

4 eggs

Salt

Black pepper

1. For basil sauce, in a small saucepan heat whipping cream over medium-high heat until boiling; reduce heat. Simmer, uncovered, about 10 minutes or until whipping cream is slightly thickened, stirring occasionally. Remove from heat and stir in the basil, 2 tablespoons of the Parmesan cheese, the ⅛ teaspoon salt, and the ⅛ teaspoon pepper.

2. Coat four 8- to 10-ounce round baking dishes or 6-ounce custard cups with cooking spray. To assemble, spoon about 2 tablespoons basil sauce into each dish. Gently break an egg into the center of each dish; sprinkle lightly with additional salt and pepper. Spoon remaining sauce over eggs. Bake, uncovered, in a 350° oven for 18 to 20 minutes or until eggs are set. Sprinkle with remaining 4 tablespoons Parmesan cheese.

3g carbs   **0**g fiber   **3**g net carbs

Nutrition Facts per serving: 437 cal., 35 g total fat (21 g sat. fat), 309 mg chol., 1,042 mg sodium, 3 g carbo., 0 g fiber, 26 g pro.

Veggie-Filled Baked Omelets

Prep: 30 minutes Bake: 7 minutes Oven: 400°F Makes: 6 servings

1. Lightly coat a 15×10×1-inch baking pan with cooking spray; set aside.

2. In a large skillet melt butter over medium heat. Add desired vegetables, onion, and dried basil (if using). Cook and stir for 5 to 8 minutes or until vegetables are crisp-tender. Stir in fresh basil (if using), ¼ teaspoon *salt,* and ⅛ teaspoon *pepper.* Remove from heat; stir in the 3 tablespoons tomato sauce; keep warm.

3. In a medium mixing bowl beat egg whites, eggs, water, and ¼ teaspoon *salt* with a whisk or rotary beater until combined but not frothy. Place the prepared baking pan on an oven rack. Carefully pour the egg mixture into the pan. Bake, uncovered, in a 400° oven about 7 minutes or until egg mixture is set but still has a glossy surface.

4. Meanwhile, in a small bowl combine mozzarella cheese and Parmesan cheese; set aside.

5. Cut the baked egg mixture into six 5-inch squares. Using a large spatula, lift each omelet square from baking pan and invert onto warm serving plate. Divide warm vegetable mixture among omelets. Top with cheese mixture. Fold omelets diagonally in half, forming triangles. If desired, drizzle with additional warm tomato sauce; serve immediately.

See photo, page 35.

Nonstick cooking spray

2 tablespoons butter

3 cups bite-size strips red or green sweet pepper, sliced fresh mushrooms, thinly sliced zucchini, and/or chopped tomato

⅓ cup chopped onion (1 small)

2 teaspoons snipped fresh basil or ½ teaspoon dried basil, crushed

3 tablespoons tomato sauce

10 egg whites

5 eggs

¼ cup water

¼ cup shredded mozzarella cheese

2 tablespoons grated Parmesan cheese

Tomato sauce, warmed (optional)

7 g carbs   **2** g fiber   **5** g net carbs

Nutrition Facts per serving: 170 cal., 10 g total fat (4 g sat. fat), 191 mg chol., 481 mg sodium, 7 g carbo., 2 g fiber, 14 g pro.

Asparagus, Zucchini & Yellow Pepper Frittata

Prep: 30 minutes Bake: 35 minutes Stand: 10 minutes
Oven: 350°F Makes: 8 servings

1½ pounds fresh asparagus

  or two 9-ounce or 10-ounce

  packages frozen cut asparagus

1 medium yellow sweet pepper,

  cut into ¼-inch strips

⅓ cup chopped onion (1 small)

1 small zucchini, halved

  lengthwise and sliced ¼ inch

  thick (about 1 cup)

10 eggs, slightly beaten

1 cup half-and-half or light cream

2 tablespoons snipped fresh

  flat-leaf parsley

1¼ teaspoons salt

¼ to ½ teaspoon black pepper

1. *Butter* a 2-quart rectangular baking dish; set aside.

2. If using fresh asparagus, snap off and discard woody bases. If desired, scrape off scales. Cut into 1-inch pieces.

3. In a saucepan, bring about 1 inch of water to boiling. Add asparagus, sweet pepper strips, and onion. Bring just to boiling; reduce heat. Simmer, covered, about 1 minute or until crisp-tender. Drain well, reserving some asparagus tips for garnish. Spread asparagus mixture in baking dish. Layer zucchini slices over top.

4. In a medium mixing bowl whisk together eggs, half-and-half, parsley, salt, and black pepper. Pour over vegetables in baking dish. Bake, uncovered, in a 350° oven about 35 minutes or until a knife inserted near the center comes out clean. Let stand 10 minutes before serving. If desired, garnish each serving with asparagus tips.

6g carbs   **1**g fiber   **5**g net carbs

Nutrition Facts per serving: 160 cal., 10 g total fat (4 g sat. fat),
277 mg chol., 465 mg sodium, 6 g carbo., 1 g fiber, 11 g pro.

Cheesy Vegetable Baked Eggs

Prep: 20 minutes Bake: 20 minutes Stand: 5 minutes
Oven: 350°F Makes: 4 servings

1. In a medium skillet melt 1 tablespoon butter over medium heat. Add vegetables; cook and stir for 3 to 4 minutes or until vegetables are tender. Sprinkle with salt and black pepper; set vegetables aside.

2. Grease a 3-quart rectangular baking dish with the remaining 1 tablespoon butter. Spread cooked vegetable mixture over the bottom of the prepared dish. Carefully break eggs into pan on top of vegetables. Sprinkle with dill and, if desired, additional salt and black pepper.

3. Bake, covered, in a 350° oven about 20 minutes or until egg whites are opaque and yolks are firm. Sprinkle cheese over eggs. Cover and let stand about 5 minutes or until cheese is melted.

2 tablespoons butter

2 cups chopped onion, chopped sweet pepper, sliced button mushrooms, seeded and chopped tomatoes, and/or chopped zucchini

¼ teaspoon salt

⅛ teaspoon black pepper

8 eggs

¾ teaspoon snipped fresh dill or 1 tablespoon snipped fresh chives or parsley

⅔ cup shredded Swiss, smoked mozzarella, or smoked cheddar cheese

5g carbs   **1**g fiber   **4**g net carbs

Nutrition Facts per serving: 290 cal., 22 g total fat (10 g sat. fat), 458 mg chol., 231 mg sodium, 5 g carbo., 1 g fiber, 19 g pro.

Easy Cheesy Quesadillas with Avocado, Spinach & Pepper

Prep: 20 minutes Cook: 2 minutes Oven: 300°F Makes: 4 servings

1 cup lightly packed fresh
 spinach, chopped

½ cup bottled roasted red sweet
 peppers, drained and
 thinly sliced

½ cup chopped fresh cilantro

¼ cup chopped sweet onion

½ teaspoon chili powder

½ teaspoon ground cumin

1 cup shredded cheddar cheese

1 cup shredded Monterey
 Jack cheese

1 medium avocado, halved,
 seeded, peeled, and chopped

4 8-inch low-carb whole
 wheat tortillas

1. In a large bowl combine spinach, peppers, cilantro, onion, chili powder, and cumin. Stir in cheddar and Monterey Jack cheeses. Gently stir in avocado.

2. Spoon 1 cup spinach mixture over half of each tortilla. Fold tortillas in half, pressing gently.

3. In a 10-inch skillet cook quesadillas, one at a time, over medium heat for 2 to 3 minutes or until lightly browned, turning once. Remove quesadillas from skillet; place on baking sheet. Keep warm in a 300° oven. Repeat with remaining quesadillas. To serve, cut quesadillas into wedges.

See photo, page 33.

19 g
carbs

12 g
fiber

7 g
net carbs

Nutrition Facts per serving: 385 cal., 27 g total fat (12 g sat. fat),
55 mg chol., 585 mg sodium, 19 g carbo., 12 g fiber, 18 g pro.

Easy Cheesy Quesadillas with Avocado, Spinach, & Pepper
p. 32

Roasted
Vegetable
Frittata
p. 16

Veggie-Filled
Baked
Omelets
p. 29

Poached Eggs with Grainy Mustard Vinaigrette p. 45

Colorful
Quiche
Lorraine
Bake
p. 51

Handy Egg
Wraps
p. 52

Celebrate
Spring
Crustless
Quiche
p. 53

Layered Egg
Salad with
Avocado
p. 41

Layered Egg Salad with Avocado

Start to Finish: 30 minutes Makes: 4 servings

1. In a medium bowl combine mayonnaise and mustard. Stir in eggs; add salt and pepper to taste.

2. Divide lettuce evenly among 4 salad plates. Top with egg mixture and red onion.

3. In a small bowl gently toss avocado with lemon juice. Spoon avocado over egg and onion. If desired, spoon sour cream over avocado. Sprinkle with bacon pieces. Serve immediately.

*Hard-cooked eggs: Place eggs in a single layer in a medium saucepan. Add enough cold water to just cover the eggs. Bring to a rapid boil over high heat (water will have large rapidly breaking bubbles). Remove from heat, cover, and let stand for 15 minutes; drain. Run cold water over the eggs or place them in ice water until cool enough to handle; drain. To peel eggs, gently tap each egg on the countertop. Roll the egg between the palms of your hands. Peel off eggshell, starting at the large end.

See photo, page 40.

¼ cup mayonnaise

2 teaspoons Dijon-style mustard

8 hard-cooked eggs*, peeled
   and chopped
   Salt and black pepper

4 cups torn Boston lettuce

½ cup chopped red onion (1 medium)

1 avocado, halved, seeded, peeled,
   and coarsely chopped

1 tablespoon lemon juice

⅓ cup dairy sour cream (optional)

6 slices bacon, crisp-cooked,
   drained, and crumbled

8g carbs **4**g fiber **4**g net carbs

Nutrition Facts per serving: 411 cal., 34 g total fat (8 g sat. fat), 444 mg chol., 540 mg sodium, 8 g carbo., 4 g fiber, 18 g pro.

Baked Breakfast Portobellos

Prep: 15 minutes Bake: 15 minutes Oven: 350°F Makes: 4 servings

4 fresh portobello mushrooms

   (3 to 5 ounces each)

4 eggs

3 tablespoons water

⅛ teaspoon salt

⅛ teaspoon black pepper

   Nonstick cooking spray

2 tablespoons sliced green

   onion (1)

2 tablespoons chopped bottled

   roasted red sweet peppers

1. Clean and remove stems from mushrooms. Place mushroom caps, stem side up, in an ungreased shallow baking pan. Bake, uncovered, in a 350° oven for 15 to 20 minutes or until tender.

2. Meanwhile, in a medium mixing bowl whisk together eggs, water, salt, and black pepper; set egg mixture aside. Lightly coat a large nonstick skillet with cooking spray. Heat skillet over medium heat. Add green onion to skillet; cook and stir for 30 seconds. Pour egg mixture into skillet. Cook over medium heat, without stirring, until mixture begins to set on the bottom and around edge.

3. With a spatula or a large spoon, lift and fold partially cooked egg mixture so that the uncooked portion flows underneath. Continue cooking over medium heat for 2 to 3 minutes or until egg mixture is cooked through but is still glossy and moist. Remove from heat.

4. Fill mushrooms with scrambled eggs. Top with roasted sweet peppers.

7 g carbs   **2** g fiber   **5** g net carbs

Nutrition Facts per serving: 106 cal., 5 g total fat (2 g sat. fat), 213 mg chol., 143 mg sodium, 7 g carbo., 2 g fiber, 9 g pro.

French Onion Omelet

Prep: 25 minutes   Bake: 10 minutes   Stand: 5 minutes   Oven: 375°F   Makes: 4 to 6 servings

1. In a 10-inch ovenproof skillet heat oil over medium heat. Add red onion; cook and stir about 5 minutes or until tender and golden brown. Remove 1 tablespoon of the cooked onion mixture; set aside.

2. In a medium mixing bowl whisk together eggs, water, salt, and white pepper. Stir in ³⁄₄ cup of the cheese, the green onions, mustard, and thyme. Pour egg mixture into skillet over red onion mixture. Bake, uncovered, in a 375° oven for 10 to 12 minutes or until egg mixture is set but still has a glossy surface. Top with remaining ¹⁄₄ cup cheese and the reserved onion mixture. Let stand 5 minutes before serving. To serve, cut into wedges.

1   tablespoon olive oil

½   cup coarsely chopped red
      onion (1 medium)

6   eggs

¼   cup water

¼   teaspoon salt

¼   teaspoon ground white pepper

1   cup shredded Swiss or white
      cheddar cheese

¼   cup sliced green onions (4)

2   teaspoons Dijon-style mustard

½   teaspoon dried thyme, crushed

Nutrition Facts per serving: 262 cal., 19 g total fat (8 g sat. fat),
343 mg chol., 366 mg sodium, 5 g carbo., 1 g fiber, 18 g pro.

43

Spinach-&-Feta Omelet

Start to Finish: 30 minutes Oven: 300°F Makes: 2 servings

4 cups lightly packed chopped
   fresh spinach

6 eggs

⅛ teaspoon salt

⅛ teaspoon black pepper

1 tablespoon butter

½ cup crumbled feta cheese

1. In a medium saucepan cook spinach, covered, in a small amount of boiling salted water for 2 to 3 minutes or until tender. (Or place spinach in a microwave-safe casserole with 1 tablespoon water. Microwave, covered, on 100 percent power [high] for 1 to 2 minutes or until tender, stirring once.) Drain well in a colander, pressing with the back of a spoon to force out excess moisture.

2. In a medium mixing bowl beat eggs. Stir in drained spinach, salt, and pepper; mix well.

3. In a 10-inch omelet pan or skillet with flared sides melt half the butter over medium-high heat. Pour half of the egg mixture into pan. Reduce heat to medium. As mixture sets, run a spatula around edge of skillet, lifting egg mixture so uncooked portion flows underneath. Continue cooking and lifting edges until egg mixture is almost set (surface will be moist). Sprinkle with half of the cheese. Cook about 1 minute more or until cheese is melted.

4. Fold omelet in half and transfer to a warm serving plate. Cover and keep the omelet warm in a 300° oven. Repeat with remaining butter, egg mixture, and cheese to make a second omelet.

5g carbs **1**g fiber **4**g net carbs

Nutrition Facts per serving: 362 cal., 27 g total fat (12 g sat. fat), 676 mg chol., 758 mg sodium, 5 g carbo., 1 g fiber, 25 g pro.

Poached Eggs with Grainy Mustard Vinaigrette

Start to Finish: 20 minutes Makes: 4 servings

1. In a small saucepan combine vinegar, oil, and mustard. Bring to boiling over medium-high heat, stirring to combine. Reduce heat to low and keep warm, stirring again just before serving.

2. Lightly grease 4 cups of an egg-poaching pan with oil. Place poacher cups over the pan of boiling water (water should not touch bottoms of cups); reduce heat to simmering. Break an egg into a measuring cup. Carefully slide egg into a poacher cup. Repeat with remaining eggs. Cover and cook 4 to 5 minutes or until the whites are completely set and yolks begin to thicken but are not hard.

3. Run a knife around edges to loosen eggs. Arrange spinach on serving plates. Top with poached egg by inverting poaching cups. Top with grainy mustard vinaigrette. Season with salt and pepper.

See photo, page 36.

2 **tablespoons vinegar**

2 **tablespoons olive oil**

1 **tablespoon coarse grain**
   brown mustard

4 **large eggs**

8 **cups lightly packed, torn**
   fresh spinach sautéed in
   1 tablespoon butter

Salt and black pepper

3g carbs   **1**g fiber   **2**g net carbs

Nutrition Facts per serving: 179 cal., 15 g total fat (4 g sat. fat), 220 mg chol., 340 mg sodium, 3 g carbo., 1 g fiber, 8 g pro.

Creamy Scrambled Eggs with Spinach & Shrimp

Start to Finish: 20 minutes Makes: 4 servings

8   ounces fresh or frozen peeled and deveined shrimp

8   eggs

½   cup half-and-half or light cream

¼   teaspoon salt

¼   teaspoon black pepper

     Nonstick cooking spray

2½ cups lightly packed fresh baby spinach

1   5-ounce container semisoft cheese with garlic and herb, crumbled

1. Thaw shrimp, if frozen. Rinse shrimp; pat dry with paper towels. Halve shrimp lengthwise; set aside.

2. In a medium mixing bowl whisk together eggs, half-and-half, salt, and pepper; set aside.

3. Lightly coat a large nonstick skillet with cooking spray. Heat skillet over medium heat. Add shrimp and spinach to skillet; cook and stir for 2 to 3 minutes or until shrimp turn opaque.

4. Pour egg mixture into skillet. Cook over medium heat, without stirring, until mixture begins to set on the bottom and around edge. With a spatula or a large spoon, lift and fold the partially cooked egg mixture so that the uncooked portion flows underneath. Continue cooking over medium heat for 2 to 3 minutes or until egg mixture is cooked through but is still glossy and moist.

5. Remove from heat immediately; sprinkle with cheese. Let stand 3 to 4 minutes or until cheese melts.

5 g carbs   **0** g fiber   **5** g net carbs

Nutrition Facts per serving: 382 cal., 26 g total fat (13 g sat. fat), 553 mg chol., 396 mg sodium, 5 g carbo., 0 g fiber, 28 g pro.

Amazing Artichoke Dip

Prep: 15 minutes Chill: up to 2 days Makes: about 1 cup (8 servings)

1. In a food processor bowl or blender container combine the drained artichoke hearts, cream cheese, sour cream, oil, lemon juice, mustard, and pepper; cover and process or blend until nearly smooth and well combined. Transfer dip to a small bowl and stir in basil.

2. If desired, serve immediately with vegetable sticks and/or low-carb crackers, or cover and refrigerate for up to 2 days.

1 6-ounce jar marinated artichoke
   hearts, drained

½ of an 8-ounce package cream
   cheese, softened

2 tablespoons dairy sour cream

1 tablespoon salad oil

1 tablespoon lemon juice

½ teaspoon dry mustard

⅛ teaspoon pepper

¼ cup chopped fresh basil leaves

   Assorted vegetable sticks
    and/or low-carb crackers
   (optional)

3g carbs   **0**g fiber   **3**g net carbs

Nutrition Facts per serving: 90 cal., 9 g total fat (4 g sat. fat), 17 mg chol., 110 mg sodium, 3 g carbo., 0 g fiber, 2 g pro.

Baked Brie with Roasted Red Pepper Tapenade

Prep: 20 minutes Bake: 15 minutes Oven: 350°F Makes: 8 servings

2 tablespoons chopped bottled roasted red sweet peppers, drained

1 tablespoon chopped pitted kalamata olives

1 teaspoon capers, drained

1 teaspoon olive oil

¼ teaspoon black pepper

1 8-ounce round Brie cheese

1 tablespoon snipped fresh basil

1¼ cups thinly bias-sliced zucchini (1 medium)

1. Line a baking sheet with parchment paper or foil; set aside.

2. In a small bowl combine roasted red sweet peppers, olives, capers, oil, and black pepper; set aside.

3. Cut off and discard a very thin slice from the top of the Brie to remove the rind. Spread sweet pepper mixture over top of Brie. Place Brie on prepared baking sheet. Bake in a 350° oven about 15 minutes or until cheese is softened and warm but not runny. Sprinkle with basil. Cut into wedges. Serve warm with sliced zucchini.

1 g carbs   0 g fiber   1 g net carbs

Nutrition Facts per serving: 105 cal., 9 g total fat (5 g sat. fat),
28 mg chol., 203 mg sodium, 1 g carbo., 0 g fiber, 6 g pro.

Very Veggie Bake

Prep: 20 minutes Bake: 45 to 50 minutes Stand: 10 minutes
Oven: 400°F Makes: 6 servings

1. Lightly coat an 8-inch square baking dish with cooking spray; set aside.

2. In a small bowl combine onion, garlic, thyme, salt, and black pepper. In another small bowl combine Swiss and mozzarella cheeses.

3. Arrange half of the eggplant slices in the bottom of prepared dish. Arrange half the sweet pepper rings on top of eggplant. Layer half the onion mixture, half the tomato, half the mushrooms, and half the cheese mixture over sweet pepper rings. Spoon half of the cream cheese over all.

4. Repeat layering, except do not top with the remaining Swiss cheese mixture or the cream cheese.

5. Bake, uncovered, in a 400° oven for 40 minutes. Top with remaining Swiss cheese mixture and cream cheese. Bake for 5 to 10 minutes more or until cheeses have melted and vegetables are just tender. Let stand for 10 minutes before serving.

Nonstick cooking spray

½ cup chopped onion (1 medium)

1 clove garlic, minced

2 teaspoons snipped fresh thyme

¾ teaspoon salt

½ teaspoon black pepper

¾ cup shredded Swiss cheese

½ cup shredded mozzarella cheese

1 medium eggplant (about 1 pound),
   trimmed and cut into ¼-inch slices

2 medium red, green, and/or yellow sweet
   peppers, seeded and sliced into rings

1 cup chopped tomato (1 medium)

½ cup sliced fresh mushrooms

½ of an 8-ounce container cream cheese
   with garden vegetables

11g carbs   **3**g fiber   **8**g net carbs

Nutrition Facts per serving: 182 cal., 12 g total fat (7 g sat. fat),
36 mg chol., 486 mg sodium, 11 g carbo., 3 g fiber, 8 g pro.

Mega-Mushroom Caps

Prep: 25 minutes Bake: 20 minutes Oven: 350°F Makes: 8 servings

8 4-inch portobello
   mushrooms, stems
   and gills removed

1 tablespoon butter,
   melted

   Salt and black pepper

½ cup shredded
   mozzarella cheese

½ cup finely shredded
   Parmesan cheese

½ cup shredded
   fontina cheese

3 tablespoons butter

1 cup chopped onion
   (1 large)

1 clove garlic, minced

1½ cups lightly packed
    fresh spinach,
    coarsely chopped

1 tablespoon snipped fresh
   oregano or 1 teaspoon
   dried oregano, crushed

7 eggs

¼ teaspoon salt

½ cup chopped bottled
   roasted red sweet
   peppers

1. Place mushrooms on a 15×10×1-inch baking pan, stem side down. Brush mushrooms with 1 tablespoon melted butter. Season with salt and pepper. Bake in a 350° oven for 15 minutes or until tender.

2. Meanwhile, in a bowl combine mozzarella, Parmesan, and fontina cheeses; set aside. Melt 2 tablespoons butter in a skillet over medium heat. Add onion and garlic; cook and stir for 5 minutes or until onion is tender. Stir in spinach and oregano. Cook and stir for 1 minute more or until spinach is wilted. Transfer to a small bowl; cover and keep warm.

3. In a mixing bowl whisk together eggs and ¼ teaspoon salt. In the same skillet melt the remaining 1 tablespoon butter over medium heat; pour in egg mixture. Cook, without stirring, until mixture begins to set on the bottom and around edge. With a spatula, lift and fold the partially cooked egg mixture so that the uncooked portion flows underneath. Continue cooking over medium heat for 2 to 3 minutes or until egg mixture is cooked through but is still glossy and moist. Fold in chopped roasted sweet pepper; remove from heat.

4. Turn mushrooms stem side up; sprinkle with half of cheese mixture. Spoon spinach mixture over cheese. Mound egg mixture over spinach mixture; sprinkle with remaining cheese.

5. Bake, uncovered, 5 minutes more or until cheese is melted.

7 g carbs   **1** g fiber   **6** g net carbs

Nutrition Facts per serving: 237 cal., 18 g total fat (8 g sat. fat), 219 mg chol., 444 mg sodium, 7 g carbo., 1 g fiber, 16 g pro.

Colorful Quiche Lorraine Bake

Prep: 15 minutes Bake: 30 minutes Stand: 10 minutes Oven: 350°F Makes: 6 servings

1. Lightly coat a 2-quart square baking dish with cooking spray; set aside.

2. In a medium bowl stir together eggs, cream, nutmeg, mustard, salt, and black pepper; set aside.

3. In a small bowl combine cheese, bacon, sweet pepper strips, and green onions. Spread the cheese mixture in the bottom of the prepared baking dish. Pour the egg mixture over the filling.

4. Bake, uncovered, in a 350° oven about 30 minutes or until a knife inserted near the center comes out clean. Let stand 10 minutes before serving.

See photo, page 37.

Nonstick cooking spray

4 eggs, beaten

1½ cups whipping cream

¼ teaspoon ground nutmeg

¼ teaspoon dry mustard

¼ teaspoon salt

⅛ teaspoon black pepper

1 cup shredded Swiss cheese

6 slices bacon, crisp-cooked, drained, and crumbled

½ cup bite-size strips red and/or green sweet pepper (1 small)

¼ cup finely chopped green onions (2)

4 g carbs   0 g fiber   4 g net carbs

Nutrition Facts per serving: 379 cal., 35 g total fat (20 g sat. fat), 247 mg chol., 331 mg sodium, 4 g carbo., 0 g fiber, 13 g pro.

Handy Egg Wraps

Prep: 20 minutes Cook: 20 minutes Makes: 4 servings

4 eggs

⅓ cup finely chopped zucchini

⅓ cup finely chopped onion

⅓ cup finely chopped red

   sweet pepper

¼ cup bottled salsa

¼ teaspoon dried basil, crushed

¼ teaspoon dried oregano,

   crushed

¼ teaspoon salt

⅛ teaspoon black pepper

2 tablespoons butter, cut into

   4 pieces

4 6-inch low-carb whole

   wheat tortillas

   Bottled salsa (optional)

1. In a medium mixing bowl beat eggs slightly. Stir in zucchini, onion, sweet pepper, ¼ cup salsa, the basil, oregano, salt, and black pepper.

2. Heat an 8-inch nonstick skillet with flared sides over medium-high heat until skillet is hot. Add 1 piece of the butter to the skillet. When butter has melted, add ½ cup egg mixture to skillet; lower heat to medium. Immediately begin stirring egg mixture gently but continuously with a wooden spoon or plastic spatula until mixture resembles small pieces of cooked egg surrounded by liquid egg. Stop stirring. Cook 30 to 60 seconds more or until egg mixture is set but shiny.

3. Carefully slide omelet from skillet onto one of the tortillas. If desired, top with a spoonful of salsa. Carefully roll up. Repeat for each egg wrap, adding 1 piece of the butter to the skillet before adding ½ cup egg mixture.

See photo, page 38.

10g carbs **5**g fiber **5**g net carbs

Nutrition Facts per serving: 185 cal., 12 g total fat (5 g sat. fat), 228 mg chol., 430 mg sodium, 10 g carbo., 5 g fiber, 9 g pro.

Celebrate Spring Crustless Quiche

Prep: 25 minutes Cook: 10 minutes Bake: 40 minutes Oven: 350°F Makes: 6 to 8 servings

1. Lightly coat a 2-quart rectangular baking dish with cooking spray; set aside.

2. In a large skillet melt butter over medium-high heat. Add mushrooms and garlic; cook and stir for 7 to 8 minutes or until tender and most of the liquid has evaporated. Remove from heat; set aside.

3. Snap off and discard woody bases from asparagus. If desired, scrape off scales. Cut asparagus into 1-inch pieces. Cook asparagus, covered, in a small amount of boiling lightly salted water for 3 to 5 minutes or until crisp-tender. Drain well; rinse with cold running water until cool; drain again. Set aside.

4. In a large mixing bowl whisk together eggs, whipping cream, mustard, salt, black pepper, and cayenne pepper. Stir in mushrooms, asparagus, and ½ cup cheese.

5. Pour mixture into prepared baking dish. Sprinkle evenly with remaining cheese. Bake, uncovered, in a 350° oven for 40 to 45 minutes or until a knife inserted near the center comes out clean.

See photo, page 39.

Nonstick cooking spray

1 tablespoon butter

3 cups thickly sliced fresh
   mushrooms, such as cremini,
   shiitake, and/or portobello

1 clove garlic, minced

12 ounces asparagus spears

4 eggs, beaten

1½ cups whipping cream

2 teaspoons Dijon-style mustard

½ teaspoon salt

¼ teaspoon black pepper

⅛ teaspoon cayenne pepper

1 cup shredded Swiss or
   Emmentaler cheese

6 g carbs   **1** g fiber   **5** g net carbs

Nutrition Facts per serving: 370 cal., 34 g total fat (19 g sat. fat), 246 mg chol., 361 mg sodium, 6 g carbo., 1 g fiber, 13 g pro.

Salmon-Filled Puffy Omelet

Start to Finish: 25 minutes Bake: 4 minutes Oven: 350°F Makes: 2 servings

3 eggs, separated

1 tablespoon snipped fresh dill
    or chives

   Dash salt

   Dash black pepper

1 tablespoon cooking oil

2 ounces thinly sliced smoked
    salmon (lox-style), smoked
    turkey, or cooked ham,
    chopped

½ of a 3-ounce package cream
    cheese, cut into cubes

1. In a medium mixing bowl beat egg whites, dill, salt, and pepper with an electric mixer on medium speed until stiff peaks form (tips stand straight). In a small bowl lightly beat egg yolks with a fork. Fold yolks into beaten egg white mixture.

2. Heat oil in a 10-inch cast-iron or ovenproof skillet over medium heat. Spread egg mixture in pan; cook for 3 to 5 minutes or until bottom is set. Bake, uncovered, in a 350° oven about 3 minutes or until top is dry and set. Sprinkle salmon and cream cheese evenly over top. Bake for 1 minute more or until cheese is softened.

3. To serve, fold omelet in half. Transfer to a serving plate; cut in half. Serve immediately.

1g carbs   **0**g fiber   **1**g net carbs

Nutrition Facts per serving: 278 cal., 23 g total fat (8 g sat. fat),
347 mg chol., 805 mg sodium, 1 g carbo., 0 g fiber, 16 g pro.

Spinach & Cheese Casserole

Prep: 25 minutes Bake: 45 minutes Oven: 350°F Makes: 8 side-dish servings

1. Lightly coat a 1 1/2-quart casserole with cooking spray; set aside. In a large bowl combine cottage cheese, spinach, feta cheese, eggs, butter, flour, onion, and nutmeg; mix well. Pour mixture into the prepared casserole. Bake, uncovered, in a 350° oven about 45 minutes or until center is almost set and the internal temperature registers 160° on an instant-read thermometer.

Nonstick cooking spray

2 cups cottage cheese

1 10-ounce package frozen chopped spinach, thawed and well drained

1/3 cup crumbled feta cheese

3 eggs, beaten

1/4 cup butter, melted

3 tablespoons whole wheat flour

2 teaspoons dried minced onion

Dash ground nutmeg

5_g carbs 1_g fiber 4_g net carbs

Nutrition Facts per serving: 171 cal., 12 g total fat (6 g sat. fat), 109 mg chol., 400 mg sodium, 5 g carbo., 1 g fiber, 11 g pro.

Crabmeat-Stuffed Deviled Eggs

Start to Finish: 30 minutes Makes: 6 appetizer servings

6   hard-cooked eggs*, peeled

¼   cup mayonnaise

2   tablespoons finely
    chopped celery

2   tablespoons snipped
    fresh parsley

2   teaspoons Dijon-style mustard

1   teaspoon finely
    chopped shallot

⅛   teaspoon cayenne pepper

1   6½-ounce can crabmeat,
    drained, flaked, and
    cartilage removed

    Fresh dill (optional)

1. Halve hard-cooked eggs lengthwise and remove yolks. Set whites aside. Place yolks in a bowl; mash with a fork.

2. Add mayonnaise, celery, parsley, mustard, shallot, and cayenne pepper to the yolks; mix well. Stir in crabmeat.

3. Stuff egg white halves with yolk mixture. If desired, garnish with fresh dill. Serve immediately or cover and chill up to 24 hours.

*Hard-cooked eggs: Place eggs in a single layer in a medium saucepan. Add enough cold water to just cover the eggs. Bring to a rapid boil over high heat (water will have large rapidly breaking bubbles). Remove from heat, cover, and let stand for 15 minutes; drain. Run cold water over the eggs or place them in ice water until cool enough to handle; drain. To peel eggs, gently tap each egg on the countertop. Roll the egg between the palms of your hands. Peel off eggshell, starting at the large end.

1 g carbs   **0** g fiber   **1** g net carbs

Nutrition Facts per serving: 177 cal., 13 g total fat (3 g sat. fat),
246 mg chol., 262 mg sodium, 1 g carbo., 0 g fiber, 13 g pro.

Soups & Salads

Robustly or delicately flavored, soups and salads are ideal choices for every season and mood. North Sea Chowder (p. 67) is perfect for sipping by the fire on the coldest of winter days. Tangy Asparagus–Crabmeat Salad (p. 82) beckons to be eaten on the patio on the first warm day of spring.

Tri-Mushroom Soup

Prep: 15 minutes Cook: 32 minutes Makes: 6 servings

1 tablespoon olive oil or
   cooking oil

1 8-ounce package sliced button
   mushrooms (3 cups)

2 ounces portobello mushroom,
   sliced into ½-inch-thick pieces

2 ounces shiitake, porcini, or
   other mushrooms, sliced into
   ½-inch-thick pieces

3 cloves garlic, minced

⅓ cup dry sherry (optional)

3 14-ounce cans reduced-sodium
   chicken broth

½ teaspoon dried thyme, crushed,
   or 1 tablespoon snipped
   fresh thyme

1. In a large saucepan heat olive oil over medium heat. Add all of the mushrooms and the garlic. Cook about 10 minutes or until mushrooms have softened and most of the liquid has evaporated, stirring occasionally. If desired, stir in sherry. Cook for 2 minutes more.

2. Add the chicken broth and dried thyme (if using). Bring to boiling; reduce heat. Simmer, covered, for 20 minutes. Stir in the snipped fresh thyme (if using).

4 g carbs   1 g fiber   3 g net carbs

Nutrition Facts per serving: 58 cal., 4 g total fat (0 g sat. fat), 0 mg chol., 580 mg sodium, 4 g carbo., 1 g fiber, 3 g pro.

Squash & Caraway Soup

Prep: 20 minutes Cook: 35 minutes Makes: 4 side-dish servings

1. Reserve 1 cup of the chopped squash; set aside. In a large saucepan heat oil over medium-high heat. Add remaining squash, onion, the 1 tablespoon caraway seeds, and the chile pepper. Cook for 10 minutes, stirring occasionally. Add broth. Bring to boiling; reduce heat. Cook, uncovered, for 20 minutes. Remove from heat; cool slightly.

2. Pour one-third of mixture into a blender container or food processor bowl. Cover and blend or process until smooth. Strain into a medium saucepan (discard pulp). Repeat with remaining cooked squash mixture, blending half at a time. Add reserved 1 cup squash to strained mixture. Heat just to boiling. Ladle into soup bowls. If desired, sprinkle with additional caraway seeds.

Tip: Hot chile peppers contain oils that can burn your eyes, lips, and skin. Wear plastic gloves while preparing chile peppers and be sure to thoroughly wash your hands and nails in hot, soapy water afterward.

6 cups chopped yellow
   summer squash or zucchini
   (1½ pounds)

2 tablespoons cooking oil

½ cup chopped onion (1 medium)

1 tablespoon caraway
   seeds, crushed

1 serrano chile pepper or small
   jalapeño chile pepper, seeded
   and chopped (see tip, left)

4 cups reduced-sodium
   chicken broth
   Caraway seeds (optional)

9g carbs **2**g fiber **7**g net carbs

Nutrition Facts per serving: 121 cal., 8 g total fat (1 g sat. fat), 0 mg chol., 482 mg sodium, 9 g carbo., 2 g fiber, 5 g pro.

Chicken Broth

Prep: 25 minutes   Cook: 2 ½ hours   Makes: about 6 cups broth

3 pounds bony chicken pieces

    (wings, backs, and/or necks)

3 stalks celery with leaves, cut up

2 carrots, cut up

1 large onion, unpeeled, and cut up

1 teaspoon salt

1 teaspoon dried thyme,

    sage, or basil, crushed

½ teaspoon whole black

    peppercorns or ¼ teaspoon

    ground black pepper

4 sprigs fresh parsley

2 bay leaves

2 garlic cloves, unpeeled

    and halved

6 cups cold water

1. If using wings, cut each wing at joints into 3 pieces. Place chicken pieces in a 6-quart Dutch oven. Add celery, carrots, onion, salt, thyme, peppercorns, parsley, bay leaves, and garlic. Add water. Bring to boiling; reduce heat. Simmer, covered, for $2\frac{1}{2}$ hours. Remove chicken pieces from broth.

2. Strain broth (see tip, below). Discard vegetables and seasonings. If desired, clarify broth (see tip, below). If using the broth while hot, remove fat by using a large metal spoon to skim fat that rises to the top. Or chill broth; lift off fat. If desired, when bones are cool enough to handle, remove meat; reserve meat for another use. Discard bones. Place broth and reserved meat in separate containers. Cover and chill for up to 3 days or freeze for up to 6 months.

To strain broth: Line a large colander or sieve with 2 layers of 100%-cotton cheesecloth. Set colander in a large heatproof bowl; carefully pour broth mixture into the lined colander.

To clarify broth: Return hot strained broth to the Dutch oven. Combine ¼ cup cold water and 1 beaten egg white. Stir water mixture into broth. Bring to boiling. Remove from heat; let stand for 5 minutes and strain.

1 g carbs

0 g fiber

1 g net carbs

Nutrition Facts per 1 cup: 30 cal., 2 g total fat (1 g sat. fat), 5 mg chol., 435 mg sodium, 1 g carbo., 0 g fiber, 2 g pro.

Beef Broth

Prep: 30 minutes Bake: 30 minutes Cook: 3½ hours Oven: 450°F Makes: 8 to 9 cups broth

1. Place soup bones in a large shallow roasting pan. Bake in a 450° oven about 30 minutes or until well browned, turning once. Place soup bones in a large Dutch oven. Pour the ½ cup water into the roasting pan and scrape up browned bits; add water mixture to Dutch oven. Stir in carrots, onions, celery, basil, salt, peppercorns, parsley, bay leaves, and garlic. Add the 10 cups water. Bring to boiling; reduce heat. Simmer, covered, for 3½ hours. Remove soup bones.

2. Strain broth (see tip, below). Discard vegetables and seasonings. If desired, clarify broth (see tip, below). If using the broth while hot, remove fat by using a large metal spoon to skim fat that rises to the top. Or chill broth; lift off fat. If desired, when bones are cool enough to handle, remove meat; reserve meat for another use. Discard bones. Place broth and reserved meat in separate containers. Cover and chill for up to 3 days or freeze for up to 6 months.

To strain broth: Line a large colander or sieve with 2 layers of 100%-cotton cheesecloth. Set colander in a large heatproof bowl; carefully pour broth mixture into the lined colander.

To clarify broth: Return hot strained broth to the Dutch oven. Combine ¼ cup cold water and 1 beaten egg white. Stir water mixture into broth. Bring to boiling. Remove from heat; let stand for 5 minutes and strain.

4 pounds meaty beef soup bones
   (beef shank cross cuts or
   short ribs)

½ cup water

3 carrots, cut up

2 medium onions, unpeeled
   and cut up

2 stalks celery with leaves, cut up

1 tablespoon dried basil or
   thyme, crushed

1½ teaspoons salt

10 whole black peppercorns

8 sprigs fresh parsley

4 bay leaves

2 cloves garlic, unpeeled and halved

10 cups water

1g carbs   **0**g fiber   **1**g net carbs

Nutrition Facts per 1 cup: 20 cal., 1 g total fat (1 g sat. fat),
5 mg chol., 409 mg sodium, 1 g carbo., 0 g fiber, 2 g pro.

Creole Chicken Soup

Start to Finish: 25 minutes Makes: 6 servings

12 ounces skinless, boneless chicken thighs, cut into 1-inch pieces

⅔ cup finely chopped cooked ham (4 ounces)

1 tablespoon olive oil

1 cup coarsely chopped onion (1 medium)

¾ cup coarsely chopped green sweet pepper (1 medium)

3 cups reduced-sodium chicken broth

1 10-ounce can chopped tomatoes and green chile peppers

1 cup frozen cut okra, thawed

1 tablespoon chopped fresh parsley

1. In a Dutch oven cook and stir chicken and ham in hot oil over medium high heat for 2 to 3 minutes or until chicken is browned.

2. Add onion and sweet pepper to Dutch oven; cook and stir for 2 minutes or until vegetables are nearly tender. Add chicken broth, undrained tomatoes and green chile peppers, and okra. Bring to boiling; reduce heat. Simmer, covered, for 6 to 8 minutes or until chicken is no longer pink. Stir in parsley.

8 g
carbs

2 g
fiber

6 g
net carbs

Nutrition Facts per serving: 157 cal., 6 g total fat (1 g sat. fat), 56 mg chol., 769 mg sodium, 8 g carbo., 2 g fiber, 17 g pro.

Asian Vegetable, Chicken & Shrimp Soup

Start to Finish: 45 minutes Makes: 6 to 8 main-dish servings

1. In a 4-quart Dutch oven combine chicken and water; bring to boiling; reduce heat. Simmer, covered, for 20 to 25 minutes or until no longer pink. Remove chicken; cool slightly and chop chicken, discarding skin and bones. Strain the cooking liquid. Wipe out Dutch oven and return strained liquid to it. Add chicken broth.

2. Bring to boiling; add chopped cooked chicken, soy sauce, shrimp, bean sprouts, broccoli, mushrooms, sweet pepper, and green onions. Return to boiling; boil gently, uncovered, for 5 minutes. Season with black pepper.

2 small chicken breast halves (12 ounces)

2 cups water

4 cups chicken broth

1 tablespoon soy sauce

8 ounces peeled and deveined

    small shrimp

8 ounces fresh bean sprouts

1 cup broccoli florets

½ of a 15-ounce jar straw mushrooms

    or one 8-ounce can

    mushrooms, drained

½ cup chopped red and/or green

    sweet pepper (1 small)

4 green onions, diagonally sliced

    into 1-inch pieces

    Freshly ground black pepper

7g carbs   **2**g fiber   **5**g net carbs

Nutrition Facts per serving: 152 cal., 3 g total fat (1 g sat. fat), 76 mg chol., 849 mg sodium, 7 g carbo., 2 g fiber, 26 g pro.

Cinnamon-Spiced Pumpkin Soup

Start to Finish: 10 minutes Makes: 6 side-dish servings

1 15-ounce can pumpkin

1 14-ounce can chicken broth

¾ cup half-and-half or

   light cream

½ teaspoon ground cinnamon

⅛ to ¼ teaspoon ground nutmeg

⅛ teaspoon salt

   Dairy sour cream (optional)

   Snipped fresh chives or green

   onion tops (optional)

1. In a medium saucepan combine pumpkin, broth, half-and-half, cinnamon, nutmeg, and salt. Bring just to boiling.

2. Ladle into soup bowls or mugs. If desired, top with sour cream and sprinkle with chives.

See photo, page 74.

7 g
carbs

2 g
fiber

5 g
net carbs

Nutrition Facts per serving: 68 cal., 4 g total fat (2 g sat. fat), 12 mg chol., 334 mg sodium, 7 g carbo., 2 g fiber, 2 g pro.

Lemongrass Chicken Soup

Prep: 15 minutes   Cook: 12 minutes   Makes: 4 servings

1. Cut lemongrass pieces in half lengthwise. Tie pieces into a bundle with 100%-cotton string. In a medium saucepan combine lemongrass bundle, broth, mushrooms, and pepper. Bring mixture just to boiling; reduce heat. Simmer, uncovered, for 10 minutes.

2. Remove and discard lemongrass bundle. Add cooked chicken and asparagus. Simmer, uncovered, for 2 to 3 minutes or until chicken is heated through and asparagus is crisp-tender. Remove from heat. Stir in green onions. To serve, ladle soup into bowls. If desired, top with fresh basil leaves.

2 large stalks lemongrass, peeled, trimmed, and cut into 4-inch pieces

3 cups chicken broth

¼ cup sliced fresh shiitake or button mushrooms

⅛ teaspoon cracked black pepper

½ cup cubed cooked chicken breast

6 thin asparagus spears, trimmed and cut into 1-inch pieces (⅓ cup)

¼ cup bias-sliced green onions (2)

Fresh basil leaves (optional)

2 g carbs   **1** g fiber   **1** g net carbs

Nutrition Facts per serving: 52 cal., 1 g total fat (0 g sat. fat), 17 mg chol., 753 mg sodium, 2 g carbo., 1 g fiber, 8 g pro.

Thai Lime Custard Soup

Prep: 15 minutes Cook: 9 minutes Makes: 5 servings

2 baby eggplants or Japanese eggplants (1 pound), halved and sliced (about 5 cups)

1 tablespoon grated fresh ginger

¼ teaspoon crushed red pepper

2 to 3 cloves garlic, minced (optional)

1 tablespoon cooking oil

3½ cups chicken broth or two 14-ounce cans chicken broth

3 eggs, slightly beaten

2 cups chopped fresh spinach

¼ cup lime juice

¼ cup fresh basil leaves, cut into thin strips

1. In a large saucepan cook and stir eggplants, ginger, red pepper, and, if desired, garlic in hot oil over medium-high heat for 2 minutes. Stir in broth. Bring to boiling; reduce heat. Simmer, covered, for 5 minutes.

2. Place eggs in a small bowl. Gradually stir about ½ cup of the hot broth into eggs. Return all to saucepan. Add spinach. Cook and stir over medium-low heat about 2 minutes or until soup is slightly thickened and spinach is wilted. Stir in lime juice and basil; heat through.

Thai Lime Custard-Chicken Soup: Prepare as directed above, except add 1½ cups chopped cooked chicken with the spinach.

Thai Lime Custard-Shrimp Soup: Prepare as directed above, except add 8 ounces cooked, peeled, and deveined shrimp with the spinach.

7 g carbs   **3** g fiber   **4** g net carbs

Nutrition Facts per serving: 114 cal., 6 g total fat (1 g sat. fat), 138 mg chol., 482 mg sodium, 7 g carbo., 3 g fiber, 8 g pro .

North Sea Chowder

Prep: 10 minutes Cook: 10 minutes Makes: 4 to 6 servings

1. In a large saucepan cook and stir onion and garlic in butter over medium heat until tender. Stir in the water, fish bouillon cubes, lemon juice, chicken bouillon granules, thyme, fennel seeds, saffron (if desired), and bay leaf. Cook and stir until boiling.

2. Add fish and tomatoes. Return to boiling; reduce heat. Simmer, covered, for 10 minutes. Remove and discard bay leaf. If desired, garnish with fresh thyme sprigs.

½ cup chopped onion (1 medium)

2 cloves garlic, minced

1 tablespoon butter or olive oil

4 cups water

2 fish bouillon cubes

1 tablespoon lemon juice

½ teaspoon instant chicken bouillon granules

½ teaspoon dried thyme, crushed

¼ teaspoon fennel seeds

Dash powdered saffron (optional)

1 bay leaf

1 pound skinless, boneless sea bass, red snapper, and/or catfish fillets, cut into ¾-inch cubes

4 plum tomatoes, halved lengthwise and thinly sliced

Fresh thyme sprigs (optional)

6g carbs   **1**g fiber   **5**g net carbs

Nutrition Facts per serving: 160 cal., 5 g total fat (2 g sat. fat), 55 mg chol., 683 mg sodium, 6 g carbo., 1 g fiber, 22 g pro.

Mexican Chicken Soup

Prep: 20 minutes Cook: 1 hour Bake: 20 minutes Oven: 425°F Makes: 6 servings

2 to 2½ pounds meaty chicken pieces (breast halves, thighs, and drumsticks)

6 cups water

2 cups coarsely chopped onion (2 medium)

2 cups coarsely chopped celery (4 stalks)

1 cup coarsely chopped tomato (1 large)

½ cup snipped fresh cilantro

1½ teaspoons salt

1 teaspoon ground cumin

¼ to ½ teaspoon cayenne pepper

¼ to ½ teaspoon black pepper

1½ cups chopped carrots (3 medium)

1 or 2 poblano chile peppers (see tip, page 59)

Sliced avocado (optional)

Chopped fresh cilantro (optional)

Sliced green onions (optional)

1. Skin chicken. In a 4½-quart Dutch oven combine chicken pieces, water, 1 cup onion, 1 cup celery, the tomato, cilantro, salt, cumin, cayenne pepper, and black pepper. Bring to boiling; reduce heat. Simmer, covered, for 40 to 50 minutes or until chicken is tender. Remove chicken pieces and set aside to cool slightly. Strain the broth mixture, reserving broth and discarding the vegetables. Return the broth to the Dutch oven. Add the remaining 1 cup onion, 1 cup celery, and the carrots. Bring to boiling; reduce heat. Simmer, covered, for 20 minutes or until vegetables are tender.

2. Meanwhile, cut chile peppers in half lengthwise and remove seeds, stems, and veins. Place pepper halves, cut side down, on a foil-lined baking sheet. Bake in a 425° oven for 20 to 25 minutes or until skins are blistered and dark. Wrap in the foil; let stand about 15 minutes or until cool enough to handle. Use a sharp knife to loosen the edges of the skins from the pepper halves; gently and slowly pull off the skin in strips. Discard skin. Chop peppers.

3. Remove chicken from bones; discard bones. Chop the chicken. Stir chicken and poblano peppers into broth mixture. Heat through. To serve, ladle soup into bowls. If desired, garnish with avocado, cilantro, and green onions.

7 g carbs   **2** g fiber   **5** g net carbs

Nutrition Facts per serving: 158 cal., 5 g total fat (1 g sat. fat), 61 mg chol., 638 mg sodium, 7 g carbo., 2 g fiber, 21 g pro.

Yucatan Soup with Lime

Start to Finish: 30 minutes   Makes: 4 servings

1. In a Dutch oven cook the chicken and garlic in hot oil over medium-high heat until chicken is no longer pink. Stir in chile powder, cumin seeds, and, if desired, crushed red pepper. Cook and stir for 30 seconds. Stir in the chicken broth and green onions.

2. Bring to boiling; reduce heat. Simmer, uncovered, for 10 minutes. Remove from heat. Stir in tomato and the lime juice.

2 to 3 skinless, boneless chicken
    breast halves (12 ounces), cut
    into bite-size pieces

3 cloves garlic, minced

1 tablespoon olive oil or cooking oil

1 tablespoon hot chile powder

½ teaspoon cumin seeds, crushed,
    or ¼ teaspoon ground cumin

¼ to ½ teaspoon crushed
    red pepper (optional)

2 14-ounce cans chicken broth

½ cup chopped green onions (4)

1 cup chopped tomato (1 large)

3 tablespoons lime juice

6 g carbs   **1** g fiber   **5** g net carbs

Nutrition Facts per serving: 163 cal., 6 g total fat (1 g sat. fat),
51 mg chol., 881 mg sodium, 6 g carbo., 1 g fiber, 22 g pro.

Chilled Avocado Soup

Prep: 15 minutes Chill: 3 hours Makes: 6 side-dish servings

3 ripe avocados, halved, seeded, and peeled (1¼ pounds)

1 cup chicken broth

¼ cup water

1 cup half-and-half or light cream

¼ teaspoon salt

⅛ teaspoon onion powder

Dash ground white pepper

1 tablespoon lemon juice

Lemon slices (optional)

1. Place avocados in a blender container or food processor bowl. Add chicken broth and water; cover and blend or process until smooth. Add half-and-half, salt, onion powder, and white pepper. Cover and blend or process until combined. Transfer to a glass bowl. Stir in lemon juice. Cover and chill for at least 3 hours or up to 24 hours. Stir before serving. If desired, garnish with lemon slices.

See photo, page 75.

8g carbs   4g fiber   4g net carbs

Nutrition Facts per serving: 210 cal., 20 g total fat (5 g sat. fat), 15 mg chol., 253 mg sodium, 8 g carbo., 4 g fiber, 4 g pro.

Asparagus Salad with Tarragon Vinaigrette

Start to Finish: 25 minutes Makes: 6 servings

1. Snap off and discard woody bases from asparagus. If desired, scrape off scales. Cook asparagus, covered, in a small amount of boiling lightly salted water for 3 to 5 minutes or until crisp-tender. Transfer asparagus spears to a medium bowl half-filled with ice water; set aside.

2. For dressing, in a screw-top jar combine oil, vinegar, water, tarragon, mustard, salt, and pepper. Cover and shake well.

3. To serve, drizzle about half of the dressing over the greens in a large bowl; toss to coat. Divide greens among 6 salad plates. Drain asparagus; pat dry with paper towels. Arrange asparagus on top of greens. Drizzle asparagus with remaining dressing. Sprinkle with sesame seeds.

See photo, page 76.

1 pound asparagus spears

3 tablespoons olive oil

2 tablespoons rice vinegar

1 tablespoon water

1 teaspoon snipped fresh tarragon or ¼ teaspoon dried tarragon, crushed

½ teaspoon Dijon-style mustard

¼ teaspoon salt

⅛ teaspoon black pepper

6 cups torn mixed salad greens

1 tablespoon sesame seeds, toasted

3g carbs   **1**g fiber   **2**g net carbs

Nutrition Facts per serving: 88 cal., 8 g total fat (1 g sat. fat), 0 mg chol., 120 mg sodium, 3 g carbo., 1 g fiber, 2 g pro.

Mediterranean Beef Salad with Lemon Vinaigrette

Prep: 20 minutes Broil: 15 minutes Makes: 4 main-dish servings

1 pound boneless beef sirloin
    steak, cut 1 inch thick
    Salt and ground black pepper

4 cups torn romaine lettuce

½ of a small red onion, thinly
    sliced and separated into
    rings (½ cup)

1 cup halved cherry or grape
    tomatoes

½ cup crumbled feta cheese
    Lemon Vinaigrette
    (see recipe, right)
    Fresh oregano sprigs
    (optional)

1. Preheat broiler. Trim fat from steak. Lightly sprinkle steak with salt and pepper. Place steak on the unheated rack of a broiler pan. Broil 3 to 4 inches from the heat to desired doneness, turning once. Allow 15 to 17 minutes for medium rare (145°F) or 20 to 22 minutes for medium (160°F). Thinly slice the meat.

2. Divide torn romaine among 4 dinner plates. Top with sliced meat, onion, tomatoes, and feta cheese. Drizzle with Lemon Vinaigrette. If desired, garnish with oregano sprigs.

Lemon Vinaigrette: In a screw-top jar combine ¼ cup olive oil, ½ teaspoon finely shredded lemon peel, 3 tablespoons lemon juice, 1 tablespoon snipped fresh oregano, and 2 cloves garlic, minced. Cover and shake well. Season to taste with salt and black pepper. Makes about ½ cup.

See photo, page 73.

5g carbs   **2**g fiber   **3**g net carbs

Nutrition Facts per serving: 198 cal., 7 g total fat (3 g sat. fat), 81 mg chol., 365 mg sodium, 5 g carbo., 2 g fiber, 27 g pro.

Mediterranean
Beef Salad
with Lemon
Vinaigrette
p. 72

Cinnamon-
Spiced
Pumpkin
Soup
p. 64

Chilled
Avocado
Soup
p .70

Asparagus Salad with Tarragon Vinaigrette p. 71

Grilled
Tomato &
Mozzarella
Salad
p. 84

Romaine &
Radicchio
Salad
p. 86

Ginger-Lime Chicken Salad p. 100

Shiitake &
Lemongrass
Soup
p. 81

Shiitake & Lemongrass Soup

Prep: 20 minutes Cook: 25 minutes Makes: 4 appetizer servings

1. Cut lemongrass pieces in half lengthwise. Tie pieces into a bundle with 100%-cotton string; set aside. In a large saucepan melt 1 tablespoon of the butter over medium-high heat. Add onion; cook and stir about 5 minutes or until onion is tender. Add the broth and lemongrass bundle. Bring to boiling; reduce heat. Simmer, uncovered, for 15 minutes. Remove and discard the lemongrass bundle.

2. Meanwhile, in a large skillet melt the remaining 1 tablespoon butter over medium-high heat. Add mushrooms; cook and stir about 5 minutes or until mushrooms are lightly browned around the edges. Remove from heat; set mushrooms aside.

3. Stir vinegar and pepper into broth. Stir in spinach. To serve, ladle soup into bowls. Top with cooked mushrooms.

See photo, page 80.

2 large stalks lemongrass, peeled, trimmed, and cut into 4-inch pieces

2 tablespoons butter

⅓ cup finely chopped onion (1 small)

3 cups vegetable broth

3 ounces fresh shiitake mushrooms, stemmed and sliced (1 cup)

1 tablespoon rice vinegar

⅛ teaspoon ground white pepper

¾ cup coarsely chopped fresh spinach

8g carbs   **1**g fiber   **7**g net carbs

Nutrition Facts per serving: 94 cal., 7 g total fat (3 g sat. fat), 16 mg chol., 777 mg sodium, 8 g carbo., 1 g fiber, 1 g pro.

Tangy Asparagus-Crabmeat Salad

Start to Finish: 25 minutes   Makes: 4 servings

6   ounces asparagus spears

8   ounces cooked crabmeat

    (about 1½ cups)

½   cup sliced celery (1 stalk)

8   to 12 romaine lettuce leaves

    or 6 cups torn mixed greens

½   cup olive oil

¼   cup lemon juice

¼   cup red wine vinegar

1   tablespoon finely

    chopped onion

2   teaspoons Dijon-style mustard

1   teaspoon snipped fresh parsley

1   teaspoon snipped fresh chives

1   teaspoon snipped fresh dill

½   teaspoon black pepper

1. Snap off and discard woody bases from asparagus. If desired, scrape off scales. Cut asparagus into 1-inch pieces. Cook asparagus, covered, in a small amount of boiling water for 2 minutes. Transfer asparagus to a medium bowl half-filled with ice water; drain well.

2. In a medium bowl combine asparagus, crabmeat, and celery. Line 4 salad plates with romaine leaves. Top with asparagus mixture.

3. For dressing, in a screw-top jar combine oil, lemon juice, vinegar, onion, mustard, parsley, chives, dill, and pepper. Cover and shake well. Drizzle dressing over salads.

7 g carbs   **3** g fiber   **4** g net carbs

Nutrition Facts per serving: 317 cal., 28 g total fat (4 g sat. fat), 68 mg chol., 298 mg sodium, 7 g carbo., 3 g fiber, 12 g pro.

Spring Asparagus Slaw

Prep: 25 minutes Cook: 4 minutes Makes: 8 to 10 side-dish servings

1. Snap off and discard woody bases from asparagus. If desired, scrape off scales. Cook asparagus, covered, in a small amount of boiling lightly salted water for 3 to 5 minutes or until crisp-tender. Transfer asparagus spears to a medium bowl half-filled with ice water; drain well.

2. In a large bowl combine green cabbage, radicchio, mint, parsley, and onion. Divide asparagus spears among 8 salad plates; top with cabbage mixture.

3. For dressing, in a screw-top jar combine oil, vinegar, lemon peel, lemon juice, garlic, and pepper. Cover and shake well. Pour over cabbage mixture. Top with cheese.

- 1 pound asparagus spears
- 4 cups shredded green cabbage
- 1 cup torn radicchio or red cabbage
- ¼ cup snipped fresh mint
- ¼ cup snipped fresh parsley
- ¼ of a small red onion, thinly sliced
- 2 tablespoons olive oil
- 2 tablespoons balsamic vinegar
- ½ teaspoon finely shredded lemon peel
- 1 tablespoon lemon juice
- 1 clove garlic, minced
- ½ teaspoon black pepper
- ¼ cup finely shredded Parmesan cheese

5g carbs   **1**g fiber   **4**g net carbs

Nutrition Facts per serving: 72 cal., 5 g total fat (1 g sat. fat), 3 mg chol., 75 mg sodium, 5 g carbo., 1 g fiber, 3 g pro.

Grilled Tomato & Mozzarella Salad

Prep: 30 minutes Grill: 7 minutes Makes: 4 servings

1 tablespoon balsamic vinegar or red
wine vinegar

1 tablespoon olive oil or salad oil

1 tablespoon water

1 medium yellow summer squash,
bias-cut into ¼-inch slices
(1¼ cups)

2 large red and/or yellow tomatoes,
cut into ½-inch-thick slices

4 ounces mozzarella cheese, thinly
sliced and cut into triangles
Salt and black pepper

2 tablespoons assorted snipped fresh
herbs (such as oregano, basil,
thyme, and sage)
Fresh oregano sprigs (optional)

1. For dressing, in a screw-top jar combine vinegar, oil, water, ⅛ teaspoon *salt,* and ⅛ teaspoon *black pepper.* Cover and shake well; set aside.

2. For a charcoal grill, grill squash on the greased rack of an uncovered grill directly over medium coals (see tip, page 107) for 5 to 6 minutes or until crisp-tender, turning once halfway through grilling. Add tomato slices to rack; grill 2 to 4 minutes or until heated through but still slightly firm, turning once. (For a gas grill, preheat grill. Reduce heat to medium. Grill, covered, as above.)

3. On a shallow serving platter, alternately place slices of tomato, squash, and mozzarella cheese. Sprinkle with salt and pepper. Drizzle dressing over vegetables. Sprinkle snipped fresh herbs over the salad. If desired, garnish with fresh oregano sprigs.

See photo, page 77.

6 g carbs   1 g fiber   5 g net carbs

Nutrition Facts per serving: 126 cal., 8 g total fat (3 g sat. fat),
18 mg chol., 324 mg sodium, 6 g carbo., 1 g fiber, 8 g pro.

Fresh Herb Tuna Salad

Start to Finish: 15 minutes Makes: 2 servings

1. In a small bowl combine mayonnaise, French sorrel, chives, lovage, tarragon, curry powder, and black pepper.

2. If desired, add dill. Fold in tuna. Serve immediately, or cover and chill for up to 6 hours. If desired, spoon mixture into sweet pepper halves and garnish with greens and herbs.

*Note: If desired, substitute 1 tablespoon flat-leaf parsley for the sorrel and lovage.

½ cup mayonnaise

2 tablespoons snipped fresh French sorrel leaves*

1 tablespoon snipped fresh chives

1 tablespoon snipped fresh lovage*

1 teaspoon snipped fresh tarragon

¼ teaspoon curry powder

Dash black pepper

1 teaspoon snipped fresh dill (optional)

1 9- or 9¼-ounce can chunk or solid white tuna (water pack), drained and flaked

1 yellow sweet pepper, halved and seeded (optional)

Assorted salad greens and fresh herbs (optional)

1g carbs   **0**g fiber   **1**g net carbs

Nutrition Facts per serving: 568 cal., 48 g total fat (7 g sat. fat), 94 mg chol., 822 mg sodium, 1 g carbo., 0 g fiber, 31 g pro.

Romaine & Radicchio Salad

Start to Finish: 15 minutes Makes: 8 servings

3 tablespoons white wine

   vinegar

3 anchovy fillets, finely chopped

¼ teaspoon black pepper

⅛ teaspoon salt

¼ cup olive oil

1 10-ounce package Italian-

   blend salad greens (romaine

   and radicchio)

2 ounces Parmesan

   cheese, shaved

¼ cup chopped pecans or

   walnuts, toasted

1. For dressing, in a medium mixing bowl whisk together vinegar, anchovies, pepper, and salt; gradually whisk in oil. Season to taste with additional salt and pepper. Toss salad greens with dressing. Top greens with Parmesan cheese and nuts.

See photo, page 78.

2 g carbs   **1** g fiber   **1** g net carbs

Nutrition Facts per serving: 125 cal., 11 g total fat (2 g sat. fat), 6 mg chol., 216 mg sodium, 2 g carbo., 1 g fiber, 4 g pro.

Tomato & Zucchini Salad

Start to Finish: 20 minutes Makes: 4 servings

1. In a medium bowl combine tomato, zucchini, green onion, dressing, and basil. Toss lightly to coat.

2. Line 4 salad plates with lettuce. Divide tomato mixture among plates. Sprinkle each serving with cheese.

1 cup coarsely chopped tomato
   (1 large)

1 cup thinly sliced zucchini (1 small)

2 tablespoons sliced green onion (1)

2 tablespoons bottled low-carb
   Italian salad dressing

1 teaspoon snipped fresh basil or
   ¼ teaspoon dried basil, crushed

4 lettuce leaves

2 tablespoons crumbled feta cheese
   or shredded mozzarella cheese

3g carbs   **1**g fiber   **2**g net carbs

Nutrition Facts per serving: 44 cal., 3 g total fat (1 g sat. fat),
4 mg chol., 147 mg sodium, 3 g carbo., 1 g fiber, 2 g pro.

Beef & Veggie Plate

Start to Finish: 20 minutes Makes: 4 servings

1 cup finely chopped button mushrooms

¼ cup sliced green onions (2)

2 tablespoons Worcestershire

    sauce for chicken

1 tablespoon hazelnut oil,

    walnut oil, or salad oil

¼ teaspoon ground white pepper

3 cups beet greens or other

    leafy greens

1 pound thinly sliced cooked beef

4 red and/or yellow plum tomatoes,

    chopped, or 8 grape, cherry, or pear-

    shape tomatoes, halved

½ of a small red onion, thinly sliced

    Snipped fresh rosemary (optional)

1. In a medium bowl combine mushrooms, green onions, Worcestershire sauce, oil, and pepper. If desired, cover and chill for 2 to 24 hours.

2. To serve, line 4 chilled salad plates with greens. Top with beef, tomatoes, and red onion. Spoon mushroom mixture onto plates. If desired, sprinkle with rosemary.

9 g carbs **3** g fiber **6** g net carbs

Nutrition Facts per serving: 321 cal., 17 g total fat (6 g sat. fat),
90 mg chol., 249 mg sodium, 9 g carbo., 3 g fiber, 33 g pro.

Lemon-Tarragon Asparagus Salad

Prep: 20 minutes Chill: 2 hours Makes: 6 to 8 side-dish servings

1. Snap off and discard woody bases from asparagus. If desired, scrape off scales. Cut asparagus into 1-inch pieces. Cook asparagus, covered, in a small amount of boiling water for 2 minutes. Transfer asparagus to a medium bowl half-filled with ice water; drain well.

2. In a salad bowl combine asparagus, radishes, oil, green onion, tarragon, lemon peel, and salt. Toss to combine. Cover and chill for 2 to 3 hours.

3. Just before serving, stir in almonds and vinegar.

1½ pounds asparagus spears

1 cup sliced radishes

2 tablespoons olive oil

1 tablespoon thinly sliced green onion

2 teaspoons snipped fresh tarragon or ½ teaspoon dried tarragon, crushed

1 teaspoon finely shredded lemon peel

¼ teaspoon salt

¼ cup slivered almonds, toasted

2 tablespoons white wine vinegar

3g carbs **2**g fiber **1**g net carbs

Nutrition Facts per serving: 95 cal., 8 g total fat (1 g sat. fat), 0 mg chol., 115 mg sodium, 3 g carbo., 2 g fiber, 3 g pro.

Tomato-Crab Salad

Prep: 15 minutes Chill: up to 8 hours Makes: 6 side-dish servings

2 pounds assorted tomatoes,
  such as Brandywine, Green
  Zebra, and/or yellow cherry

3 tablespoons tarragon vinegar
  or white wine vinegar

2 tablespoons olive oil

¼ cup snipped fresh tarragon

¾ teaspoon Herb-Salt Sprinkle
  (see recipe, right) or salt

½ teaspoon cracked black
  pepper

½ cup cooked crabmeat
  Fresh tarragon sprigs
  (optional)

1. Cut larger tomatoes into slices or wedges; halve cherry tomatoes. Arrange tomatoes on a serving platter. For dressing, in a screw-top jar combine vinegar, oil, and 3 tablespoons of the snipped tarragon. Cover and shake well. Drizzle dressing over tomatoes. Sprinkle with remaining 1 tablespoon snipped tarragon. Cover and chill up to 8 hours.

2. Just before serving, sprinkle Herb-Salt Sprinkle and the cracked pepper over salad. Top with crabmeat. If desired, garnish with tarragon sprigs.

Herb-Salt Sprinkle: In a 1-pint screw-top jar place 1 tablespoon coarse-grained sea salt or kosher salt. Sprinkle about 2 tablespoons snipped fresh herbs (such as basil, tarragon, thyme, dill, savory, or rosemary) over the salt. Sprinkle an additional 1 tablespoon coarse-grained sea salt or kosher salt over herbs. Sprinkle an additional 2 tablespoons snipped fresh herbs over salt and top with an additional 2 tablespoons coarse-grained sea salt or kosher salt. Screw on the lid. Let stand for 24 hours or up to 6 months. Shake to mix before serving.

7 g carbs

2 g fiber

5 g net carbs

Nutrition Facts per serving: 89 cal., 5 g total fat (1 g sat. fat),
8 mg chol., 166 mg sodium, 7 g carbo., 2 g fiber, 4 g pro.

Curried Egg Salad

Prep: 15 minutes Chill: 4 hours Makes: 12 servings

1. In a medium bowl combine chopped eggs, mayonnaise, olives, green onion, curry powder, and salt; mix well. Cover and chill for 4 to 24 hours.

*Hard-cooked eggs: Place eggs in a single layer in a medium saucepan. Add enough cold water to just cover the eggs. Bring to a rapid boil over high heat (water will have large rapidly breaking bubbles). Remove from heat, cover, and let stand for 15 minutes; drain. Run cold water over the eggs or place them in ice water until cool enough to handle; drain. To peel eggs, gently tap each egg on the countertop. Roll the egg between the palms of your hands. Peel off eggshell, starting at the large end.

8 hard-cooked eggs*, peeled and chopped

½ cup mayonnaise

¼ cup finely chopped pitted ripe olives

2 tablespoons finely chopped green onion (1)

½ to 1 teaspoon curry powder

¼ teaspoon salt

2 g carbs   0 g fiber   2 g net carbs

Nutrition Facts per serving: 243 cal., 22 g total fat (4 g sat. fat), 294 mg chol., 333 mg sodium, 2 g carbo., 0 g fiber, 9 g pro.

Beef-Vegetable Salad

Start to Finish: 30 minutes Makes: 4 servings

¼ cup olive oil

4 teaspoons tarragon
   vinegar or white wine
   vinegar

2 teaspoons Dijon-style
   mustard

2 teaspoons snipped fresh
   tarragon or ½ teaspoon
   dried tarragon, crushed

¼ teaspoon salt

1 pound boneless beef
   sirloin steak, cut 1 inch
   thick

1 cup cauliflower florets

1 cup broccoli florets

1 small red sweet pepper,
   cut into 1-inch pieces
   (¾ cup)

1 small yellow sweet
   pepper, cut into 1-inch
   pieces (¾ cup)

1 small red onion, halved
   and thinly sliced (½ cup)

2 slices bacon, crisp-
   cooked, drained, and
   crumbled

4 cups torn mixed
   salad greens

¼ cup finely shredded
   Parmesan cheese

1. For dressing, in a screw-top jar combine oil, vinegar, mustard, tarragon, and salt. Cover and shake well; set aside.

2. Preheat broiler. Slash fat on edges of steak at 1-inch intervals. Place steak on the unheated rack of a broiler pan. Broil 3 to 4 inches from the heat to desired doneness, turning once. Allow 15 to 17 minutes for medium rare (145°F) and 20 to 22 minutes for medium (160°F). Cut the meat into 1-inch cubes.

3. In a large bowl combine the beef, cauliflower, broccoli, sweet peppers, onion, and bacon.

4. Shake the dressing and pour it over the beef mixture; toss lightly to coat. Divide greens among 4 dinner plates. Top with beef mixture. Sprinkle with Parmesan.

10g carbs   **3**g fiber   **7**g net carbs

Nutrition Facts per serving: 472 cal., 30 g total fat (10 g sat. fat),
96 mg chol., 912 mg sodium, 10 g carbo., 3 g fiber, 41 g pro.

Tomato & Onion Salad

Start to Finish: 20 minutes Makes: 4 to 6 servings

1. In a serving bowl combine tomatoes, onion, and parsley.

2. In a small mixing bowl whisk together oil, lemon juice, salt, and pepper. Pour over tomato mixture; lightly toss to coat. Season to taste with additional salt and pepper. Serve immediately, or cover and chill up to 2 hours. (If chilled, let stand at room temperature for 30 minutes before serving.)

2 cups chopped seeded

tomatoes (2 large)

1 small onion, halved and thinly

sliced (⅓ cup)

¼ cup snipped fresh parsley

2 tablespoons olive oil

2 tablespoons lemon juice

¼ teaspoon salt

⅛ teaspoon black pepper

7 g carbs   **1** g fiber   **6** g net carbs

Nutrition Facts per serving: 94 cal., 7 g total fat (1 g sat. fat), 0.0 mg chol., 159 mg sodium, 7 g carbo., 1 g fiber, 1 g pro.

Hot Italian Beef Salad

Start to Finish: 20 minutes Makes: 4 servings

1 12-ounce beef flank steak or
   beef top round steak, cut
   1 inch thick

2 teaspoons olive oil or
   cooking oil

1 medium red or green sweet
   pepper, seeded and cut into
   bite-size strips

½ cup bottled low-carb Italian
   salad dressing

6 cups torn mixed salad greens

¼ cup finely shredded
   Parmesan cheese
   Coarsely ground black pepper

1. Trim fat from steak. Thinly slice steak across the grain into bite-size strips*.

2. In a large nonstick skillet heat oil over medium-high heat. Add steak and sweet pepper strips. Cook and stir for 3 to 5 minutes or until steak is desired doneness and pepper is crisp-tender; drain. Add dressing to skillet. Cook and stir until heated through.

3. Divide the salad greens among 4 salad plates. Top with the beef mixture. Sprinkle with Parmesan and black pepper. Serve immediately.

***Note:** Partially freeze beef for easier slicing.

5 g carbs   **1** g fiber   **4** g net carbs

Nutrition Facts per serving: 376 cal., 25 g total fat (10 g sat. fat), 58 mg chol., 968 mg sodium, 5 g carbo., 1 g fiber, 32 g pro.

Plum Tomato Salad

Prep: 10 minutes Stand: 5 minutes Makes: 6 servings

1. In a medium bowl combine tomatoes, mozzarella cheese, and olives. Pour dressing over tomato mixture; toss lightly to coat. Let stand for 5 minutes before serving.

1 pound plum tomatoes,
   coarsely chopped

4 ounces mozzarella or provolone
   cheese, cubed

⅔ cup pimiento-stuffed green olives

¼ cup bottled low-carb Italian
   salad dressing

4 g carbs   **1** g fiber   **3** g net carbs

Nutrition Facts per serving: 101 cal., 8 g total fat (2 g sat. fat), 12 mg chol., 575 mg sodium, 4 g carbo., 1 g fiber, 5 g pro.

Marinated Beef & Garden Vegetable Salad

Prep: 15 minutes Marinate: 4 hours Makes: 2 servings

1 cup sliced cooked beef or pork, cut into thin strips (4 ounces)

1 medium tomato, cut into thin wedges

½ cup cubed Edam or Gouda cheese

½ of a small onion, thinly sliced and separated into rings

½ of a small green or yellow sweet pepper, seeded and cut into thin strips (⅓ cup)

3 tablespoons olive oil or salad oil

3 tablespoons red or white wine vinegar

1 tablespoon snipped fresh basil or 1 teaspoon dried basil, crushed

1 tablespoon mayonnaise

1 clove garlic, minced

⅛ teaspoon salt

⅛ teaspoon black pepper

2 leaves romaine lettuce

2 tablespoons pine nuts or chopped walnuts, toasted

1. In a medium bowl combine beef, tomato, cheese, onion, and sweet pepper; set aside.

2. For dressing, in a screw-top jar combine oil, vinegar, basil, mayonnaise, garlic, salt, and black pepper. Cover and shake well. Pour over meat and vegetable mixture; toss lightly to coat. Cover and chill for 4 to 24 hours, stirring occasionally.

3. To serve, line 2 dinner plates with lettuce leaves. Using a slotted spoon, spoon meat mixture onto lettuce-lined plates. Sprinkle with nuts.

8_g carbs 1_g fiber 7_g net carbs

Nutrition Facts per serving: 426 cal., 33 g total fat (9 g sat. fat), 68 mg chol., 437 mg sodium, 8 g carbo., 1 g fiber, 27 g pro.

Potpourri Chicken Salad

Prep: 30 minutes Chill: 2 hours Makes: 8 main-dish servings

1. In a large bowl combine chicken, celery, onion, water chestnuts, olives, and sunflower seeds. Add mayonnaise and mustard; mix well. Cover and chill for 2 to 24 hours. Serve chicken salad on a lettuce-lined plate, or roll salad up in a lettuce leaf.

3 cups chopped cooked chicken

1½ cups finely chopped celery (3 stalks)

½ cup finely chopped onion (1 medium)

½ cup water chestnuts, drained and
finely chopped

½ cup pitted ripe olives, finely chopped

½ cup shelled sunflower seeds

1 cup mayonnaise or salad dressing

2 tablespoons Dijon-style mustard

8 lettuce leaves

6 g carbs   2 g fiber   4 g net carbs

Nutrition Facts per serving: 387 cal., 32 g total fat (5 g sat. fat),
70 mg chol., 403 mg sodium, 6 g carbo., 2 g fiber, 20 g pro.

Roasted Pepper & Eggplant Salad with Goat Cheese

Prep: 30 minutes Roast: 20 minutes Oven: 425°F Makes: 8 servings

2 medium red and/or yellow sweet peppers

1 small eggplant (12 ounces)

⅓ cup olive oil

¼ cup white wine vinegar

2 teaspoons Dijon-style mustard

2 cloves garlic, minced

¼ teaspoon salt

⅛ teaspoon black pepper

1 5-ounce package baby salad greens (mesclun) or other torn salad greens (8 cups)

2 4-ounce logs semi-soft goat cheese (chèvre), cut into ½-inch rounds

1. Halve sweet peppers lengthwise; remove stems, seeds, and membranes. Place sweet pepper halves, cut sides down, on a foil-lined baking sheet. Cut eggplant in half lengthwise. Place eggplant halves, cut side down, on the baking sheet with the sweet peppers. Roast in a 425° oven for 20 to 25 minutes or until skins are blistered and dark. Carefully bring the foil up and around the sweet pepper and eggplant halves to enclose. Let stand about 15 minutes or until cool enough to handle. Use a sharp knife to loosen the edges of the skins from the sweet pepper and eggplant halves; gently and slowly pull off the skin in strips. Discard skin.

2. Meanwhile, for dressing, in a screw-top jar combine olive oil, vinegar, mustard, garlic, salt, and black pepper. Cover and shake well; set aside.

3. Cut sweet peppers into long strips; place in a medium bowl. Cut eggplant into bite-size pieces; add to sweet peppers in bowl. Add 2 tablespoons of the dressing to the eggplant mixture; toss to coat.

4. Divide the salad greens among 8 serving plates. Spoon eggplant mixture over greens. Top with cheese rounds. Drizzle remaining dressing over salads.

5 g carbs **2** g fiber **3** g net carbs

Nutrition Facts per serving: 176 cal., 15 g total fat (5 g sat. fat), 13 mg chol., 180 mg sodium, 5 g carbo., 2 g fiber, 6 g pro.

Summer Tomato Salad

Start to Finish: 30 minutes Makes: 6 servings

1. For dressing, in a screw-top jar combine oil, vinegar, tarragon, chives, and mustard. Cover and shake well; set aside.

2. Divide the salad greens among 6 salad plates. Arrange the tomatoes on and around the greens. Top with onion slices. Sprinkle with salt and pepper. Drizzle with desired amount of dressing. Store any remaining dressing, covered, in the refrigerator for up to 1 week.

½ cup olive oil

¼ cup red or white wine vinegar

1 tablespoon snipped fresh tarragon

1 tablespoon snipped fresh chives

½ teaspoon Dijon-style mustard

3 cups baby salad greens
   (mesclun)

2 medium red tomatoes, cut into
   wedges or sliced

2 medium yellow or heirloom green
   tomatoes, cut into 8 wedges each

1 cup red or yellow cherry tomatoes,
   halved if desired

1 small red onion, thinly sliced

¼ teaspoon coarse salt

¼ teaspoon black pepper

7g carbs **2**g fiber **5**g net carbs

Nutrition Facts per serving: 192 cal., 19 g total fat (3 g sat. fat),
0 mg chol., 109 mg sodium, 7 g carbo., 2 g fiber, 2 g pro.

Ginger-Lime Chicken Salad

Prep: 10 minutes Chill: 30 minutes Makes: 4 servings

¼ cup dairy sour cream

2 tablespoons lime juice

2 teaspoons grated fresh ginger

2 cups chopped cooked chicken

1 cup snow pea pods,

   long-bias cut

1 cup thinly sliced celery

   (2 stalks)

2 tablespoons slivered red

   onion

1. In a medium bowl combine sour cream, lime juice, and ginger. Add chicken; stir to coat. Cover and chill for at least 30 minutes. In a second medium bowl combine pea pods, celery, and onion. Divide vegetable mixture among 4 salad plates. Top with chicken mixture.

See photo, page 79.

5 g
carbs

1 g
fiber

4 g
net carbs

Nutrition Facts per serving: 188 cal., 8 g total fat (3 g sat. fat), 73 mg chol., 98 mg sodium, 5 g carbo., 1 g fiber, 23 g pro.

Fish & Seafood

Americans are eating more fish and seafood than ever before and for good reason. You've finally hooked up to its enormous health benefits and learned that simple preparation enhances its naturally fresh flavors. Whether you catch it yourself or are a regular customer at the fish market, use these recipes for luscious, low-carb enticements.

Whitefish with Roasted Asparagus

Prep: 20 minutes Bake: 15 minutes Oven: 450°F Makes: 4 servings

1 pound fresh or frozen skinless
  whitefish fillets or other white-
  fleshed fish fillets, about
  ½ inch thick

½ cup chopped onion (1 medium)

½ cup chopped red sweet
  pepper (1 small)

¼ cup reduced-sodium chicken broth

2 cloves garlic, minced

¼ teaspoon salt

¼ teaspoon smoked paprika or paprika

¼ teaspoon black pepper

12 ounces asparagus spears,
  trimmed and bias-sliced into
  1-inch pieces (1½ cups)

1. Thaw fish, if frozen. Rinse fish; pat dry. Cut fish into 4 serving-size pieces, if necessary; set aside. In a 2-quart rectangular baking dish combine onion, sweet pepper, broth, and garlic. Top with fish, turning under thin edges. Sprinkle with salt, paprika, and black pepper. Top with asparagus.

2. Bake, covered, in a 450° oven for 15 to 20 minutes or until fish flakes easily when tested with a fork.

5g carbs   **1**g fiber   **4**g net carbs

Nutrition Facts per serving: 184 cal., 7 g total fat (2 g sat. fat), 62 mg chol., 248 mg sodium, 5 g carbo., 1 g fiber, 24 g pro.

Roasted Salmon & Tomatoes

Prep: 15 minutes Bake: 12 minutes Oven: 450°F Makes: 4 servings

1. Thaw fish, if frozen. Rinse fish; pat dry. Cut fish into 4 serving-size pieces. Lightly coat a 13×9×2-inch baking pan with cooking spray. Arrange fish, skin side up, in prepared pan, turning under thin edges. Sprinkle fish with the 1/8 teaspoon salt.

2. Arrange tomatoes around fish. Sprinkle tomatoes with Worcestershire sauce, pepper, and 1/8 teaspoon salt.

3. Bake, uncovered, in a 450° oven for 12 to 16 minutes or until fish flakes easily when tested with a fork. Remove skin from fish; discard skin. Transfer fish to serving platter. Stir mustard and marjoram into tomatoes. Serve tomato mixture with fish. If desired, garnish with oregano sprigs.

1   1¼-pound fresh or frozen
      salmon fillet, about 1 inch thick
      Nonstick cooking spray
1/8 teaspoon salt
2   cups chopped seeded plum
      tomatoes (6 medium)
1   tablespoon Worcestershire sauce
      for chicken
1/4 teaspoon black pepper
1/8 teaspoon salt
1   tablespoon Dijon-style mustard
1   tablespoon snipped fresh
      marjoram or oregano
      Fresh oregano sprigs (optional)

6g carbs   **1**g fiber   **5**g net carbs

Nutrition Facts per serving: 231 cal., 10 g total fat (2 g sat. fat), 75 mg chol., 370 mg sodium, 6 g carbo., 1 g fiber, 30 g pro.

Pan-Seared Tilapia with Almond Browned Butter & Snow Peas

Start to Finish: 20 minutes Makes: 4 servings

Snipped fresh parsley (optional)

3 cups fresh snow pea
  pods, trimmed

4 4- to 5-ounce fresh skinless
  tilapia fillets

  Sea salt and freshly ground
  black pepper

1 tablespoon olive oil

2 tablespoons butter

¼ cup coarsely chopped
  almonds

1 tablespoon snipped fresh
  parsley

1. Cook pea pods in boiling lightly salted water for 2 minutes. Drain and set aside.

2. Meanwhile, season one side of fish with salt and pepper. Heat a large skillet over medium–high heat. When hot (a drop of water should sizzle or roll), remove skillet from heat and carefully add oil, tilting pan to coat with oil. Return pan to heat and add fish, seasoned side up, in a single layer. Cook fish for 4 to 5 minutes or until it is easy to lift with a spatula. Gently turn fish and cook for 2 to 3 minutes more or until fish flakes easily when tested with a fork. Arrange peas on a serving platter; top with fish. Cover and keep warm.

3. Reduce heat to medium. Add butter to skillet. When butter begins to melt, stir in almonds. Cook for 30 to 60 seconds or until butter is melted and nuts are lightly toasted (do not let butter burn). Spoon nuts and butter over fish. Sprinkle with parsley.

8 g carbs   **3** g fiber   **5** g net carbs

Nutrition Facts per serving: 277 cal., 17 g total fat (4 g sat. fat),
16 mg chol., 251 mg sodium, 8 g carbo., 3 g fiber, 22 g pro.

Snapper Veracruz

Start to Finish: 30 minutes Makes: 6 servings

1. Thaw fish, if frozen. Rinse fish; pat dry. Cut fish into 6 serving-size pieces, if necessary. Sprinkle fish with ⅛ teaspoon *salt* and ⅛ teaspoon *black pepper*.

2. In a large skillet cook onion and garlic in hot oil until onion is tender. Stir in tomatoes, olives, wine, capers, chile peppers, and bay leaf. Bring to boiling. Add fish to skillet. Return to boiling; reduce heat. Simmer, uncovered, for 6 to 10 minutes or until fish flakes easily when tested with a fork.

3. Using a slotted spatula, carefully transfer fish to a serving platter. Cover and keep warm.

4. Continue simmering sauce in skillet for 5 to 6 minutes or until reduced to about 2 cups, stirring occasionally. Discard bay leaf. Spoon sauce over fish. If desired, sprinkle with some parsley.

1½ pounds fresh or frozen skinless red snapper or other fish fillets

1 large onion, sliced and separated into rings

2 cloves garlic, minced

1 tablespoon cooking oil

2 cups chopped tomatoes (2 medium)

¼ cup sliced pimiento-stuffed green olives

¼ cup dry white wine

2 tablespoons capers, drained

1 to 2 fresh jalapeño chile peppers or serrano chile peppers, seeded and chopped, or 1 to 2 canned jalapeño chile peppers, rinsed, drained, seeded, and chopped (see tip, page 59)

1 bay leaf

Snipped fresh parsley (optional)

6 g carbs   **1** g fiber   **5** g net carbs

Nutrition Facts per serving: 177 cal., 6 g total fat (1 g sat. fat), 41 mg chol., 361 mg sodium, 6 g carbo., 1 g fiber, 25 g pro.

Poached Salmon with Dilled Sour Cream

Prep: 10 minutes Cook: 4 minutes Chill: 2 hours Makes: 6 servings

1½ pounds fresh or frozen skinless
      salmon fillets, about ½ inch thick

⅛ teaspoon ground white pepper

⅔ cup dry white wine

⅓ cup water

½ lemon, cut into thick slices

1 teaspoon coriander seeds

3 star anise or ½ teaspoon anise seeds

½ cup light dairy sour cream

1 tablespoon snipped fresh dill

1 tablespoon lime juice

   Salt and black pepper

1 head Bibb or Boston lettuce, torn
      into large pieces

   Fresh dill sprigs (optional)

   Cucumber slices

1. Thaw fish, if frozen. Rinse fish; pat dry. Cut into serving-size pieces, if necessary. Sprinkle fish with white pepper.

2. In a large skillet combine wine, water, lemon slices, coriander seeds, and star anise. Bring to boiling; reduce heat. Add fish in a single layer. Cover and simmer for 4 to 6 minutes or until fish flakes easily when tested with a fork. Using a slotted spatula, carefully transfer fish to a platter. Cover and chill for 2 hours or overnight.

3. In a small bowl combine sour cream, snipped dill, and lime juice. Add salt and black pepper to taste. Cover and chill for 1 hour or until serving time.

4. Arrange lettuce on 6 dinner plates. Top with fish. Spoon sour cream mixture over fish. Garnish with dill sprigs, if desired, and cucumber slices.

4g carbs   1g fiber   3g net carbs

Nutrition Facts per serving: 230 cal., 12 g total fat (3 g sat. fat),
76 mg chol., 118 mg sodium, 4 g carbo., 1 g fiber, 26 g pro.

Trout with Pepper Salad

Prep: 20 minutes Grill: 16 minutes Makes: 4 servings

1. Thaw fish, if frozen. Rinse fish; pat dry. Set aside.

2. In bowl toss sweet peppers with 1 tablespoon oil. For a charcoal grill, grill peppers on the rack of an uncovered grill directly over medium coals (see tip, below) for 8 to 10 minutes or until crisp-tender, turning once halfway through grilling. (For a gas grill, preheat grill. Reduce heat to medium. Place peppers on rack over heat. Cover; grill as above.) Cool peppers slightly; cut into strips. Return to bowl; stir in basil, capers, garlic, $\frac{1}{2}$ teaspoon salt, and $\frac{1}{8}$ teaspoon black pepper.

3. Spread fish open, skin side down. Season with $\frac{1}{2}$ teaspoon salt and $\frac{1}{4}$ teaspoon pepper. Place trout in a greased grill basket. Grill on rack of uncovered grill directly over medium coals (see tip, below) for 6 to 10 minutes or until fish flakes easily when tested with a fork, turning once halfway through grilling. Remove skin from trout and discard.

4. In a bowl toss spinach with 2 tablespoons oil and lemon juice. Divide spinach among 4 dinner plates. Arrange fish over spinach; top with sweet pepper mixture.

Tip: To test charcoal or gas grill temperatures: Hold your hand, palm side down, at cooking level and time how long you can comfortably keep it there. A hot fire allows a 2-second hand count, a medium-hot fire a 3-second hand count, a medium fire a 4-second hand count, and a low fire a 5-second hand count. When grilling indirectly, hot coals will provide medium-hot heat and medium-hot coals will provide medium heat.

4 8- to 10-ounce fresh or frozen
   pan-dressed trout

2 medium red, yellow, and/or green sweet
   peppers, halved and seeded

3 tablespoons olive oil

$\frac{1}{4}$ cup thinly sliced fresh basil leaves

1 tablespoon capers, drained

2 cloves garlic, minced

$\frac{1}{2}$ teaspoon salt

$\frac{1}{8}$ teaspoon black pepper

$\frac{1}{2}$ teaspoon salt

$\frac{1}{4}$ teaspoon black pepper

4 cups lightly packed torn fresh spinach

1 tablespoon lemon juice

6g carbs   **2**g fiber   **4**g net carbs

Nutrition Facts per serving: 429 cal., 23 g total fat (5 g sat. fat), 133 mg chol., 750 mg sodium, 6 g carbo., 2 g fiber, 49 g pro.

Pan-Dressed Trout with Lemon Butter

Prep: 15 minutes Grill: 8 minutes Makes: 4 servings

2 8- to 10-ounce fresh or frozen

pan-dressed* rainbow trout

4 teaspoons butter, softened

1 tablespoon finely chopped

shallots or onion

1 teaspoon finely shredded

lemon peel

Salt and coarsely ground

black pepper

1 tablespoon snipped

fresh rosemary

1 tablespoon lemon juice

2 teaspoons olive oil

2 medium tomatoes,

halved crosswise

Fresh parsley sprigs

1. Thaw fish, if frozen. Rinse fish; pat dry. Set aside. For lemon butter, in a small bowl combine butter, 1½ teaspoons of the shallots, and the lemon peel; season with salt and pepper. Set aside.

2. Rub remaining 1½ teaspoons shallots and the rosemary inside fish; sprinkle with additional salt and pepper and drizzle with lemon juice and oil. For a charcoal grill, grill fish on the greased rack of an uncovered grill directly over medium coals (see tip, page 107) for 8 to 10 minutes or until fish flakes easily when tested with a fork, turning once halfway through grilling.

3. Meanwhile, dot each tomato half with ¼ teaspoon of the lemon butter. Place tomatoes, cut side up, on grill rack. Grill about 5 minutes or until tomatoes are heated through. (For a gas grill, preheat grill. Reduce heat to medium. Place fish and tomatoes on greased grill rack over heat. Cover and grill as above.)

4. To serve, in a small saucepan melt remaining lemon butter. Drizzle butter mixture inside each fish. Garnish fish with parsley.

*Note: A pan-dressed fish has the scales and internal organs removed; often the head, fins, and tail have also been removed.

See photo, page 114.

4g carbs   **1**g fiber   **3**g net carbs

Nutrition Facts per serving: 206 cal., 10 g total fat (3 g sat. fat), 75 mg chol., 109 mg sodium, 4 g carbo., 1 g fiber, 24 g pro.

Grilled Blackened Redfish

Prep: 10 minutes Grill: 4 minutes Makes: 4 servings

1. Thaw fish, if frozen. Rinse fish; pat dry. Measure thickness of fish. Cut fish into 4 serving-size pieces, if necessary. In a small bowl combine onion powder, garlic powder, white pepper, cayenne pepper, black pepper, thyme, and salt. Brush fish with some of the melted butter. Coat fillets on both sides with pepper mixture.

2. Remove grill rack from charcoal grill. Place a 12-inch cast-iron skillet directly on hot coals. Heat about 5 minutes or until a drop of water sizzles in the skillet. Add fish to skillet; drizzle with remaining melted butter. Cook, uncovered, until fish flakes easily when tested with a fork, turning once halfway through grilling. Allow 2 to 3 minutes per side for $^1/_2$- to $^3/_4$-inch fillets (3 to 4 minutes per side for 1-inch fillets).

1 **pound fresh or frozen skinless redfish or red snapper fillets**

$^1/_2$ **teaspoon onion powder**

$^1/_2$ **teaspoon garlic powder**

$^1/_2$ **teaspoon ground white pepper**

$^1/_2$ **teaspoon cayenne pepper**

$^1/_2$ **teaspoon black pepper**

$^1/_2$ **teaspoon dried thyme, crushed**

$^1/_4$ **teaspoon salt**

3 **tablespoons butter, melted**

1g carbs   **0**g fiber   **1**g net carbs

Nutrition Facts per serving: 194 cal., 10 g total fat (2 g sat. fat), 42 mg chol., 151 mg sodium, 1 g carbo., 0 g fiber, 24 g pro.

Red Snapper with Pepper & Fennel

Prep: 25 minutes Bake: 4 minutes Oven: 450°F Makes: 4 servings

1 pound fresh or frozen skinless
   red snapper fillets, about
   ½ inch thick
1 cup sliced fennel bulb
½ cup chopped onion (1 medium)
½ cup chopped red sweet
   pepper (1 small)
2 cloves garlic, minced
1 tablespoon olive oil
¼ cup dry white wine or
   chicken broth
1 tablespoon snipped fresh dill
   or 1 teaspoon dried dill
¼ teaspoon salt
¼ teaspoon black pepper
   Fresh dill sprigs (optional)

1. Thaw fish, if frozen. Rinse fish; pat dry. Cut fish into 4 serving-size pieces, if necessary. In a large skillet cook and stir fennel, onion, sweet pepper, and garlic in hot oil over medium heat for 5 to 7 minutes or until vegetables are tender and lightly browned. Remove from heat. Stir in wine, dill, salt, and black pepper.

2. Spoon about 1 cup of the vegetable mixture into a 2-quart square baking dish. Place fish on top of vegetables, turning under thin edges. Spoon remaining vegetable mixture over top of fish.

3. Bake, uncovered, in a 450° oven for 4 to 6 minutes or until fish flakes easily when tested with a fork. Transfer fish and vegetables to dinner plates. If desired, garnish with dill sprigs.

See photo, page 115.

5 g carbs   **1** g fiber   **4** g net carbs

Nutrition Facts per serving: 182 cal., 6 g total fat (1 g sat. fat), 41 mg chol., 255 mg sodium, 5 g carbo., 1 g fiber, 24 g pro.

Flounder & Vegetables en Papillote

Prep: 15 minutes Bake: 10 minutes Oven: 450°F Makes: 2 servings

1. Thaw fish, if frozen. Rinse fish; pat dry. Set aside. Fold each sheet of parchment paper in half lengthwise. Then cut each folded sheet in a half-heart shape that is 6 inches longer and 2 inches wider than the fish fillets. (The fold will be the center of the heart.)

2. Open each paper heart. Place one fish fillet on the right half of each heart, turning under thin edges. Sprinkle fish with salt and black pepper. Stir together cream cheese and cilantro; spoon over fish. Top with sweet pepper and onion rings.

3. To seal, fold the left half of the paper hearts over the fish, matching edges. Starting at the top of the hearts, seal the packets by folding the edges together in a double fold. Fold only a small section at a time to ensure a tight seal. Then twist the bottom tip of the hearts to close the packets.

4. Place packets on an ungreased baking sheet. Bake in a 450° oven about 10 minutes or until paper puffs up and fish flakes easily when tested with a fork (carefully open the paper to check doneness). Transfer the packets to plates.

5. To serve, cut a large × on the top of each packet, then pull back the paper. Serve with lime wedges.

2 4-ounce fresh or frozen skinless flounder or sole fillets, about ¼ inch thick

2 15×12-inch pieces parchment paper

Salt and black pepper

2 tablespoons cream cheese, softened

1 tablespoon snipped fresh cilantro or parsley

¼ cup chopped green or red sweet pepper

1 onion, thinly sliced and separated into rings

2 lime or lemon wedges

4g carbs   **1**g fiber   **3**g net carbs

Nutrition Facts per serving: 169 cal., 6 g total fat (4 g sat. fat), 70 mg chol., 283 mg sodium, 4 g carbo., 1 g fiber, 23 g pro.

111

Halibut with Pepper Salsa

Prep: 25 minutes   Broil: 8 minutes   Makes: 4 servings

3 tablespoons rice vinegar

2 tablespoons soy sauce

½ teaspoon grated fresh ginger

¾ cup coarsely chopped and seeded
   red and/or yellow sweet pepper
   (1 medium)

½ cup chopped, seeded cucumber

2 tablespoons thinly sliced green onion

2 tablespoons snipped fresh cilantro

½ of a small jalapeño chile pepper,
   seeded and finely chopped (see
   tip, page 59)

4 4-ounce fresh or frozen halibut
   steaks, ¾ to 1 inch thick

1 teaspoon sesame seeds

Chinese cabbage leaves (optional)

1. For sweet pepper salsa, in a small bowl combine vinegar, soy sauce, and ginger. In another small bowl combine 2 tablespoons of vinegar mixture and ⅛ teaspoon *black pepper*; set aside. To the remaining vinegar mixture, add sweet pepper, cucumber, green onion, cilantro, and jalapeño pepper; toss to coat. Cover and chill up to 1 hour.

2. Thaw fish, if frozen. Rinse fish; pat dry. Preheat broiler. Place fish on the greased unheated rack of a broiler pan. Brush steaks with the reserved 2 tablespoons vinegar mixture. Sprinkle with sesame seeds. Broil 4 inches from the heat for 4 to 6 minutes per ½-inch thickness or until fish flakes easily when tested with a fork. (If steaks are 1 inch thick, turn once halfway through broiling.) If desired, line serving plates with Chinese cabbage leaves. Place fish on cabbage leaves and serve with sweet pepper salsa.

See photo, page 113.

3g carbs   **1**g fiber   **2**g net carbs

Nutrition Facts per serving: 150 cal., 3 g total fat (0 g sat. fat),
36 mg chol., 525 mg sodium, 3 g carbo., 1 g fiber, 25 g pro.

Halibut
with Pepper
Salsa
p. 112

Pan-
Dressed
Trout with
Lemon Butt
p. 108

Red Snapper with Pepper & Fennel p. 110

Grilled
Bass with
Strawberry
Salsa
p. 125

Salmon
with Herb
Crust
p. 136

Wasabi
Glazed
Whitefish with
Vegetable
Slaw
p. 140

Shrimp
Salsa Verde
p. 149

Fish
Kabobs
p. 121

Fish Kabobs

Prep: 10 minutes Marinate: 30 minutes Grill: 8 minutes Makes: 6 servings

1. Thaw fish, if frozen. Rinse fish; pat dry. Remove bones and skin, if necessary. Cut fish into 1-inch cubes. Place fish in a plastic bag set in a shallow dish.

2. For marinade, in a bowl combine lemon juice, oil, bay leaf, dill, black pepper, and hot pepper sauce. Pour over fish; seal bag. Marinate in refrigerator 30 minutes, turning bag once.

3. Drain fish, reserving marinade. On 6 long metal skewers, alternately thread the fish, cucumber, mushrooms, red sweet peppers, and olives. Brush with some of the reserved marinade.

4. For a charcoal grill, place kabobs on the greased rack of an uncovered grill directly over medium coals (see tip, page 107) for 8 to 12 minutes or until fish flakes easily when tested with a fork, turning and brushing once with reserved marinade halfway through grilling. (For a gas grill, preheat grill. Reduce heat to medium. Place kabobs on greased grill rack over heat. Cover and grill as above.)

See photo, page 120.

2 pounds fresh or frozen halibut, salmon, or swordfish steaks, 1 inch thick

½ cup lemon juice

⅓ cup olive oil

1 bay leaf

1 tablespoon snipped fresh dill

¼ teaspoon black pepper

Several drops bottled hot pepper sauce

1 large cucumber or zucchini, halved lengthwise and cut into ¾-inch slices

12 small to medium button mushrooms

½ of a 12-ounce jar roasted red sweet peppers, drained and cut into 1-inch pieces

12 pimiento-stuffed green olives

4g carbs   **1**g fiber   **3**g net carbs

Nutrition Facts per serving: 230 cal., 9 g total fat (1 g sat. fat), 48 mg chol., 241 mg sodium, 4 g carbo., 1 g fiber, 33 g pro.

121

Asian Spiced Red Snapper

Prep: 30 minutes Cook: 15 minutes Makes: 4 servings

2 1¼-pound fresh or frozen whole dressed or pan-dressed* red snapper or whitefish

1 tablespoon fish sauce

1 teaspoon finely shredded lemon peel

1 clove garlic, minced

2 tablespoons toasted sesame oil

1 tablespoon soy sauce

1 tablespoon rice vinegar

⅛ teaspoon ground ginger

Dash cayenne pepper

3 cups shredded lettuce

½ cup thinly sliced green onions (4)

1. Thaw fish, if frozen. Rinse and pat dry. Score fish by making 4 diagonal cuts on the top sides, slicing almost to the bone; set aside. In a small bowl combine fish sauce, lemon peel, and garlic; set aside.

2. Place the fish in a greased 12-inch steamer basket. Place basket into a large, deep saucepan or wok over 1 inch of boiling water. Brush fish sauce mixture over fish. Cover and steam for 15 to 20 minutes or until fish flakes easily when tested with a fork.

3. Meanwhile, in a screw-top jar combine sesame oil, soy sauce, rice vinegar, ginger, and cayenne pepper. Cover and shake well; set aside. In a medium bowl combine lettuce and green onions.

4. Transfer fish to a serving platter. Drizzle with 1 tablespoon of the sesame oil mixture. Pour remaining sesame oil mixture over lettuce mixture; toss to coat. Spoon lettuce mixture around fish on serving platter.

*Note: A pan-dressed fish has the scales and internal organs removed; often the head, fins, and tail have also been removed.

3g carbs   **1**g fiber   **2**g net carbs

Nutrition Facts per serving: 385 cal., 14 g total fat (2 g sat. fat), 103 mg chol., 825 mg sodium, 3 g carbo., 1 g fiber, 61 g pro.

Whitefish with Creamy Morel & Port Sauce

Prep: 30 minutes Cook: 6 minutes Makes: 4 servings

1. Thaw fish, if frozen. Rinse fish; pat dry. Set aside. For the sauce, halve or coarsely chop the mushrooms. In a medium saucepan melt the butter over medium heat. Add mushrooms and shallots; cook and stir until all of the liquid has cooked out of the mushrooms and the shallots are tender. Add the port wine; boil the mixture gently for 1 minute.

2. Stir in the cream and thyme; bring to boiling. Boil gently about 10 minutes or until sauce is reduced to $1\frac{1}{4}$ cups. Stir in capers; season with salt and pepper. Remove from heat; keep warm.

3. Season fish with additional salt and pepper. In a large skillet heat oil over medium heat. Add fish; cook until fish is golden brown and flakes easily when tested with a fork, carefully turning once halfway through cooking. Allow 3 to 4 minutes per side for $\frac{1}{2}$-inch fillets (5 to 6 minutes per side for 1-inch fillets).

4. Transfer the fish to warm dinner plates; spoon the mushroom sauce over the fish.

*Note: If using dried morel mushrooms, rehydrate the mushrooms according to package directions; drain the liquid and use mushrooms as directed.

4 4-ounce fresh or frozen skinless whitefish fillets or walleye fillets

1 cup fresh morel or button mushrooms or ½ cup dried morel mushrooms*

2 tablespoons butter

1 tablespoon finely chopped shallots

2 tablespoons port wine

1 cup whipping cream

½ teaspoon snipped fresh thyme

1 tablespoon capers, drained

Salt and black pepper

2 tablespoons cooking oil

4_g carbs · 0_g fiber · 4_g net carbs

Nutrition Facts per serving: 495 cal., 42 g total fat (19 g sat. fat), 160 mg chol., 335 mg sodium, 4 g carbo., 0 g fiber, 24 g pro.

Grilled Swordfish with Spicy Tomato Sauce

Prep: 15 minutes Grill: 8 minutes Makes: 4 servings

1¼ pounds fresh swordfish steaks,
   1 inch thick

4 teaspoons cooking oil

¼ teaspoon salt

¼ teaspoon black pepper

¼ cup chopped onion

1 small serrano chile pepper or
   jalapeño chile pepper, seeded
   and finely chopped (see tip, page 59)

1 clove garlic, minced

½ teaspoon ground turmeric

¼ teaspoon ground coriander

1½ cups chopped plum tomatoes
   (4 large)

¼ teaspoon salt

1 tablespoon snipped fresh cilantro

1. Rinse fish; pat dry. Cut into 4 serving-size pieces, if necessary. Drizzle 2 teaspoons of the oil over fish. Sprinkle with ¼ teaspoon salt and the black pepper. For a charcoal grill, grill fish on the greased rack of an uncovered grill directly over medium coals (see tip, page 107) for 8 to 12 minutes or until fish flakes easily when tested with a fork, turning once halfway through grilling. (For a gas grill, preheat grill. Reduce heat to medium. Place fish on greased grill rack over heat. Cover and grill as above.)

2. Meanwhile, for the spicy tomato sauce, in a skillet heat the remaining oil over medium heat. Add onion, chile pepper, garlic, turmeric, and coriander; cook and stir about 2 minutes or until onion is tender. Stir in tomatoes and ¼ teaspoon salt; cook and stir for 2 to 3 minutes or until tomatoes are just tender. Remove from heat; stir in cilantro. Serve sauce over fish.

5g
carbs

1g
fiber

4g
net carbs

Nutrition Facts per serving: 237 cal., 11 g total fat (2 g sat. fat),
56 mg chol., 402 mg sodium, 5 g carbo., 1 g fiber, 29 g pro.

Grilled Bass with Strawberry Salsa

Start to Finish: 30 minutes Makes: 4 servings

1. Thaw fish, if frozen. Rinse fish; pat dry. Finely shred lime peel. Peel, section, and chop lime; set aside. In a small bowl combine lime peel, ¼ teaspoon salt, and the cayenne pepper. Rub onto both sides of fish.

2. For a charcoal grill, arrange medium-hot coals (see tip, page 107) around a drip pan. Place fish on the greased grill rack over drip pan. Cover and grill for 7 to 9 minutes per ½-inch thickness or until fish flakes easily when tested with a fork, gently turning once halfway through grilling. (For a gas grill, preheat grill. Reduce heat to medium. Adjust for indirect cooking. Place fish on greased grill rack. Cover and grill as above.)

3. Meanwhile, in a medium bowl combine chopped lime, strawberries, poblano pepper, cilantro, cumin seeds, and ⅛ teaspoon salt. Serve with grilled fish.

*To toast cumin seeds: In a small skillet heat cumin seeds over medium heat until fragrant, shaking the pan occasionally.

See photo, page 116.

4 4- to 5-ounce fresh or frozen
    sea bass or halibut steaks,
    about 1 inch thick

1 small lime

¼ teaspoon salt

¼ teaspoon cayenne pepper

1 cup chopped strawberries

¼ cup finely chopped seeded
    fresh poblano chile pepper
    (½ of a small) (see tip, page 59)

2 tablespoons snipped fresh cilantro

½ teaspoon cumin seeds, toasted*

⅛ teaspoon salt

7 g carbs **1** g fiber **6** g net carbs

Nutrition Facts per serving: 137 cal., 3 g total fat (1 g sat. fat),
46 mg chol., 299 mg sodium, 7 g carbo., 1 g fiber, 22 g pro.

Grilled Grouper with Ham & Pepper Relish

Prep: 25 minutes Marinate: 30 minutes Grill: 4 minutes per half-inch thickness Makes: 4 servings

1½ pounds fresh or frozen skinless grouper or catfish fillets

1 tablespoon snipped fresh thyme or 1 teaspoon dried thyme, crushed

1 tablespoon olive oil

2 teaspoons olive oil

¼ cup chopped cooked ham

¼ cup chopped red sweet pepper

3 tablespoons chopped onion

3 tablespoons chopped celery

2 tablespoons snipped fresh chives

2 tablespoons snipped fresh parsley

Lemon wedges (optional)

Fresh thyme sprigs (optional)

1. Thaw fish, if frozen. Rinse fish; pat dry. Cut fish into 4 serving-size pieces, if necessary. Place fish in a shallow baking dish. In a small bowl combine thyme, 1 tablespoon olive oil, 2 to 3 teaspoons freshly *cracked black pepper*, and ¼ teaspoon *salt*. Rub onto both sides of fish. Cover and refrigerate for 30 minutes.

2. Meanwhile, for relish, in a medium skillet heat the 2 teaspoons olive oil over medium heat. Add ham, sweet pepper, onion, and celery to skillet. Cook and stir for 3 to 5 minutes or until ham is browned and vegetables are crisp-tender. Transfer mixture to a medium bowl. Stir in chives and parsley. Season with *salt*. Cool to room temperature.

3. Place fish in a greased grill basket. For a charcoal grill, place on grill rack of an uncovered grill directly over medium coals (see tip, page 107) for 4 to 6 minutes per ½-inch thickness or until fish flakes easily when tested with a fork, turning basket once halfway through grilling. (For a gas grill, preheat grill. Reduce heat to medium. Place basket on grill rack over heat. Cover and grill as above.)

4. Serve grilled fish with relish. If desired, garnish with lemon wedges and thyme sprigs.

3 g carbs   **1** g fiber   **2** g net carbs

Nutrition Facts per serving: 228 cal., 8 g total fat (1 g sat. fat), 67 mg chol., 480 mg sodium, 3 g carbo., 1 g fiber, 35 g pro.

Seafood Skewers

Prep: 20 minutes Marinate: 2 hours Grill: 8 minutes Makes: 6 servings

1. Rinse fish; pat dry. Cut fish into 1-inch cubes; set aside. Thaw shrimp, if frozen. Peel and devein shrimp, leaving tails intact. Rinse shrimp; pat dry. Set aside. Cut off and discard upper stalks of fennel, reserving some of the leafy fronds. Snip 2 tablespoons of the fronds for use in the marinade. Discard any wilted outer layers on fennel bulbs; cut off a thin slice from each base. Wash fennel and pat dry. Cut each bulb lengthwise into 6 wedges; remove core. Cook wedges, covered, in a small amount of boiling water about 5 minutes or until crisp-tender; drain.

2. Place fennel wedges, fish cubes, and shrimp in a plastic bag set in a deep bowl. For marinade, in a small bowl combine oil, lemon juice, garlic, oregano, salt, and 2 tablespoons of the snipped fennel fronds. Add marinade; seal bag. Marinate in the refrigerator for 2 hours, turning occasionally.

3. Drain seafood and fennel, discarding marinade. On 6 long metal skewers, alternately thread fennel wedges, fish, and shrimp. For a charcoal grill, place kabobs on the greased rack of an uncovered grill directly over medium coals (see tip, page 107) for 8 to 12 minutes or until fish flakes easily when tested with a fork, turning once halfway through grilling. (For a gas grill, preheat grill. Reduce heat to medium. Place kabobs on greased grill rack over heat. Cover and grill as above.)

1 pound fresh skinless fish fillets,
   1 inch thick (choose from
   salmon, halibut, sea bass, and/or
   red snapper)
8 ounces fresh or frozen medium
   shrimp in shells
2 medium fennel bulbs
¼ cup olive oil
3 tablespoons lemon juice
4 cloves garlic, minced
3 tablespoons snipped fresh oregano
¼ teaspoon salt

8g carbs   **2**g fiber   **6**g net carbs

Nutrition Facts per serving: 288 cal., 18 g total fat (3 g sat. fat), 102 mg chol., 239 mg sodium, 8 g carbo., 2 g fiber, 24 g pro.

Chilled Salmon with Lemon-Dill Mayonnaise

Prep: 30 minutes Cook: 10 minutes Chill: 4 hours Makes: 6 serving

¼ cup lemon juice

½ cup sliced onion (1 medium)

½ teaspoon salt

¼ teaspoon whole black peppercorns

2 bay leaves

6 6- to 8-ounce salmon steaks,
   about 1 inch thick

1 cup mayonnaise

⅓ cup whipping cream

2 tablespoons snipped fresh parsley

1 tablespoon snipped fresh dill or
   ½ teaspoon dried dill

1 teaspoon shredded lemon peel

1 tablespoon lemon juice

1 clove garlic, minced

1. In a 12-inch skillet, combine 2 cups of water, ¼ cup lemon juice, the onion, salt, peppercorns, and bay leaves. Bring to boiling; add the salmon steaks.

2. Return just to boiling. Simmer, covered, for 10 to 14 minutes or until fish flakes easily when tested with a fork. Using a slotted spatula carefully transfer fish to a storage container or a tray. Cool slightly. Cover and chill at least 4 hours or up to 8 hours.

3. For sauce, in a medium bowl combine mayonnaise, cream, parsley, dill, lemon peel, the 1 tablespoon lemon juice, and the garlic in a medium bowl. Cover and chill until ready to serve.

4. To serve, arrange fish on a platter. Spoon some of the sauce over the fish; if desired, garnish with *dill sprigs.* Pass remaining sauce.

1 g carbs

0 g fiber

1 g net carbs

Nutrition Facts per serving: 635 cal., 49 g total fat (11 g sat. fat), 165 mg chol., 580 mg sodium, 1 g carbo., 0 g fiber, 47 g pro.

Tuna with Pepper Mayonnaise

Prep: 15 minutes   Marinate: 30 minutes   Grill: 8 minutes   Makes: 4 servings

1. Thaw fish, if frozen. Rinse fish; pat dry. For marinade, in a blender container or food processor bowl combine onion, oil, 1 tablespoon of the lemon juice, and the lemon-pepper seasoning. Cover and blend or process until smooth. Place fish in a plastic bag set in a shallow dish. Add marinade; seal bag. Turn fish to coat. Marinate in the refrigerator for 30 minutes, turning bag occasionally.

2. Meanwhile, in a small bowl combine mayonnaise, sour cream, jalapeño peppers, half-and-half, lemon peel, the 1 teaspoon lemon juice, salt, and black pepper. Cover and chill until ready to serve.

3. Drain fish, discarding marinade. For a charcoal grill, grill fish on the greased rack of an uncovered grill directly over medium coals (see tip, page 107) for 4 to 6 minutes per $\frac{1}{2}$-inch thickness or until fish flakes easily when tested with a fork, turning once halfway through grilling. (For a gas grill, preheat grill. Reduce heat to medium. Place fish on greased grill rack over heat. Cover and grill as above.)

4. To serve, arrange fish on romaine leaves. Spoon mayonnaise mixture over fish; if desired, sprinkle with fresh cilantro.

To broil fish: Place drained tuna on greased unheated rack of a broiler pan. Broil 3 to 4 inches from heat for 4 to 6 minutes per $\frac{1}{2}$-inch thickness, turning once halfway through broiling.

4 6-ounce fresh or frozen tuna steaks, 1 inch thick

1 small onion, cut up

2 tablespoons olive oil

1 tablespoon lemon juice

$\frac{1}{2}$ teaspoon lemon-pepper seasoning

$\frac{1}{4}$ cup mayonnaise

$\frac{1}{4}$ cup dairy sour cream

1 or 2 red or green jalapeño chile peppers, seeded and finely chopped (see tip, page 59)

2 tablespoons half-and-half or light cream

$\frac{1}{2}$ teaspoon finely shredded lemon peel

1 teaspoon lemon juice

$\frac{1}{8}$ teaspoon salt

$\frac{1}{8}$ teaspoon black pepper

4 romaine lettuce leaves

Snipped fresh cilantro (optional)

3g carbs   **1**g fiber   **2**g net carbs

Nutrition Facts per serving: 358 cal., 19 g total fat (4 g sat. fat), 94 mg chol., 301 mg sodium, 3 g carbo., 1 g fiber, 41 g pro.

Tarragon Sauced Fish & Asparagus

Prep: 20 minutes Grill: 15 minutes Makes: 4 servings

4 3- to 4-ounce fresh or frozen
   sole or flounder fillets, ¼ to
   ½ inch thick

2 tablespoons mayonnaise

2 tablespoons dairy sour cream

1 teaspoon snipped fresh
   tarragon or ¼ teaspoon
   dried tarragon, crushed

1 pound asparagus spears*
   Salt and black pepper

4 thin slices lemon

¼ cup thinly sliced green
   onions (2)

4 sprigs fresh tarragon
   Fresh tarragon sprigs
   (optional)

1. Thaw fish, if frozen. Rinse fish; pat dry. For sauce, in a small bowl combine mayonnaise, sour cream, and the 1 teaspoon tarragon. Cover and chill until serving time.

2. Snap off and discard woody bases from asparagus. If desired, scrape off scales. Cut asparagus into 4-inch pieces.

3. Tear off four 24×18-inch pieces of foil. Fold each in half crosswise to make 12×18-inch rectangles. Place a fillet on each piece of foil, turning under thin edges. Sprinkle each fillet lightly with salt and pepper and top with a lemon slice. Divide green onions and asparagus among fillets. Top each with a tarragon sprig. Bring up two opposite edges of foil and seal with double fold. Then fold remaining ends to completely enclose, leaving space for steam to build.

4. For a charcoal grill, grill packets on the rack of an uncovered grill directly over medium coals (see tip, page 107) about 15 minutes or until fish flakes easily when tested with a fork. (For a gas grill, preheat grill. Reduce heat to medium. Place packets on grill rack over heat. Cover and grill as above.) Serve fish with sauce. Garnish with additional tarragon sprigs, if desired.

*****Note:** Asparagus will be crisp-tender after grilling. If you like your asparagus more tender, precook in boiling lightly salted water for 1 to 2 minutes. Drain and proceed as above.

3 g carbs   **1** g fiber   **2** g net carbs

Nutrition Facts per 4: 151 cal., 8 g total fat (2 g sat. fat), 47 mg chol., 158 mg sodium, 3 g carbo., 1 g fiber, 16 g pro.

130

Grilled Shrimp Cocktail

Prep: 25 minutes Marinate: 30 minutes Grill: 8 minutes Makes: 4 appetizer servings

1. Thaw shrimp, if frozen. Peel and devein shrimp, leaving tails intact. Rinse shrimp; pat dry. Set aside.

2. In a small food processor bowl or a blender container combine tomato, tarragon, lemon juice, garlic, salt, and pepper. Cover and process or blend with several on/off turns until mixture is coarsely chopped. Remove half of mixture (about ⅓ cup) to a small bowl and set aside. Process or blend remaining mixture until nearly smooth.

3. Place shrimp in a plastic bag set in a shallow dish. Add the smooth tomato mixture; seal bag. Turn to coat. Marinate in the refrigerator for 30 to 45 minutes, turning the bag once. On 2 long metal skewers, thread shrimp, leaving about ¼ inch between shrimp.

4. For a charcoal grill, grill skewers on the rack of an uncovered grill directly over medium coals (see tip, page 107) for 8 to 10 minutes or until shrimp are opaque, turning once halfway through grilling. (For a gas grill, preheat grill. Reduce heat to medium. Place skewers on rack over heat. Cover and grill as above.) Remove shrimp from skewers and place them in a medium bowl. Add the reserved coarsely chopped tomato mixture; toss to coat. Serve in 4 cocktail glasses.

8 ounces fresh or frozen large shrimp in shells (10 to 16)

1 cup coarsely chopped seeded tomato (2 medium)

2 tablespoons fresh tarragon leaves

2 tablespoons lemon juice

3 large cloves garlic, minced

⅛ teaspoon salt

⅛ teaspoon black pepper

4g carbs   **1**g fiber   **3**g net carbs

Nutrition Facts per serving: 50 cal., 1 g total fat (0 g sat. fat), 65 mg chol., 147 mg sodium, 4 g carbo., 1 g fiber, 8 g pro.

Poached Salmon with Shrimp Sauce

Start to Finish: 40 minutes Makes: 6 servings

6 6-ounce fresh or frozen
   skinless salmon fillets

4 cups dry white wine or
   chicken broth

1 bay leaf

1 sprig fresh parsley

1 teaspoon dried thyme

2 whole peppercorns

½ cup finely chopped green onions (8)
   or shallots (3 medium)

8 tablespoons butter

2 cups whipping cream

1 8-ounce container button
   mushrooms, quartered

8 ounces peeled and deveined
   cooked small shrimp

1. Thaw fish, if frozen. Rinse fish; pat dry. Set aside. Add 3 cups of the wine to a fish poacher or large roasting pan that has a wire rack with handles.

2. Tie bay leaf, parsley, thyme, and peppercorns in a double-thick square piece of 100%-cotton cheesecloth; add to wine in pan. Stir in ½ teaspoon *salt*. Place pan over two burners on range top. Bring to boiling; reduce heat.

3. Grease wire rack; place fish on rack and lower into pan. Simmer, covered, for 6 to 10 minutes or until fish flakes easily when tested with a fork. remove fish; keep warm.

4. For sauce, in a skillet cook onions in 1 tablespoon of the butter until tender. Add the remaining 1 cup wine; season with *salt* and black *pepper*. Bring to boiling; reduce heat. Boil gently, uncovered, about 5 minutes or until sauce is reduced by half.

5. Reduce heat. Add cream; cook and stir for 7 minutes or until thickened. Whisk in 5 tablespoons butter, 1 tablespoon at a time, until melted. Remove from heat; keep warm.

6. In a skillet, cook and stir mushrooms in the remaining 2 tablespoons butter over medium heat 5 minutes or until mushrooms are tender and liquid has evaporated. Stir mushrooms and shrimp into sauce. Serve salmon with sauce.

4g carbs   **1**g fiber   **3**g net carbs

Nutrition Facts per serving: 787 cal., 64 g total fat (30 g sat. fat), 252 mg chol., 625 mg sodium, 4 g carbo., 1 g fiber, 42 g pro.

Lime-Steamed Salmon

Prep: 15 minutes Cook: 10 minutes Makes: 3 servings

1. Thaw fish, if frozen. Rinse fish; pat dry. Cut into 3 serving-size pieces, if necessary. Finely shred 2 teaspoons peel from the limes; set aside. Thinly slice limes and place in a steamer basket. Top with fish; set aside. In a small bowl combine reserved lime peel, the sesame oil, ginger, salt, and pepper. Brush over fish in basket.

2. Place steamer basket into a large, deep skillet or saucepan over 1 inch of boiling water. Cover and steam about 10 minutes or until fish flakes easily when tested with a fork. If desired, serve fish with lime wedges.

1 pound fresh or frozen skinless salmon fillet, about 1 inch thick

2 limes

2 tablespoons toasted sesame oil

1 tablespoon grated fresh ginger

⅛ teaspoon salt

⅛ teaspoon black pepper

Lime wedges (optional)

2g carbs

0g fiber

2g net carbs

Nutrition Facts per serving: 309 cal., 20 g total fat (3 g sat. fat), 80 mg chol., 200 mg sodium, 2 g carbo., 0 g fiber, 31 g pro.

Orange Roughy
with Puttanesca Sauce

Start to Finish: 30 minutes   Makes: 4 servings

1 pound fresh or frozen skinless
   orange roughy or cod fillets

1 teaspoon dried oregano, crushed

$\frac{1}{2}$ teaspoon coarsely ground
   black pepper

1 tablespoon olive oil

$1\frac{1}{3}$ cups chopped plum tomatoes
   (4 medium)

1 small onion, cut into thin wedges

$\frac{1}{4}$ cup sliced ripe olives, drained

$\frac{1}{4}$ cup dry white wine or
   chicken broth

1 tablespoon capers, drained

2 cloves garlic, minced

1. Thaw fish, if frozen. Rinse fish; pat dry. Cut into 4 serving-size pieces, if necessary. Measure thickness of fish. Sprinkle fish with $\frac{1}{2}$ teaspoon of the oregano and $\frac{1}{4}$ teaspoon of the pepper.

2. In a large skillet heat oil over medium heat. Add fish, seasoned side down, and cook for 2 minutes, turning once. Add tomatoes, onion, olives, wine, capers, garlic, and the remaining $\frac{1}{2}$ teaspoon oregano and $\frac{1}{4}$ teaspoon pepper. Bring to boiling; reduce heat. Simmer, covered, for 4 to 6 minutes per $\frac{1}{2}$-inch thickness of fish or until fish flakes easily when tested with a fork.

3. Using a slotted spatula, transfer fish to a serving platter; keep warm. Boil sauce in skillet, uncovered, for $1\frac{1}{2}$ to 2 minutes or until slightly thickened. Spoon sauce over fish.

5g carbs   **2**g fiber   **3**g net carbs

Nutrition Facts per serving: 152 cal., 6 g total fat (1 g sat. fat),
23 mg chol., 211 mg sodium, 5 g carbo., 2 g fiber, 18 g pro.

Sicilian-Style Swordfish

Prep: 20 minutes Broil: 8 minutes Makes: 4 servings

1. Thaw fish, if frozen. Preheat broiler. Rinse fish; pat dry. Cut into 4 serving–size pieces. In a small bowl combine garlic powder, crushed fennel seeds, lemon–pepper seasoning, salt, and crushed red pepper. Rub on both sides of each fish piece.

2. Preheat broiler. Place fish on the greased unheated rack of a broiler pan. Broil 4 inches from the heat for 8 to 12 minutes or until fish flakes easily when tested with a fork, turning once halfway through broiling. Serve with Sicilian Relish. If desired, garnish with basil sprigs.

Sicilian Relish: In a small bowl toss together ³/₄ cup chopped plum tomatoes (2 large); 3 tablespoons chopped pitted Sicilian or kalamata olives; 3 tablespoons snipped fresh basil; 2 teaspoons lemon juice; 2 cloves garlic, minced; and 2 teaspoons olive oil.

2 8- to 10-ounce fresh or frozen
   swordfish steaks, 1 inch thick

1 teaspoon garlic powder

³/₄ teaspoon fennel seeds,
   crushed

¹/₂ teaspoon lemon-pepper
   seasoning

¹/₄ teaspoon salt

¹/₀ teaspoon crushed red pepper

   Sicilian Relish (see recipe, left)

   Fresh basil sprigs (optional)

4g carbs **1**g fiber **3**g net carbs

Nutrition Facts per serving: 177 cal., 8 g total fat (2 g sat. fat),
43 mg chol., 457 mg sodium, 4 g carbo., 1 g fiber, 23 g pro.

Salmon with Herb Crust

Prep: 15 minutes Grill: 6 minutes Makes: 4 servings

12 ounces fresh or frozen salmon
fillets, ¾ inch thick

⅓ cup coarsely chopped
fresh oregano

⅓ cup coarsely chopped
fresh cilantro

¼ cup sliced green onions (2)

1 clove garlic

1 tablespoon lemon juice

2 teaspoons olive oil

¼ teaspoon salt

⅛ teaspoon black pepper

Cherry tomatoes, halved
(optional)

Fresh oregano sprigs
(optional)

1. Thaw salmon, if frozen. Rinse fish; pat dry. Cut into two 6-ounce pieces, if necessary; set aside.

2. In a food processor bowl combine oregano, cilantro, green onions, garlic, lemon juice, oil, salt, and pepper. Cover and process until evenly chopped. (Or use a knife to finely chop oregano, cilantro, green onion, and garlic. Transfer to a shallow bowl. Stir in lemon juice, oil, salt, and pepper.) Generously coat top of salmon with the herb mixture.

3. For a charcoal grill, grill fish, skin side down, on the rack of an uncovered grill directly over medium coals (see tip, page 107) for 6 to 8 minutes or until fish flakes easily when tested with a fork. (For a gas grill, preheat grill. Reduce heat to medium. Place fish on grill rack over heat. Cover and grill as above.) To serve, cut each salmon piece into 2 serving-size pieces. If desired, garnish with cherry tomatoes and oregano sprigs.

See photo, page 117.

2g
carbs

0g
fiber

2g
net carbs

Nutrition Facts per serving: 126 cal., 5 g total fat (1 g sat. fat),
44 mg chol., 207 mg sodium, 2 g carbo., 0 g fiber, 17 g pro.

Basil Halibut Steaks

Prep: 25 minutes Grill: 8 minutes Makes: 4 servings

1. Thaw fish, if frozen. Rinse fish; pat dry. Set aside. In a medium skillet cook and stir onion and garlic in hot oil over medium heat until tender. Stir in tomatoes, salt, and pepper. Bring to boiling; reduce heat. Simmer, uncovered, for 15 minutes. Stir in 2 tablespoons of the basil. Set aside.

2. Meanwhile, in a small bowl combine the remaining 2 tablespoons basil and the melted butter; brush over one side of the halibut steaks.

3. For a charcoal grill, grill fish, brushed side up, on the greased rack of an uncovered grill directly over medium coals (see tip, page 107) for 8 to 12 minutes or until fish flakes easily when tested with a fork, turning once halfway through grilling. (For a gas grill, preheat grill. Reduce heat to medium. Place fish on greased grill rack over heat. Cover and grill as above.)

4. If desired, season fish with additional salt and pepper. Serve with tomato mixture.

To broil: To broil: Place fish on the greased unheated rack of a broiler pan. Broil 4 inches from the heat for 8 to 12 minutes or until fish flakes easily when tested with a fork, turning once halfway through broiling.

1½ pounds fresh or frozen halibut steaks, 1 inch thick

½ cup chopped onion (1 medium)

1 clove garlic, minced

2 tablespoons olive oil

2 to 3 cups chopped, peeled tomatoes (4 to 6 medium)

¼ teaspoon salt

¼ teaspoon black pepper

4 tablespoons snipped fresh basil

1 tablespoon butter, melted

7 g carbs   **2** g fiber   **5** g net carbs

Nutrition Facts per serving: 302 cal., 14 g total fat (3 g sat. fat), 62 mg chol., 265 mg sodium, 7 g carbo., 2 g fiber, 37 g pro.

Broiled Fish Steaks with Tarragon Cheese Sauce

Prep: 10 minutes Broil: 6½ minutes Makes: 4 servings

1¼ pounds fresh or frozen

salmon, swordfish, or tuna

steaks, about ¾ inch thick

½ cup dairy sour cream

½ cup shredded mozzarella or

Monterey Jack cheese

2 teaspoons snipped fresh

tarragon or ½ teaspoon

dried tarragon, crushed

Salt

Black pepper

Fresh tarragon sprigs

(optional)

Red sweet pepper strips

(optional)

1. Thaw fish, if frozen. Rinse fish; pat dry. Cut fish into 4 serving-size pieces, if necessary.

2. In a small bowl combine sour cream, cheese, and tarragon. Set aside.

3. Preheat broiler. Place fish on the unheated rack of a broiler pan. Sprinkle fish with salt and black pepper. Broil 4 inches from the heat for 6 to 9 minutes or until fish flakes easily when tested with a fork, turning once halfway through broiling. Spoon sour cream mixture over fish. Broil for 30 to 60 seconds more or until heated through and cheese starts to melt. If desired, garnish with fresh tarragon sprigs and sweet pepper strips.

1 g carbs   **0** g fiber   **1** g net carbs

Nutrition Facts per serving: 288 cal., 17 g total fat (7 g sat. fat),
94 mg chol., 268 mg sodium, 1 g carbo., 0 g fiber, 33 g pro.

Flounder with Zucchini Relish

Prep: 15 minutes Bake: 4 minutes per ¹/₂-inch thickness
Oven: 450°F Makes: 4 servings

1. Thaw fish, if frozen. Rinse fish; pat dry. Cut into 4 serving-size pieces, if necessary. Measure thickness of fish. Set aside. For the zucchini relish, in a medium bowl combine zucchini, sweet pepper, onion, jalapeño pepper, white wine vinegar, 1 tablespoon olive oil, and ¹/₄ teaspoon of the salt. Set aside.

2. In a small bowl combine remaining ¹/₄ teaspoon salt, the cumin, and black pepper. Arrange fish in a single layer in a 15×10×1-inch baking pan, turning under thin edges. Sprinkle cumin mixture over fish. Drizzle with 1 tablespoon oil.

3. Bake in a 450° oven for 4 to 6 minutes per ¹/₂-inch thickness of fish or until fish flakes easily when tested with a fork.

4. Serve fish with zucchini relish and, if desired, tomato wedges.

1 pound fresh or frozen skinless
    flounder fillets

1¹/₄ cups chopped zucchini (1 medium)

¹/₂ cup chopped red sweet pepper
    (1 small)

¹/₄ cup finely chopped onion

1 small fresh jalapeño chile pepper,
    seeded and finely chopped
    (2 teaspoons) (see tip, page 59)

1 tablespoon white wine vinegar

1 tablespoon olive oil

¹/₂ teaspoon salt

¹/₄ teaspoon ground cumin

¹/₄ teaspoon black pepper

1 tablespoon olive oil

    Tomato wedges (optional)

4g carbs **1**g fiber **3**g net carbs

Nutrition Facts per serving: 170 cal., 8 g total fat (1 g sat. fat),
48 mg chol., 357 mg sodium, 4 g carbo., 1 g fiber, 21 g pro.

Wasabi-Glazed Whitefish with Vegetable Slaw

Prep: 15 minutes Grill: 6 minutes Makes: 4 servings

4 4-ounce fresh or frozen
   skinless whitefish fillets or
   other white-fleshed fish
   fillets, about ¾ inch thick

2 tablespoons soy sauce

¼ teaspoon wasabi powder or
   1 tablespoon prepared
   horseradish

1 teaspoon toasted sesame oil

1⅓ cups coarsely shredded
   zucchini (1 medium)

1 cup sliced radishes

1 cup fresh snow pea pods

3 tablespoons snipped fresh
   chives

3 tablespoons rice vinegar

1. Thaw fish, if frozen. Rinse fish; pat dry. In a small bowl combine soy sauce, wasabi powder, and ½ teaspoon of the sesame oil. Brush soy sauce mixture over fish. For a charcoal grill, grill fish on the lightly greased rack of an uncovered grill directly over medium coals (see tip, page 107) for 6 to 9 minutes or until fish flakes easily when tested with a fork, turning once halfway through grilling.

2. Meanwhile, for vegetable slaw, in a medium bowl combine the zucchini, radishes, pea pods, and 2 tablespoons of the chives. In a small bowl combine the remaining ½ teaspoon sesame oil and the vinegar. Drizzle over the zucchini mixture; toss to combine. Sprinkle remaining 1 tablespoon chives over cooked fish. Serve fish with vegetable slaw.

See photo, page 118.

4g
carbs

1g
fiber

3g
net carbs

Nutrition Facts per serving: 198 cal., 8 g total fat (2 g sat. fat),
62 mg chol., 539 mg sodium, 4 g carbo., 1 g fiber, 24 g pro.

Marinated Tuna Steaks

Prep: 10 minutes Marinate: 1 hour Grill: 8 minutes Makes: 4 servings

1. Thaw fish, if frozen. Rinse fish; pat dry. Set aside.

2. For marinade, in a small bowl combine wine, lemon juice, oil, garlic, rosemary, oregano, and salt. Place fish in plastic bag set in a shallow dish. Add marinade; seal bag. Turn fish to coat. Marinate in the refrigerator for at least 1 hour or up to 2 hours, turning bag once.

3. Drain fish, discarding marinade. For a charcoal grill, grill fish on the greased rack of an uncovered grill directly over medium coals (see tip, page 107) for 8 to 12 minutes or until fish flakes easily when tested with a fork, gently turning once halfway through grilling. (For a gas grill, preheat grill. Reduce heat to medium. Place fish on greased grill rack over heat. Cover and grill as above.) If desired, garnish with lemon slices and rosemary and/or oregano.

4 6-ounce fresh or frozen tuna steaks, 1 inch thick

$\frac{1}{3}$ cup dry white wine

1 tablespoon lemon juice

1 tablespoon olive oil or cooking oil

1 clove garlic, minced

2 teaspoons snipped fresh rosemary or $\frac{1}{2}$ teaspoon dried rosemary, crushed

1 teaspoon snipped fresh oregano or $\frac{1}{4}$ teaspoon dried oregano, crushed

$\frac{1}{4}$ teaspoon salt

Lemon slices (optional)

Fresh rosemary and/or oregano (optional)

0_g carbs 0_g fiber 0_g net carbs

Nutrition Facts per serving: 277 cal., 10 g total fat (2 g sat. fat), 71 mg chol., 106 mg sodium, 0 g carbo., 0 g fiber, 43 g pro.

White Wine-Marinated Fish

Prep: 10 minutes   Marinate: 30 minutes   Grill: 8 minutes   Makes: 4 servings

4   5- to 6-ounce fresh or

    frozen swordfish, shark, or

    halibut steaks, 1 inch thick

½   cup dry white wine

3   tablespoons olive oil or

    cooking oil

2   tablespoons snipped

    fresh parsley

1   tablespoon Worcestershire

    sauce for chicken

1   tablespoon snipped fresh

    sage, basil, or marjoram, or

    1 teaspoon dried sage, basil,

    or marjoram, crushed

⅛   teaspoon black pepper

1. Thaw fish, if frozen. Rinse fish; pat dry. For marinade, combine wine, oil, parsley, Worcestershire sauce, sage, and pepper. Place fish in a plastic bag set in a shallow dish. Add marinade; seal bag. Turn to coat. Marinate in the refrigerator for 30 minutes to 1 hour, turning the bag occasionally.

2. Drain fish, reserving marinade. For a charcoal grill, grill fish on the greased rack of an uncovered grill directly over medium coals (see tip, page 107) for 8 to 12 minutes or until fish flakes easily when tested with a fork, turning once and brushing once with reserved marinade halfway through grilling. (For a gas grill, preheat grill. Reduce heat to medium. Place fish on greased grill rack over heat. Cover and grill as above.)

1 g carbs   **0** g fiber   **1** g net carbs

Nutrition Facts per serving: 223 cal., 11 g total fat (2 g sat. fat),
56 mg chol., 144 mg sodium, 1 g carbo., 0 g fiber, 28 g pro.

Spicy Shrimp Boil

Prep: 20 minutes Cook: 25 minutes Stand: 5 minutes Makes: 4 servings

1. Thaw shrimp, if frozen. To devein shrimp, use a sharp knife to make a slit through shell along the back of each shrimp. Remove the back vein, if present. Rinse shrimp and pat dry. Cover and chill shrimp.

2. Meanwhile, in Dutch oven combine water, jalapeño slices, garlic, onion, lemon, salt, bay leaves, coriander seeds, mustard seeds, peppercorns, celery seeds, and hot pepper sauce. Bring to boiling; boil, uncovered, for 20 minutes. Add shrimp; return to boiling. Remove from heat. Cover and let stand for 5 minutes.

3. Drain shrimp in a large colander. Remove and discard lemon halves and bay leaves. Divide shrimp and any remaining spices among 4 serving bowls. If desired, serve with lemon wedges.

1½ pounds fresh or frozen large
    shrimp in shells

8 cups water

¼ cup pickled jalapeño chile pepper
    slices (see tip, page 59)

4 large garlic cloves, peeled

⅓ cup chopped onion (1 small)

1 lemon, halved

2 tablespoons kosher salt

2 bay leaves

2 teaspoons coriander seeds

2 teaspoons mustard seeds

2 teaspoons whole black peppercorns

1 teaspoon celery seeds

1 teaspoon bottled hot pepper sauce

    Lemon wedges (optional)

7 g carbs **2** g fiber **5** g net carbs

Nutrition Facts per serving: 166 cal., 3 g total fat (0 g sat. fat), 194 mg chol., 1,364 mg sodium, 7 g carbo., 2 g fiber, 27 g pro.

Fiesta Shrimp with Peppers & Jalapeños

Start to Finish: 35 minutes Makes: 10 servings

2 red sweet peppers

2 yellow sweet peppers

2 whole jalapeño chile peppers

   (see tip, page 59)

¾ teaspoon salt

¼ teaspoon freshly ground

   black pepper

2 pounds fresh or frozen peeled

   and deveined large shrimp

1 tablespoon olive oil

2 tablespoons minced garlic

3 tablespoons fresh lime juice

1 tablespoon chopped

   fresh cilantro

1. Preheat broiler. Cut off ½ inch from top and bottom of red and yellow sweet peppers; cut sweet peppers in half. Remove seeds and membranes. Place sweet pepper halves, skin side up, on the unheated rack of a broiler pan. Add whole jalapeño peppers to rack. Broil 4 inches from heat for 12 to 15 minutes or until evenly charred, turning jalapeño peppers occasionally. Cover and cool for 15 minutes. Peel off skin from all peppers and remove seeds from jalapeños. Slice all peppers into ¼-inch-thick strips. In a medium bowl combine pepper strips with ¼ teaspoon salt and ⅛ teaspoon black pepper. (Can be made ahead. Cover and refrigerate up to 2 days.)

2. Thaw shrimp, if frozen. Rinse shrimp; pat dry. Sprinkle shrimp with remaining ½ teaspoon salt and ⅛ teaspoon black pepper. In a 12-inch skillet heat oil over medium-high heat. Add shrimp and garlic; cook and stir for 3 to 4 minutes or until shrimp are opaque. Stir in lime juice and bring just to boiling. Transfer shrimp mixture to serving bowl. Cover and keep warm.

3. Cook peppers in same skillet for 2 to 3 minutes or until heated through. Add peppers and cilantro to shrimp; toss to combine. Serve immediately.

6 g carbs   **1** g fiber   **5** g net carbs

Nutrition Facts per serving: 129 cal., 3 g total fat (1 g sat. fat),
138 mg chol., 311 mg sodium, 6 g carbo., 1 g fiber, 19 g pro.

Lobster with Curried Dressing

Prep: 15 minutes Cook: 6 minutes Chill: 2 hours Makes: 2 servings

1. Thaw lobster, if frozen. Set aside. In a large saucepan bring water and salt to boiling. Add lobster. Return to boiling; reduce heat. Simmer, uncovered, for 6 to 10 minutes or until lobster shells turn bright red and meat is tender. Drain. Cover and chill at least 2 hours or up to 24 hours.

2. For curried dressing, in a small bowl combine mayonnaise, sour cream, parsley, lime juice, curry powder, and hot pepper sauce. Season to taste with salt and pepper. Cover and chill at least 2 hours or up to 24 hours.

3. To serve, place one lobster tail, shell side down, on each serving plate. With scissors, cut the lobster lengthwise. Serve with the dressing.

2   5-ounce fresh or frozen rock
      lobster tails

6   cups water

1½ teaspoons salt

2   tablespoons mayonnaise

2   tablespoons dairy sour cream

1   tablespoon snipped fresh
      parsley

1   teaspoon lime juice

½   teaspoon curry powder

    Dash bottled hot pepper sauce

    Salt and black pepper

2g carbs   **0**g fiber   **2**g net carbs

Nutrition Facts per serving: 206 cal., 14 g total fat (3 g sat. fat), 96 mg chol., 1,799 mg sodium, 2 g carbo., 0 g fiber, 17 g pro.

Spring Veggies & Scallops

Prep: 25 minutes Chill: 1 hour Makes: 2 main-dish servings

8 ounces fresh or frozen
    sea scallops

½ pound asparagus spears,
    trimmed and cut into
    2-inch pieces

1 cup fresh snow pea pods

1 teaspoon cooking oil

¼ cup dairy sour cream

½ teaspoon finely shredded
    lime peel

2 teaspoons lime juice

⅛ teaspoon cayenne pepper

6 Bibb lettuce leaves

1. Thaw scallops, if frozen. Rinse scallops; pat dry. Set aside. In a large saucepan bring a small amount of salted water to boiling. Add asparagus and pea pods. Cook, uncovered, for 2 to 3 minutes or until crisp-tender. Drain vegetables. Rinse in cold water; drain again. Cover and chill for 1 hour or until serving time.

2. In a medium nonstick skillet heat oil over medium-high heat. Add scallops; cook for 2 to 3 minutes or until scallops are opaque, turning once. Remove scallops from skillet; cover and chill for 1 hour or until serving time.

3. In a small bowl combine sour cream, lime peel, lime juice, and cayenne pepper. Cover and chill for 1 hour or until serving time.

4. Divide lettuce leaves between 2 dinner plates. Arrange chilled scallops and vegetables on lettuce leaves. Spoon sour cream mixture onto scallops and vegetables.

9 g carbs   **2** g fiber   **7** g net carbs

Nutrition Facts per serving: 219 cal., 9 g total fat (4 g sat. fat),
48 mg chol., 211 mg sodium, 9 g carbo., 2 g fiber, 23 g pro.

Skewered Scallops & Swordfish with Fennel

Prep: 20 minutes Marinate: 1 hour Broil: 9 minutes Makes: 4 servings

1. Thaw scallops and fish, if frozen. Rinse scallops and fish; pat dry. Cut fish into 1-inch cubes. Cook fennel in boiling water for 4 minutes; drain and cool.

2. For marinade, in a small bowl combine oil, lime juice, green onion, thyme, fennel seeds, salt, and black pepper. Place scallops, swordfish, sweet pepper, and mushrooms in a plastic bag set in a shallow dish. Add marinade; seal bag. Turn to coat. Marinate in the refrigerator for 1 hour, turning the bag occasionally.

3. Preheat broiler. Drain fish and vegetables, reserving marinade. On 8 long metal skewers, alternately thread scallops, swordfish, fennel, sweet pepper, and mushrooms, leaving about 1/4 inch between pieces. Place skewers on the greased unheated rack of a broiler pan. Broil 4 inches from the heat for 5 minutes. Turn kabobs over and brush with reserved marinade. Broil for 4 to 5 minutes more or until fish flakes easily when tested with a fork and scallops are opaque.

8 ounces fresh or frozen sea scallops

8 ounces fresh or frozen swordfish steaks,
   1 inch thick

1 fennel bulb, trimmed and cut into thin
   wedges

1/4 cup olive oil or cooking oil

2 tablespoons lime juice or lemon juice

2 tablespoons finely chopped green onion (1)

1 tablespoon snipped fresh thyme or
   1/2 teaspoon dried thyme, crushed

1 teaspoon fennel seeds, crushed

1/4 teaspoon salt

1/4 teaspoon black pepper

1 medium red sweet pepper, cut into
   1-inch squares

8 small button mushrooms

7 g carbs   **2** g fiber   **5** g net carbs

Nutrition Facts per serving: 270 cal., 17 g total fat (3 g sat. fat),
41 mg chol., 289 mg sodium, 7 g carbo., 2 g fiber, 23 g pro.

Spicy Cajun Shrimp

Prep: 20 minutes Broil: 3 minutes Makes: 8 appetizer servings

1 pound fresh or frozen large
   shrimp in shells

½ cup mayonnaise or
   salad dressing

2 tablespoons tomato paste

1 clove garlic, minced

1 tablespoon lemon juice

2 tablespoons butter, melted

4 teaspoons Cajun seasoning
   Lemon wedges and sage
   leaves (optional)

1. Thaw shrimp, if frozen. Peel and devein shrimp, leaving tails intact. Rinse shrimp; pat dry. Set aside.

2. In a small bowl combine mayonnaise, tomato paste, garlic, and lemon juice. Cover and chill until ready to serve.

3. Preheat broiler. On 8 long metal skewers thread shrimp, leaving about ¼ inch between shrimp. Brush both sides of shrimp with melted butter. Sprinkle both sides of shrimp with Cajun seasoning.

4. Preheat broiler. Place skewers on the unheated rack of a broiler pan. Broil 4 inches from the heat for 2 minutes. Turn skewers and broil for 1 to 2 minutes more or until shrimp are opaque. Remove shrimp from skewers, if desired, and serve with mayonnaise mixture. If desired, garnish with lemon wedges and sage leaves.

2 g carbs   **0** g fiber   **2** g net carbs

Nutrition Facts per serving: 181 cal., 15 g total fat (3 g sat. fat),
83 mg chol., 264 mg sodium, 2 g carbo., 0 g fiber, 9 g pro.

Shrimp Salsa Verde

Prep: 25 minutes Grill: 7 minutes Makes: 4 servings

1. Thaw shrimp, if frozen. Peel and devein shrimp, leaving tails intact, if desired. Rinse shrimp; pat dry. Set aside.

2. For salsa verde, in a blender container or food processor bowl combine mint, parsley, shallots, oil, anchovies, water, pepper, and salt. Cover and blend or process until smooth, stopping to scrape down sides, if necessary. Set aside.

3. On 4 long metal skewers, thread shrimp; brush shrimp with ¼ cup of the salsa verde. Cover remaining salsa; set aside.

4. For a charcoal grill, place the skewers on the rack of an uncovered grill directly over medium coals (see tip, page 107) for 7 to 9 minutes or until shrimp are opaque, turning once halfway through grilling. (For a gas grill, preheat grill. Reduce heat to medium. Place skewers on the grill rack over heat. Cover and grill as above.) Serve shrimp with remaining salsa verde.

Make-AheadTip: Salsa can be made up to 24 hours ahead. Cover and refrigerate. Remove from refrigerator 30 minutes before grilling.

See photo, page 119.

1 pound fresh or frozen large
  shrimp in shells
2 cups fresh mint leaves
1 cup fresh flat-leaf parsley
  leaves
2 medium shallots, peeled
  and quartered
¼ cup olive oil
3 anchovy fillets, drained
2 tablespoons water
¼ teaspoon black pepper
  Dash salt

5 g carbs **1** g fiber **4** g net carbs

Nutrition Facts per serving: 267 cal., 16 g total fat (2 g sat. fat), 175 mg chol., 325 mg sodium, 5 g carbo., 1 g fiber, 25 g pro.

149

Garlic & Herb Shrimp Saute

Start to Finish: 25 minutes Makes: 4 servings

1 pound fresh or frozen
　　large shrimp in shells

2 tablespoons olive oil

4 cloves garlic, minced

⅓ cup thinly sliced leek
　　(1 medium) or thinly sliced
　　green onions (3)

½ teaspoon dried basil, oregano,
　　or tarragon, crushed

2 tablespoons dry sherry or dry
　　white wine

1 tablespoon lemon juice

¼ teaspoon salt

¼ teaspoon black pepper

1 tablespoon snipped
　　fresh parsley

1. Thaw shrimp, if frozen. Peel and devein shrimp, leaving tails intact. Rinse shrimp; pat dry. Set aside.

2. In a large skillet heat oil over medium heat. Add shrimp, garlic, leek, and basil. Cook and stir for 2 to 4 minutes or until shrimp are opaque. Carefully add sherry, lemon juice, salt, and pepper to skillet. Cook and stir just until heated through. Stir in parsley.

4 g carbs   **0** g fiber   **4** g net carbs

Nutrition Facts per serving: 201 cal., 9 g total fat (1 g sat. fat),
172 mg chol., 316 mg sodium, 4 g carbo., 0 g fiber, 23 g pro.

Side Dishes

Fresh vegetables are exceptional when combined with fragrant herbs, aromatic spices, robust garlic, and pungent cheeses. Rich in flavor and packed with antioxidants and phytonutrients, they're an invaluable part of any phase 2 eating plan.

Spring Greens with Lemon Sauce

Start to Finish: 25 minutes Makes: 4 servings

1 pound baby broccoli and/or

    asparagus spears and/or

    snow pea pods

2 ounces mascarpone cheese

2 tablespoons dairy sour cream

2 tablespoons whipping cream

¾ teaspoon snipped fresh thyme

½ teaspoon finely shredded

    lemon peel

1½ teaspoon lemon juice

    Salt and ground white pepper

1. Remove strings and tips from pea pods, if using. In a Dutch oven or large saucepan bring a small amount of salted water to boiling. Add vegetables; cook, covered, until crisp-tender, about 5 to 7 minutes for baby broccoli, 3 to 5 minutes for asparagus, and 2 to 4 minutes for pea pods. Drain.

2. For the lemon sauce, in a small bowl combine mascarpone cheese, sour cream, milk, thyme, lemon peel, and lemon juice. Season sauce to taste with salt and white pepper. To serve, spoon lemon sauce over the hot vegetables.

6 g
carbs

2 g
fiber

4 g
net carbs

Nutrition Facts per serving: 125 cal., 11 g total fat (6 g sat. fat),
31 mg chol., 110 mg sodium, 6 g carbo., 2 g fiber, 5 g pro.

Steamed Red Chard

Start to Finish: 45 minutes Makes: 6 servings

1. Fill a 4-quart Dutch oven with water to a depth of 1 inch. Bring water to boiling. Place a steamer basket in the Dutch oven. Place one-third of the chard in the steamer basket. Cover and steam for 5 minutes or until chard is tender. Remove chard from steamer basket and place in a colander to drain; set aside. Repeat with remaining chard.

2. In the same Dutch oven cook and stir onions in hot oil over medium heat until tender but not brown. Add steamed chard, vinegar, salt, and pepper. Cook and stir until heated through.

3 pounds red Swiss chard, stems removed and leaves cut crosswise into ½-inch-wide strips

1 cup chopped onions (2 medium)

2 tablespoons olive oil

¼ cup sherry vinegar or red wine vinegar

½ teaspoon salt

½ teaspoon black pepper

11g carbs **4**g fiber **7**g net carbs

Nutrition Facts per serving: 91 cal., 5 g total fat (1 g sat. fat), 0 mg chol., 617 mg sodium, 11 g carbo., 4 g fiber, 4 g pro.

Roasted Vegetable Antipasto Platter

Prep: 20 minutes Chill: 2 hours Roast: 45 minutes Oven: 425°F Makes: 6 servings

2 4-ounce logs soft goat cheese (chèvre)

¼ cup snipped fresh parsley

¼ cup snipped fresh basil

3 tablespoons finely chopped pine nuts, toasted

3 medium red sweet peppers, halved lengthwise, stems, seeds, and membranes removed

1 large zucchini (12 ounces), bias-sliced ¼ inch thick

1 small eggplant (12 ounces), peeled, quartered lengthwise, and cut crosswise in ½-inch pieces

¾ cup pitted green or ripe olives

1. In a small bowl, combine goat cheese, parsley, snipped basil, and ¼ teaspoon black pepper. Shape mixture into a 6-inch log. Place nuts in a shallow dish or on a sheet of waxed paper. Roll cheese log in nuts to coat. Wrap cheese log in plastic wrap. Chill for 2 hours.

2. Meanwhile, place sweet pepper halves, cut side down, on a foil-lined baking sheet. Roast in a 425° oven for 20 to 25 minutes or until skins are blistered and slightly charred. Carefully bring the foil up and around the sweet pepper halves to enclose. Set aside.

3. In a roasting pan toss together zucchini, eggplant, 2 tablespoons *olive oil,* ½ teaspoon *salt,* and ¼ teaspoon *black pepper.* Roast, uncovered, in a 425° oven for 25 to 30 minutes or until tender, stirring once. Remove from oven; cool mixture to room temperature. Use a sharp knife to gently and slowly pull off the sweet pepper skins; discard skins. Cut sweet peppers into 1-inch strips.

4. On a large serving platter, arrange eggplant mixture, sweet pepper strips, cheese log, and olives.

9 g carbs   **4** g fiber   **5** g net carbs

Nutrition Facts per serving: 223 cal., 18 g total fat (7 g sat. fat), 17 mg chol., 747 mg sodium, 9 g carbo., 4 g fiber, 10 g pro.

Zucchini Alfredo

Prep: 30 minutes Stand: 1 hour Makes: 8 servings

1. Cut zucchini in half crosswise. Cut lengthwise into 1/4-inch slices and then lengthwise into long, thin strips about 1/4 inch wide (fettuccine-like strips). You should have about 8 cups. In a large colander toss the zucchini with the salt. Allow to drain for 1 hour. Rinse and drain; pat dry.

2. In a 12-inch skillet cook the zucchini and garlic in hot oil over medium-high heat for 2 to 4 minutes or until crisp-tender. Transfer mixture to a large bowl.

3. In the skillet heat the cream cheese and half-and-half over medium-low heat until smooth. Stir in 1/2 cup Parmesan cheese. Stir in zucchini; heat through. Transfer to a serving dish. Sprinkle with pepper, nutmeg, and additional Parmesan cheese.

5   large zucchini (about 2½ pounds)

1   teaspoon salt

2   to 3 cloves garlic, minced

2   tablespoons olive oil

1   8-ounce package cream cheese, cubed and softened

¾   cup half-and-half or light cream

½   cup finely shredded Parmesan cheese

    Coarsely ground black pepper

    Ground nutmeg

    Finely shredded Parmesan cheese

7g carbs   **2**g fiber   **5**g net carbs

Nutrition Facts per serving: 351 cal., 27 g total fat (16 g sat. fat), 69 mg chol., 876 mg sodium, 7 g carbo., 2 g fiber, 20 g pro.

Red & Green Gazpacho

Prep: 30 minutes Chill: 1 hour Makes: 6 servings

3 cups chopped red and/or partially
 green tomatoes (3 large)

½ cup chopped tomatillos (2 medium)

1 16-ounce can tomato juice

½ cup chopped cucumber

1 large jalapeño chile pepper,
 seeded and finely chopped
 (see tip, page 59)

¼ cup finely chopped green onions (2)

¼ teaspoon bottled green pepper sauce

1 tablespoon lime juice

¼ cup finely snipped fresh cilantro

6 ounces peeled and deveined
 cooked medium shrimp (12 to 15)

Dairy sour cream (optional)

Green onion curls (optional)

1. In a large bowl combine tomatoes; tomatillos; tomato juice; cucumber; jalapeño pepper; green onions; 1 clove *garlic, minced;* pepper sauce; 1 tablespoon *olive oil;* lime juice; and cilantro. Cover; chill at least 1 hour.

2. To serve, reserve 6 shrimp. Coarsely chop remaining shrimp. Stir chopped shrimp into gazpacho. Spoon gazpacho into chilled bowls. Top each serving with 1 whole shrimp. If desired, garnish with sour cream and green onion curls.

10 g
carbs

2 g
fiber

8 g
net carbs

Nutrition Facts per serving: 90 cal., 3 g total fat (0 g sat. fat),
55 mg chol., 371 mg sodium, 10 g carbo., 2 g fiber, 8 g pro.

Ginger-Cream Asparagus

Start to Finish: 15 minutes   Makes: 4 servings

1. Snap off and discard woody bases from asparagus. If desired, scrape off scales. In a large skillet cook asparagus spears, uncovered, in boiling salted water for 3 to 5 minutes or until crisp-tender. Drain.

2. Meanwhile, for sauce, in a small saucepan combine the half-and-half, arrowroot, ginger, and lemon peel. Cook and stir over medium heat until heated through and thickened (do not boil). Season to taste with salt and pepper. Serve sauce over asparagus.

12   ounces asparagus spears

½   cup half-and-half or light cream

1   teaspoon arrowroot

¼   teaspoon ground ginger

¼   teaspoon finely shredded
       lemon peel

     Salt and black pepper

3g carbs   **1**g fiber   **2**g net carbs

Nutrition Facts per serving: 53 cal., 4 g total fat (2 g sat. fat), 11 mg chol., 165 mg sodium, 3 g carbo., 1 g fiber, 2 g pro.

Green Beans with Shallot Butter

Prep: 10 minutes Cook: 15 minutes Makes: 4 servings

8 ounces fresh green beans, ends trimmed

1 tablespoon butter

1 tablespoon finely chopped shallot

⅛ teaspoon salt

⅛ teaspoon black pepper

1. Place a steamer basket in a large skillet; add enough water to come just below the bottom of the basket. Bring to boiling. Add beans to basket. Cover and steam about 15 minutes or until crisp-tender. Remove basket from skillet; set aside. Drain water from skillet.

2. In the same skillet melt butter over medium heat. Add shallots, salt, and pepper. Cook and stir for 2 minutes. Add beans to skillet and toss until heated through.

5g carbs

2g fiber

3g net carbs

Nutrition Facts per serving: 46 cal., 3 g total fat (2 g sat. fat), 8 mg chol., 98 mg sodium, 5 g carbo., 2 g fiber, 1 g pro.

Melted Tomato Salad

Prep: 10 minutes Bake: 1½ hours Oven: 300°F Makes: 6 servings

1. Place tomatoes in an even layer in a large shallow glass baking dish. Drizzle with oil; sprinkle with basil, salt, and pepper. Bake, uncovered, in a 300° oven for 1½ to 2 hours or until tomatoes are slightly dried and charred. Cool slightly.

2. Arrange spinach on a large serving platter. Spoon tomatoes and the pan juices over spinach.

4 cups quartered medium
    tomatoes (about 2 pounds) or
    halved cherry tomatoes

3 tablespoons olive oil

¼ cup snipped fresh basil

¼ teaspoon salt

¼ teaspoon black pepper

6 cups baby spinach

6 g carbs **4** g fiber **2** g net carbs

Nutrition Facts per serving: 89 cal., 7 g total fat (1 g sat. fat), 0 mg chol., 146 mg sodium, 6 g carbo., 4 g fiber, 2 g pro.

Roasted Asparagus Parmesan

Prep: 10 minutes Roast: 15 minutes Oven: 400°F Makes: 6 servings

2 pounds asparagus spears

2 tablespoons olive oil

   Salt

   Black pepper

½ cup finely shredded
   Parmesan cheese

1. Snap off and discard woody bases from asparagus spears. If desired, scrape off scales. Place asparagus in a 15×10×1-inch baking pan. Drizzle with olive oil, tossing gently to coat. Spread out into a single layer. Sprinkle with salt and pepper.

2. Roast in a 400° oven about 15 minutes or until asparagus is crisp-tender. Transfer to a serving platter; sprinkle with Parmesan cheese.

4 g carbs   2 g fiber   2 g net carbs

Nutrition Facts per serving: 95 cal., 7 g total fat (2 g sat. fat), 8 mg chol., 102 mg sodium, 4 g carbo., 2 g fiber, 5 g pro.

Lemon-Almond Broccoli

Start to Finish: 20 minutes Makes: 4 servings

1. If using fresh broccoli, cook, covered, in a small amount of boiling lightly salted water about 8 minutes or until crisp-tender. If using frozen broccoli, cook according to package directions. Drain.

2. Meanwhile, for sauce, in a small saucepan cook the mushrooms and green onion in hot butter over medium heat until tender, stirring occasionally. Remove from heat. Stir in almonds and lemon peel. Toss with broccoli.

8 ounces broccoli, cut into ¾-inch
    pieces, or 2 cups loose-pack
    frozen broccoli cuts

¾ cup sliced fresh mushrooms

2 tablespoons thinly sliced green
    onion (1)

1 tablespoon butter

2 tablespoons slivered almonds
    or chopped pecans, toasted

½ teaspoon finely shredded
    lemon peel

4g
carbs

2g
fiber

2g
net carbs

Nutrition Facts per serving: 69 cal., 6 g total fat (2 g sat. fat),
8 mg chol., 34 mg sodium, 4 g carbo., 2 g fiber, 3 g pro.

Garlic-Mustard Beans

Start to Finish: 20 minutes Makes: 8 servings

3 9-ounce packages frozen cut

   green beans or asparagus

2 slices bacon

½ cup thinly sliced onion

2 cloves garlic, minced

1 tablespoon brown mustard

½ teaspoon lemon-pepper

   seasoning or ¼ teaspoon

   black pepper

⅛ teaspoon salt

1. Cook beans according to package directions. Drain.

2. Meanwhile, in a medium skillet cook bacon until crisp. Drain, reserving drippings in skillet. Crumble bacon; set aside. Cook and stir onion and garlic in drippings over medium heat about 3 minutes or until tender. Stir in mustard, lemon-pepper, and salt. Cook for 30 seconds more. Toss onion mixture with beans. Sprinkle bacon over beans.

6 g
carbs

3 g
fiber

3 g
net carbs

Nutrition Facts per serving: 49 cal., 1 g total fat (0 g sat. fat),
2 mg chol., 181 mg sodium, 6 g carbo., 3 g fiber, 2 g pro.

Brussels Sprouts with Lemon Sauce

Start to Finish: 25 minutes Makes: 6 servings

1. Trim stems and remove any wilted outer leaves from Brussels sprouts; wash. Cut any large sprouts in half lengthwise.

2. In a medium saucepan combine Brussels sprouts, ¾ cup broth, the butter, and garlic. Bring to boiling; reduce heat. Simmer, covered, for 7 to 10 minutes or until Brussels sprouts are crisp-tender. Using a slotted spoon, transfer sprouts to a serving bowl. Keep warm.

3. Meanwhile, in a small bowl combine 2 tablespoons chicken broth, the arrowroot, lemon peel, lemon juice, and pepper. Gradually add lemon mixture to hot broth in saucepan. Cook and stir over medium heat until mixture is just thickened (do not boil). Stir in dill.

4. Pour lemon sauce over Brussels sprouts.

3 cups Brussels sprouts
(12 ounces)
¾ cup chicken broth
1 teaspoon butter
1 clove garlic, minced
2 tablespoons chicken broth
1½ teaspoons arrowroot
½ teaspoon finely shredded
lemon peel
1 tablespoon lemon juice
⅛ teaspoon black pepper
2 teaspoons snipped fresh dill

5g carbs **2**g fiber **3**g net carbs

Nutrition Facts per serving: 29 cal., 1 g total fat (0 g sat. fat),
2 mg chol., 159 mg sodium, 5 g carbo., 2 g fiber, 2 g pro.

Herbed Yellow Summer Squash with Parmesan

Prep: 20 minutes Bake: 30 minutes Oven: 375°F Makes: 6 to 8 servings

3 tablespoons snipped fresh chives

2 tablespoons snipped fresh parsley

2 tablespoons snipped fresh basil and/or summer savory

2 teaspoons snipped fresh rosemary or thyme

4 cups coarsely chopped yellow summer squash (about 3 medium)

⅔ cup chopped seeded plum tomatoes (2 medium)

½ cup chopped green sweet pepper (1 small)

1 cup finely shredded Parmesan cheese

2 tablespoons butter

1. Grease a 2-quart shallow baking dish; set aside. In a large bowl combine chives, parsley, basil, and rosemary.

2. Stir in squash, tomatoes, sweet pepper, and ½ cup of the Parmesan cheese. Spoon vegetable mixture into prepared baking dish. Dot with butter. Sprinkle with remaining ½ cup cheese.

3. Bake, covered, in a 375° oven for about 25 minutes or until squash is crisp-tender. Uncover dish and bake 5 minutes more.

6 g carbs   **2** g fiber   **4** g net carbs

Nutrition Facts per serving: 134 cal., 9 g total fat (6 g sat. fat), 28 mg chol., 246 mg sodium, 6 g carbo., 2 g fiber, 7 g pro.

Zucchini with Onions

Prep: 10 minutes Cook: 6 minutes Makes: 4 to 6 servings

1. Rinse and trim zucchini. If using medium zucchini, cut in half lengthwise and then into $1/2$-inch slices.

2. In a large nonstick skillet heat oil over medium heat. Add zucchini and onion. Cook for 6 to 8 minutes or until vegetables are just tender, stirring occasionally.

3. Add walnuts, oregano, salt, and pepper. Cook and stir for 1 minute more.

1 pound baby zucchini or
　　3 medium zucchini

1 tablespoon olive oil

1 small onion, cut into thin wedges

$1/4$ cup chopped walnuts

$1/2$ teaspoon dried oregano, crushed

$1/4$ teaspoon salt

$1/4$ teaspoon black pepper

6_g carbs 1_g fiber 5_g net carbs

Nutrition Facts per serving: 106 cal., 9 g total fat (1 g sat. fat),
0 mg chol., 146 mg sodium, 6 g carbo., 1 g fiber, 4 g pro.

Vegetable Curry

Start to Finish: 45 minutes Makes: 4 servings

1 tablespoon cooking oil

½ cup chopped onion

  (1 medium)

1 teaspoon thinly sliced

  fresh ginger

1 teaspoon curry powder

¼ teaspoon salt

1 cup coarsely chopped plum

  tomatoes (3 medium)

¼ cup chicken broth

4 ounces fresh green beans

1 small yellow summer squash

  or zucchini, cut into

  ¾-inch pieces

1. Heat oil in a large skillet over medium heat. Add onion and ginger; cook and stir about 5 minutes or until tender. Stir in curry powder and salt; cook and stir for 2 minutes. Stir in tomatoes until they are coated with spices. Add broth. Bring to boiling; reduce heat to medium-low. Add green beans. Simmer, uncovered, about 10 minutes or just until green beans are tender.

2. Add squash to skillet; simmer, covered, for 8 to 10 minutes or just until squash is tender but still retains its shape.

7 g
carbs

2 g
fiber

5 g
net carbs

Nutrition Facts per serving: 63 cal., 4 g total fat (1 g sat. fat),
0 mg chol., 212 mg sodium, 7 g carbo., 2 g fiber, 2 g pro.

Grilled Balsamic Vegetables

Prep: 20 minutes Grill: 8 minutes Makes: 8 servings

1. In a medium bowl combine vinegar, oil, garlic, black pepper, and salt. Add sweet peppers, mushrooms, and tomatoes; toss gently to coat.

2. For a charcoal grill, grill vegetables on the rack of an uncovered grill directly over medium coals (see tip, page 107) for 8 to 10 minutes or until sweet peppers and mushrooms are tender and tomatoes begin to soften, turning once halfway through grilling. (For a gas grill, preheat grill. Reduce heat to medium. Cover and grill as above.)

1 tablespoon balsamic vinegar

1 tablespoon olive oil

1 clove garlic, minced

1/4 teaspoon black pepper

1/8 teaspoon salt

2 green or yellow sweet peppers,
  seeded and cut into quarters

4 3- to 4-ounce fresh portobello
  mushrooms

4 plum tomatoes, halved
  lengthwise

Nutrition Facts per serving: 44 cal., 3 g total fat (0 g sat. fat),
0 mg chol., 42 mg sodium, 5 g carbo., 1 g fiber, 2 g pro.

167

Vegetables in Spicy Sour Cream

Prep: 15 minutes Chill: 1 hour Makes: 6 servings

½ cup dairy sour cream

1 tablespoon white wine vinegar

   or lemon juice

½ teaspoon salt

⅛ teaspoon cayenne pepper

1 medium cucumber, halved

   lengthwise and thinly sliced

   (about 1½ cups)

1¼ cups sliced yellow summer

   squash or zucchini

   (1 medium)

½ of a medium onion, halved

   lengthwise and thinly sliced

¼ cup chopped red sweet

   pepper

1. In a large bowl combine sour cream, vinegar, salt, and cayenne pepper.

2. Add cucumber, squash, onion, and sweet pepper; toss gently to coat. Cover and chill for at least 1 hour or up to 6 hours. Stir before serving.

4g carbs   **1**g fiber   **3**g net carbs

Nutrition Facts per serving: 48 cal., 3 g total fat (2 g sat. fat),
7 mg chol., 204 mg sodium, 4 g carbo., 1 g fiber, 1 g pro.

Sautéed Broccoli Rabe

Start to Finish: 20 minutes Makes: 6 servings

1. Wash broccoli rabe; remove and discard woody stems. Cut into 2-inch pieces. In a very large skillet cook and stir broccoli rabe, garlic, and salt in hot oil over medium-high heat for 3 to 4 minutes or until broccoli rabe is crisp-tender. (If using broccoli florets, cook and stir for 5 to 6 minutes or until crisp-tender). If desired, sprinkle with crushed red pepper.

2 pounds broccoli rabe or

    6 cups coarsely chopped

    broccoli florets

3 cloves garlic, minced

¼ teaspoon salt

4 teaspoons olive oil

    Crushed red pepper (optional)

8g carbs **5**g fiber **3**g net carbs

Nutrition Facts per serving: 71 cal., 4 g total fat (0 g sat. fat), 0 mg chol., 128 mg sodium, 8 g carbo., 5 g fiber, 5 g pro.

Braised Seasoned Brussels Sprouts

Prep: 15 minutes Cook: 12 minutes Makes: 4 servings

Olive oil or nonstick cooking

  spray

½ teaspoon mustard seeds

½ teaspoon cumin seeds

½ teaspoon fennel seeds

2 cups halved Brussels sprouts

  (8 ounces)

2 teaspoons grated fresh ginger

1 dried Thai red pepper, crushed, or

  ¼ teaspoon crushed red pepper

⅓ cup chicken or vegetable broth

1 tablespoon coarsely chopped

  cashews or peanuts

2 teaspoons sherry vinegar or red

  wine vinegar

¼ teaspoon salt

1. Lightly coat a medium saucepan with olive oil; heat saucepan over medium-high heat. Add mustard seeds, cumin seeds, and fennel seeds. Cook and stir for 30 seconds. Reduce heat to medium. Stir in Brussels sprouts, ginger, and crushed red pepper. Add broth and cook, covered, for 10 to 12 minutes or until Brussels sprouts are tender, stirring occasionally.

2. Stir in cashews, vinegar, and salt.

6 g carbs   **2** g fiber   **4** g net carbs

Nutrition Facts per serving: 51 cal., 3 g total fat (0 g sat. fat),
0 mg chol., 225 mg sodium, 6 g carbo., 2 g fiber, 2 g pro.

Roasted Summer Vegetables

Prep: 15 minutes Bake: 25 minutes Oven: 425°F Makes: 8 servings

1. In a 13×9×2-inch baking pan combine the onions, yellow squash, zucchini, sweet peppers, and garlic.

2. In a screw-top jar combine parsley, vinegar, oil, oregano, salt, and black pepper. Cover and shake well. Pour over the vegetables and toss to coat.

3. Bake the vegetables in a 425° oven for about 25 minutes or until crisp-tender, stirring twice.

2 medium red onions, cut into 8 wedges

2 small yellow summer squash, cut into ½-inch slices

2 small zucchini, cut into ½-inch strips

3 red, yellow, and/or green sweet peppers, seeded and cut into ½-inch strips

4 cloves garlic, thinly sliced

2 tablespoons snipped fresh parsley

2 tablespoons balsamic vinegar

1 tablespoon olive oil

1 teaspoon dried oregano, crushed

½ teaspoon salt

¼ teaspoon black pepper

7g carbs **1**g fiber **6**g net carbs

Nutrition Facts per serving: 45 cal., 2 g total fat (0.0 g sat. fat), 0 mg chol., 137 mg sodium, 7 g carbo., 1 g fiber, 1 g pro.

Asparagus with Fresh Mozzarella

Start to Finish: 10 minutes   Makes: 4 servings

1 pound thin asparagus spears

4 ounces fresh mozzarella
    cheese, cut or torn into
    pieces

   Salt

   Freshly ground black pepper

   Fresh lemon verbena leaves or
    ½ teaspoon finely shredded
    lemon peel

1. Snap off and discard woody bases from asparagus. If desired, scrape off scales.

2. Place a steamer basket in a large skillet; add enough water to come just below the bottom of the basket. Bring water to boiling. Place asparagus in steamer basket. Cover and steam for 2 minutes.

3. Preheat broiler. Transfer asparagus to an 8×8×2-inch baking pan. Top with cheese. Season with salt and pepper. Broil 4 inches from heat for 1 minute or until cheese melts. Top with lemon verbena.

2 g carbs   **1** g fiber   **1** g net carbs

Nutrition Facts per serving: 102 cal., 7 g total fat (4 g sat. fat),
22 mg chol., 331 mg sodium, 2 g carbo., 1 g fiber, 8 g pro.

Eggplant with Herbed Goat Cheese

Prep: 30 minutes Broil: 9 minutes Makes: 16 servings

1. Cut the eggplant crosswise into about sixteen $\frac{1}{2}$-inch slices. Sprinkle each side of the eggplant slices lightly with salt. Place them on paper towels; let stand for 20 minutes. Blot the surfaces of the slices with paper towels.

2. In a small bowl combine the cheese, 1 tablespoon basil, the onion powder, and dash black pepper.

3. Preheat broiler. Brush the eggplant slices with oil. Place the eggplant in a single layer on the unheated rack of a broiler pan. Broil 4 to 5 inches from heat for 8 to 9 minutes or until tender, turning once halfway through broiling.

4. Remove eggplant slices from oven and spread with the cheese mixture. Sprinkle with lemon-pepper seasoning. Broil for about 1 minute more or until cheese is heated through.

5. To serve, top eggplant with chopped tomato and additional snipped basil.

1 small eggplant (about 12 ounces)

Salt

1 5½- or 6-ounce package soft goat cheese (chèvre)

1 tablespoon snipped fresh basil or 1 teaspoon dried basil, crushed

1 teaspoon onion powder

Dash black pepper

2 tablespoons olive oil

Lemon-pepper seasoning or black pepper

⅓ cup chopped seeded tomato (1 small)

Snipped fresh basil

2g carbs   **1**g fiber   **1**g net carbs

Nutrition Facts per serving: 58 cal., 5 g total fat (2 g sat. fat), 8 mg chol., 88 mg sodium, 2 g carbo., 1 g fiber, 2 g pro.

173

Roasted Herbes de Provence Tomatoes

Prep: 10 minutes Roast: 25 minutes Cool: 10 minutes
Oven: 425°F Makes: 4 servings

2 tablespoons olive oil

8 medium plum tomatoes
   (about 1 pound)

1 teaspoon herbes de Provence

   Coarse salt or salt

   Freshly ground black pepper

1. Line a shallow baking pan with foil; brush foil with 1 tablespoon olive oil. Cut off and discard the stem ends of the tomatoes. Cut tomatoes in half lengthwise; remove and discard seeds. Place tomato halves, cut side up, on prepared pan. Roast, uncovered, in a 425° oven for 25 to 30 minutes or until edges of tomatoes begin to char.

2. Drizzle tomatoes with remaining 1 tablespoon olive oil and sprinkle with herbes de Provence. Let tomatoes cool for 10 minutes. Season with salt and pepper.

5g carbs   **1**g fiber   **4**g net carbs

Nutrition Facts per serving: 81 cal., 7 g total fat (1 g sat. fat), 0 mg chol., 127 mg sodium, 5 g carbo., 1 g fiber, 1 g pro.

Savory Grilled Vegetables

Prep: 25 minutes Grill: 8 minutes Makes: 8 servings

1. In a small bowl combine olive oil, balsamic vinegar, garlic, 1 teaspoon *salt*, black pepper, and oregano. Brush vegetables with oil mixture; reserve any remaining oil mixture.

2. For a charcoal grill, grill portobellos on the rack of an uncovered grill directly over medium-high coals (see tip, page 107) for 8 to 10 minutes or until tender, turning and brushing with reserved oil mixture once. Grill remaining vegetables for 3 to 4 minutes or until tender, turning and brushing with reserved oil mixture once. (For a gas grill, preheat grill. Reduce heat to medium-high. Cover and grill as above.) Discard any remaining oil mixture.

3. To serve, slice portobellos. Arrange portobello slices and grilled vegetables on a platter. Top with feta cheese.

½ cup olive oil

2 tablespoons balsamic vinegar

4 cloves garlic, minced

1 teaspoon black pepper

1 teaspoon snipped fresh oregano

6 portobello mushroom caps

16 asparagus spears, trimmed

3 small zucchini, cut lengthwise
    into ½-inch slices

3 small yellow summer squash,
    cut lengthwise into
    ½-inch slices

1 medium red sweet pepper, cut
    into 8 wedges

1 medium onion, cut into ½-inch slices

½ cup crumbled feta cheese

11 g carbs   **5** g fiber   **6** g net carbs

Nutrition Facts per serving: 199 cal., 16 g total fat (3 g sat. fat), 8 mg chol., 406 mg sodium, 11 g carbo., 5 g fiber, 5 g pro.

175

Marinated Baby Vegetable Kabobs

Prep: 20 minutes Marinate: 1 hour Grill: 8 minutes Makes: 6 servings

8   green onions

12 baby green pattypan squash

12 baby zucchini

1   cup green beans, trimmed and

cut into 2-inch pieces

⅓   cup olive oil

⅓   cup finely shredded

Parmesan cheese

3   tablespoons red wine vinegar

3   tablespoons snipped fresh

oregano or 1½ teaspoons

dried oregano, crushed

¼   teaspoon salt

¼   teaspoon black pepper

1. Rinse and trim vegetables. Cut a 3-inch portion from the bottom of 6 of the green onions. Save remaining onion tops for another use. Place 3-inch green onion portions, pattypan squash, zucchini, and green beans in a plastic bag set in a shallow dish.

2. Finely chop remaining 2 green onions. For marinade, in a screw-top jar combine chopped green onions, oil, Parmesan cheese, vinegar, oregano, salt, and pepper. Cover and shake well. Pour over vegetables; seal bag. Marinate vegetables in the refrigerator for 1 to 24 hours, turning occasionally.

3. Drain vegetables, reserving marinade. On 6 long bamboo* or metal skewers, alternately skewer vegetables. For a charcoal grill, place kabobs on the rack of an uncovered grill directly over medium coals (see tip, page 107) for 8 to 10 minutes or until browned and tender, turning and brushing with reserved marinade occasionally. (For a gas grill, preheat grill. Reduce heat to medium. Place kabobs on grill rack over heat. Cover and grill as above.)

*__Note:__ If using bamboo skewers, keep them from catching fire by soaking them in water for at least 30 minutes before use.

7g carbs

2g fiber

5g net carbs

Nutrition Facts per serving: 153 cal., 13 g total fat (2 g sat. fat), 4 mg chol., 173 mg sodium, 7 g carbo., 2 g fiber, 4 g pro.

Wild Mushrooms with Herbs & Shallots

Prep: 15 minutes Cook: 12 minutes Makes: 6 to 8 servings

1. In a large skillet cook and stir shallots and garlic in hot oil over medium-high heat for 2 minutes. Add matsutake mushrooms. Cook for 10 to 12 minutes or until tender, stirring occasionally. If using oyster or button mushrooms, add them during the last 6 to 8 minutes. Add shiitakes during last 4 minutes. Stir in herbs, salt, and pepper.

3 shallots, peeled and cut into
 thin wedges

3 cloves garlic, minced

2 tablespoons olive oil or
 canola oil

1¼ pounds fresh matsutake,
 oyster, white button, and/or
 shiitake mushrooms, broken
 into clusters or sliced
 (about 8 cups)

¼ cup snipped fresh mixed herbs,
 such as tarragon, rosemary,
 basil, oregano, and/or parsley

¼ teaspoon coarse salt or salt

¼ teaspoon cracked black pepper

6g carbs   **1**g fiber   **5**g net carbs

Nutrition Facts per serving: 74 cal., 5 g total fat (1 g sat. fat),
0 mg chol., 86 mg sodium, 6 g carbo., 1 g fiber, 3 g pro.

Grilled Tomatoes with Pesto

Prep: 5 minutes Grill: 13 minutes Makes: 6 servings

3   medium tomatoes, cored and

halved crosswise

¼   cup bottled pesto sauce

6   very thin onion slices

½   cup shredded Monterey

Jack cheese

⅓   cup smoked almonds,

chopped

2   tablespoons snipped

fresh parsley

Salt and black pepper

(optional)

1. Hollow out the top ¼ inch of tomato halves with a spoon. Top each tomato half with 2 teaspoons pesto sauce and an onion slice. Arrange tomatoes in 2 foil pie pans.

2. For a charcoal grill, place pie pans in center of grill rack directly over medium coals (see tip, page 107). Cover and grill for 8 to 10 minutes or until tomatoes are heated through. (For a gas grill, preheat grill. Reduce heat to medium. Cover and grill as above.)

3. In a small bowl combine the cheese, almonds, and parsley. Sprinkle mixture over tomatoes. Cover and grill for 5 minutes more or until cheese melts. If desired, season with salt and pepper.

6 g carbs   **2** g fiber   **4** g net carbs

Nutrition Facts per serving: 145 cal., 12 g total fat (3 g sat. fat),
11 mg chol., 166 mg sodium, 6 g carbo., 2 g fiber, 6 g pro.

Mustard Greens Salad

Start to Finish: 10 minutes Makes: 4 to 6 servings

1. In a large skillet heat oil over medium heat. Add sweet pepper; cook and stir for 2 minutes. Add vinegar and mustard. Cook and stir just until bubbly; remove from heat. In a large salad bowl combine greens and walnuts. Add warm dressing; toss to coat. Serve immediately.

1 tablespoon cooking oil

1 small red sweet pepper, seeded and cut into bite-size strips

2 tablespoons rice vinegar

4 teaspoons green peppercorn mustard, tarragon mustard, or Dijon-style mustard

4 cups shredded fresh mustard greens

3 tablespoons chopped walnuts

6g carbs   **3**g fiber   **3**g net carbs

Nutrition Facts per serving: 95 cal., 7 g total fat (1 g sat. fat), 0 mg chol., 135 mg sodium, 6 g carbo., 3 g fiber, 4 g pro.

Green Beans & Fennel

Start to Finish: 30 minutes Makes: 10 to 12 servings

2 tablespoons butter, softened

1½ teaspoons fennel seeds,

crushed

1½ teaspoons finely shredded

lemon peel

¾ teaspoon black pepper

¼ teaspoon salt

3 large fennel bulbs

(about 3 pounds)

1¾ pounds fresh green beans

1. In a large bowl, combine butter, fennel seeds, lemon peel, pepper, and salt.

2. Cut off and discard upper stalks of fennel bulbs. Remove any wilted outer layers and cut a thin slice from the fennel base. Wash fennel and cut into quarters lengthwise; remove cores. Cut lengthwise into ¼-inch-wide strips.

3. Place beans in a 4-quart Dutch oven. Cook beans, covered, in a small amount of boiling salted water for 4 to 5 minutes. Add fennel strips. Cook for 6 to 10 minutes more or until vegetables are crisp-tender. Drain. Add beans and fennel to bowl with the seasoned butter; toss to coat. Transfer to a serving dish.

11 g carbs

5 g fiber

6 g net carbs

Nutrition Facts per serving: 69 cal., 3 g total fat (1 g sat. fat), 6 mg chol., 117 mg sodium, 11 g carbo., 5 g fiber, 2 g pro.

Beet Greens with Walnuts & Blue Cheese

Prep: 10 minutes Cook: 3 minutes Makes: 4 servings

1. Thoroughly clean beet greens; drain well. Cut greens into 1-inch strips; set aside. In a large skillet heat oil over medium-high heat. Add walnuts; cook and stir for 2 minutes. Add beet greens. Cook and stir for 1 minute or just until wilted. Remove from heat. Serve immediately. Top each serving with some crumbled blue cheese and pepper.

*Note: This recipe can also be prepared with spinach or chard. Whichever greens you choose to use, be sure to clean them well under cold running water to remove any dirt or sand. Drain well.

8 ounces beet greens*

2 teaspoons cooking oil

2 tablespoons chopped walnuts

1 tablespoon crumbled blue
cheese, such as Gorgonzola,
Stilton, French, or Danish blue

¼ teaspoon coarsely ground
black pepper

3g carbs **2**g fiber **1**g net carbs

Nutrition Facts per serving: 55 cal., 5 g total fat (1 g sat. fat),
0 mg chol., 109 mg sodium, 3 g carbo., 2 g fiber, 2 g pro.

Brussels Sprouts with Bacon

Start to Finish: 40 minutes Makes: 8 servings

1¼ pounds Brussels sprouts

  3 slices slab bacon or

      bacon, diced

1½ teaspoons snipped fresh

      thyme or ½ teaspoon dried

      thyme, crushed

  ¼ teaspoon salt

  ¼ teaspoon black pepper

1. Trim stems and remove any wilted outer leaves from Brussels sprouts; wash. Cut any large sprouts in half lengthwise. In a medium saucepan cook Brussels sprouts, covered, in a small amount of boiling salted water for 8 to 10 minutes or until tender. Drain; rinse under cold water. Pat dry with paper towels. Set aside.

2. In a large skillet cook bacon over medium heat for 3 to 5 minutes or just until cooked through but not crisp; drain fat. Reduce heat to medium-low.

3. Add Brussels sprouts, thyme, salt, and pepper to bacon in skillet. Cook about 2 minutes or until sprouts are heated through.

6g carbs   **3**g fiber   **3**g net carbs

Nutrition Facts per serving: 45 cal., 2 g total fat (1 g sat. fat),
3 mg chol., 136 mg sodium, 6 g carbo., 3 g fiber, 3 g pro.

Sautéed Artichoke Hearts with Creamy Green Salsa

Start to Finish: 15 minutes Makes: 6 servings

1. Drain artichokes; coarsely chop. In a small saucepan combine chopped artichokes, green onions, and salsa. Cook over medium heat until heated through, stirring frequently. Remove from heat. Stir in cheese, sour cream, and cilantro. Serve immediately.

1   12-ounce jar or 2 6-ounce jars
    marinated artichoke hearts

⅓ cup sliced green onions (3)

2   tablespoons bottled green
    salsa

½ cup shredded Monterey Jack
    or white cheddar cheese

¼ cup dairy sour cream

¼ cup snipped fresh cilantro

5g carbs   **0**g fiber   **5**g net carbs

Nutrition Facts per serving: 144 cal., 13 g total fat (5 g sat. fat),
12 mg chol., 256 mg sodium, 5 g carbo., 0 g fiber, 3 g pro.

Pea Pods & Onions with Dill Butter

Start to Finish: 15 minutes Makes: 10 to 12 servings

1 16-ounce package frozen

    small whole onions

2 6-ounce packages frozen

    snow pea pods

2 cloves garlic, minced

3 tablespoons butter

1 tablespoon snipped fresh dill

    or 1 teaspoon dried dill

½ teaspoon salt

¼ teaspoon ground white

    pepper

    Fresh dill sprigs (optional)

1. In a large saucepan cook onions in a small amount of boiling water for 2 minutes. Add pea pods; cook for 2 to 3 minutes more or just until tender, stirring occasionally. Drain.

2. Meanwhile, in a small saucepan cook and stir garlic in hot butter over medium heat for 30 seconds. Stir in dill, salt, and white pepper. Drizzle butter mixture over vegetables, tossing to coat. If desired, garnish with fresh dill sprigs.

7 g carbs **2** g fiber **5** g net carbs

Nutrition Facts per serving: 64 cal., 4 g total fat (2 g sat. fat),
9 mg chol., 144 mg sodium, 7 g carbo., 2 g fiber, 2 g pro.

Cheese-Crusted Cauliflower

Prep: 15 minutes Broil: 4 minutes Makes: 4 servings

1. Preheat broiler. In a large ovenproof skillet melt butter over medium heat. Add cauliflower, leek, garlic, salt, nutmeg, and pepper. Cook and stir for 5 minutes. Carefully add water; reduce heat, cover, and cook about 5 minutes more or until cauliflower is crisp-tender. Remove from heat. Sprinkle with cheese.

2. Broil 4 to 5 inches from the heat for 4 to 5 minutes or until cheese is browned.

2 tablespoons butter

3 cups cauliflower florets

    (about 1 small head)

⅓ cup thinly sliced leek

    (1 medium)

1 clove garlic, minced

¼ teaspoon salt

⅛ teaspoon ground nutmeg

⅛ teaspoon black pepper

2 tablespoons water

½ cup finely shredded Gruyère or

    Swiss cheese, finely shredded

5g carbs   **1**g fiber   **4**g net carbs

Nutrition Facts per serving: 137 cal., 11 g total fat (6 g sat. fat), 32 mg chol., 261 mg sodium, 5 g carbo., 1 g fiber, 6 g pro.

Cheesy Mashed Turnips

Prep: 20 minutes Bake: 20 minutes Oven: 350°F Makes: 4 to 6 servings

1½ pounds turnips, peeled and
      cut into 1-inch cubes

2 tablespoons butter

¼ cup whipping cream

⅛ teaspoon salt

⅛ teaspoon ground white
      pepper

1 cup finely shredded smoked
      Gouda or provolone cheese

2 tablespoons snipped fresh
      chives

2 slices bacon, crisp-cooked,
      drained, and crumbled
      Snipped fresh chives
      (optional)

1. In a large saucepan cook turnips, covered, in boiling lightly salted water for 12 to 15 minutes or until tender. Drain. Return turnips to saucepan. Add butter, cream, salt, and pepper. Mash turnips with a potato masher or beat with an electric mixer on low speed until nearly smooth. Stir in cheese and 2 tablespoons chives.

2. Transfer turnip mixture to a 1-quart au gratin dish or casserole. Bake, uncovered, in a 350° oven for 20 minutes. Sprinkle turnips with crumbled bacon and, if desired, additional chives.

11 g carbs   **3** g fiber   **8** g net carbs

Nutrition Facts per serving: 258 cal., 21 g total fat (12 g sat. fat),
64 mg chol., 743 mg sodium, 11 g carbo., 3 g fiber, 8 g pro.

Feta-Stuffed Celery

Start to Finish: 15 minutes Makes: 6 servings

1. Remove tops and wide ends from celery; set stalks aside. In a small bowl combine sour cream, feta cheese, 2 tablespoons almonds, and the dill. Spread or spoon cheese mixture into celery. Sprinkle with remaining 2 tablespoons almonds and, if desired, additional dill.

2. Cut each filled stalk of celery crosswise into 4 pieces.

6 sttalks celery

¼ cup dairy sour cream

¼ cup crumbled feta cheese

¼ cup chopped almonds, toasted

¼ teaspoon dried dill

   Dried dill (optional)

4g carbs   **2**g fiber   **2**g net carbs

Nutrition Facts per serving: 86 cal., 7 g total fat (3 g sat. fat), 11 mg chol., 109 mg sodium, 4 g carbo., 2 g fiber, 3 g pro.

Ginger Peas & Pecans

Start to Finish: 20 minutes Makes: 4 servings

3 cups fresh snow pea pods

⅓ cup chopped pecans

1 tablespoon chopped shallot

2 tablespoons butter

1 to 1½ teaspoons grated
   fresh ginger

1. Remove strings and tips from pea pods; set aside.

2. In a large skillet cook and stir pecans and shallot in hot butter over medium heat for 1 minute. Add pea pods and ginger. Cook and stir for 2 to 3 minutes or until pea pods are crisp-tender.

6 g
carbs

2 g
fiber

4 g
net carbs

Nutrition Facts per serving: 155 cal., 13 g total fat (4 g sat. fat), 16 mg chol., 51 mg sodium, 6 g carbo., 2 g fiber, 2 g pro.

Marinated Eggplant with Lemon-Caper Aïoli

Prep: 20 minutes Marinate: 30 minutes Broil: 14 minutes Makes: 4 servings

1. Place eggplant slices in a plastic bag set in a shallow dish. In a screw-top jar combine oil, lemon juice, Greek seasoning, salt, and pepper. Cover and shake well. Pour over eggplant; seal bag. Marinate at room temperature for 30 minutes, turning occasionally. Drain eggplant, discarding marinade.

2. Preheat broiler. Place eggplant slices on the unheated rack of a broiler pan. Broil 4 to 5 inches from heat for 14 to 16 minutes or until tender, turning once halfway through broiling. Serve eggplant slices with Lemon-Caper Aïoli.

Lemon-Caper Aïoli: In a small bowl combine ⅓ cup mayonnaise; 2 tablespoons olive oil; 2 teaspoons drained capers; 2 to 3 cloves garlic, minced; 1 teaspoon lemon juice; and ⅛ teaspoon salt.

1 small eggplant (12 ounces),

    cut into 1-inch slices

¼ cup olive oil

2 tablespoons lemon juice

1 teaspoon Greek seasoning

¼ teaspoon salt

⅛ teaspoon black pepper

    Lemon-Caper Aïoli

    (see recipe, left)

5 g carbs   **2** g fiber   **3** g net carbs

Nutrition Facts per serving: 332 cal., 35 g total fat (5 g sat. fat), 13 mg chol., 395 mg sodium, 5 g carbo., 2 g fiber, 1 g pro.

Pesto-Stuffed Portobellos

Prep: 10 minutes Bake: 8 minutes Oven: 400°F Makes: 4 servings

4 medium portobello

mushrooms (about 1 pound)

Olive oil

⅓ cup purchased dried tomato

pesto

¼ cup chopped almonds or

pine nuts

2 slices bacon, crisp-cooked,

drained, and crumbled

¼ cup crème fraîche* or sour

cream

1 tablespoon snipped fresh

flat-leaf parsley

1. Clean mushrooms with a damp paper towel. Cut mushroom stems flush with caps. Discard stems. Scrape gills from caps using a spoon; discard. Place mushrooms, stem side down, in a 15×10×1-inch baking pan. Brush tops lightly with olive oil.

2. Bake mushrooms in a 400° oven for 5 minutes. Turn mushrooms stem-sides up. Meanwhile, in a small bowl combine pesto, almonds, and bacon. Spoon pesto mixture into mushroom caps. Bake for 3 to 4 minutes more or until mushrooms are heated through.

3. To serve, spoon crème fraîche on mushrooms and sprinkle with parsley.

*Note: If you can't find crème fraîche in your supermarket, make your own by combining ½ cup whipping cream (do not use ultra-pasteurized cream) and ½ cup dairy sour cream. Cover the mixture and let it stand at room temperature for 2 to 5 hours or until it thickens. Cover and refrigerate for up to 1 week.

11g
carbs

3g
fiber

8g
net carbs

Nutrition Facts per serving: 242 cal., 20 g total fat (7 g sat. fat),
25 mg chol., 225 mg sodium, 11 g carbo., 3 g fiber, 8 g pro.

Pumpkin with Caramelized Onions & Mushrooms

Prep: 15 minutes Cook: 30 minutes Makes: 6 servings

1. In a large skillet cook onion in 2 tablespoons butter over medium-low heat for 20 to 25 minutes or until very tender and lightly browned, stirring occasionally. Add remaining 2 tablespoons butter, the mushrooms, garlic, salt, and pepper. Cook and stir about 5 minutes more or until mushrooms are tender and onions are golden brown. If desired, carefully add sherry to skillet; cook and stir for 1 minute.

2. Add pumpkin to skillet. Reduce heat to low; cook and stir until heated through. Season with salt and pepper. Sprinkle with toasted pecans.

1   large onion, cut in half
        lengthwise and thinly sliced
        (1 cup)
¼   cup butter
½   cup sliced fresh shiitake,
        cremini, or button mushrooms
1   clove garlic, minced
½   teaspoon salt
⅛   teaspoon black pepper
2   tablespoons dry sherry
        (optional)
1   15-ounce can pumpkin
    Salt and black pepper
¼   cup chopped pecans, toasted

11g
carbs

3g
fiber

8g
net carbs

Nutrition Facts per serving: 146 cal., 12 g total fat (4 g sat. fat), 22 mg chol., 353 mg sodium, 11 g carbo., 3 g fiber, 2 g pro.

Tender Red Cabbage with Onion & Bacon

Prep: 15 minutes Cook: 12 minutes Makes: 4 servings

2 tablespoons butter

5 cups shredded red cabbage

    (1 small head)

½ cup chopped onion

    (1 medium)

2 cloves garlic, minced

¾ teaspoon dried thyme,

    crushed

¼ teaspoon salt

⅛ teaspoon black pepper

¼ cup dry red wine

2 slices bacon, crisp-cooked,

    drained, and crumbled

1. In a large skillet heat butter over medium heat. Add cabbage, onion, garlic, thyme, salt, and pepper. Cook for 10 to 15 minutes or just until cabbage is tender, stirring occasionally. Add wine to skillet. Bring to boiling; reduce heat. Simmer, uncovered, about 2 minutes or until most of the liquid is evaporated, stirring occasionally. Remove from heat. Sprinkle with bacon.

8 g carbs   **2** g fiber   **6** g net carbs

Nutrition Facts per serving: 71 cal., 2 g total fat (1 g sat. fat),
3 mg chol., 227 mg sodium, 8 g carbo., 2 g fiber, 3 g pro.

Sherried Fennel & Tomatoes

Prep: 15 minutes Cook: 10 minutes Makes: 4 to 6 servings

1. Remove feathery tops from fennel; snip enough of the tops to make 1 tablespoon. Set aside. Cut off and discard upper stalks. Remove any wilted outer layers and cut and discard a thin slice from the fennel base. Cut fennel bulb into thin slices, removing the core.

2. In a large skillet cook fennel slices in hot butter over medium heat until nearly tender, stirring occasionally. Add tomatoes, garlic, salt, and pepper. Cook and stir for 1 to 2 minutes or until fennel is tender and tomato halves are softened. Stir in sherry. Cook and stir for 1 minute. Sprinkle with reserved fennel tops.

2 medium fennel bulbs with tops

3 tablespoons butter

1 cup halved cherry tomatoes

2 cloves garlic, minced

¼ teaspoon salt

⅛ teaspoon black pepper

2 tablespoons dry sherry

6g carbs   **2**g fiber   **4**g net carbs

Nutrition Facts per serving: 115 cal., 9 g total fat (5 g sat. fat), 24 mg chol., 235 mg sodium, 6 g carbo., 2 g fiber, 1 g pro.

Sesame-Ginger Spinach with Fennel

Start to Finish: 20 minutes Makes: 4 servings

¾ cup coarsely chopped fennel

2 tablespoons toasted

    sesame oil

2 cloves garlic, minced

1 teaspoon grated fresh ginger

1 tablespoon sherry vinegar

1 tablespoon soy sauce

    Dash cayenne pepper

1 6-ounce package prewashed

    baby spinach

2 teaspoons sesame seeds,

    toasted

1. In a very large skillet cook fennel in hot sesame oil over medium heat about 3 minutes or until nearly tender stirring occasionally. Add garlic and ginger; cook and stir 1 minute more. Stir in vinegar, soy sauce, and cayenne pepper; heat through. Remove from heat.

2. Add spinach to fennel mixture. Toss just until wilted. Sprinkle with sesame seeds. Serve immediately.

4g carbs   **2**g fiber   **2**g net carbs

Nutrition Facts per serving: 90 cal., 8 g total fat (1 g sat. fat),
0 mg chol., 300 mg sodium, 4 g carbo., 2 g fiber, 2 g pro.

Spinach with Creamy Goat Cheese Sauce

Start to Finish: 20 minutes Makes: 4 servings

1. Drain spinach well, squeezing out excess liquid. Pat dry with paper towels; set aside.

2. In a medium saucepan cook and stir shallots and garlic in hot butter over medium heat about 3 minutes or until tender. Add goat cheese, cream, mustard, salt, and pepper. Cook and stir until sauce is smooth and heated through. Stir in spinach; heat through.

2 10-ounce packages frozen chopped spinach, thawed

¼ cup finely chopped shallots (2 medium)

2 cloves garlic, minced

2 tablespoons butter

1 4-ounce package soft goat cheese (chèvre)

½ cup whipping cream

1 tablespoon Dijon-style mustard

¼ teaspoon salt

¼ teaspoon ground black pepper

8g carbs **3**g fiber **5**g net carbs

Nutrition Facts per serving: 281 cal., 23 g total fat (14 g sat. fat), 70 mg chol., 592 mg sodium, 8 g carbo., 3 g fiber, 10 g pro.

Italian Tofu & Tomatoes

Prep: 15 minutes   Cook: 3 minutes   Makes: 6 servings

1   16-ounce package extra-firm
    tub-style tofu (fresh bean curd),
    drained and cut into ½-inch cubes

1   cup halved cherry tomatoes or
    coarsely chopped plum tomatoes
    (3 medium)

⅓   cup olive oil

⅓   cup white wine vinegar

2   cloves garlic, minced

2   tablespoons snipped fresh basil
    or oregano or 2 teaspoons dried
    basil or oregano, crushed

1   tablespoon olive oil

¼   cup finely shredded Asiago or
    Parmesan cheese

    Snipped fresh basil or oregano (optional)

1. Place tofu and tomatoes in a plastic bag set in a deep bowl. In a screw-top jar combine ⅓ cup oil, the vinegar, garlic, 2 tablespoons basil, ¼ teaspoon *salt,* and ⅛ teaspoon *black pepper.* Cover and shake well. Pour over tofu and tomatoes; seal bag. Marinate in the refrigerator for 30 to 60 minutes, gently turning bag once or twice. Gently drain tofu and tomatoes; discard marinade.

2. In a large skillet cook and stir tofu and tomatoes in 1 tablespoon hot oil over medium heat for 3 to 5 minutes or until heated through, gently stirring occasionally. If desired, use a slotted spoon to transfer to serving dish. Sprinkle with Asiago cheese. Let stand about 1 minute or until cheese is slightly melted. If desired, sprinkle with additional basil just before serving.

4g carbs   **1**g fiber   **3**g net carbs

Nutrition Facts per serving: 235 cal., 20 g total fat (4 g sat. fat),
5 mg chol., 152 mg sodium, 4 g carbo., 1 g fiber, 9 g pro.

Beef & Veal

Roasted, grilled, fried, or braised, beef and veal are incredibly versatile and delicious. Better yet, they're "legal" on a low-carb diet, so you don't have to avoid temptations like Beef with Morel–Bourbon Cream Sauce (p. 209) or Stuffed Veal Chops with Gorgonzola (p. 250).

Company-Style Steaks

Start to Finish: 30 minutes Makes: 4 servings

4 beef tenderloin steaks, cut ¾ inch
   thick (1 pound), or a 1-pound
   beef top sirloin steak, cut
   ¾ inch thick

1 tablespoon Dijon-style mustard or
   coarse-grain brown mustard

2 tablespoons olive oil

1 8-ounce package sliced fresh
   mushrooms (3 cups)

⅓ cup dry red wine, dry sherry, or
   beef broth

1 tablespoon Worcestershire sauce
   for chicken

½ cup beef broth

1 teaspoon arrowroot

2 teaspoons snipped fresh thymer

1. If using top sirloin, cut meat into 4 serving-size pieces. Spread mustard over both sides of steaks. In a large skillet heat 1 tablespoon oil over medium–high heat. Add steaks; reduce heat to medium. Cook to desired doneness, turning once. Allow 7 to 9 minutes for medium rare (145°F) to medium (160°F). Transfer to a serving platter; keep warm.

2. Add remaining 1 tablespoon oil to drippings in skillet. Add mushrooms; cook and stir for 4 minutes. Stir in wine and Worcestershire sauce. Bring to boiling; reduce heat. Simmer, uncovered, for 3 minutes. In a small bowl combine broth and arrowroot. Stir into mushroom mixture. Cook and stir until slightly thickened (do not boil). Stir in thyme and season with *salt and pepper*. Spoon mushroom mixture over steaks.

4g carbs

1g fiber

3g net carbs

Nutrition Facts per serving: 283 cal., 17 g total fat (4 g sat. fat),
70 mg chol., 452 mg sodium, 4 g carbo., 1 g fiber, 27 g pro.

Beef with Mushroom-Tomato Sauce

Prep: 20 minutes Grill: 14 minutes Makes: 4 servings

1. Trim fat from meat. Sprinkle both sides of meat with salt and pepper. For a charcoal grill, grill steaks on the rack of an uncovered grill directly over medium coals (see tip, page 107) until desired doneness, turning once halfway through grilling. Allow 14 to 18 minutes for medium rare (145°F) and 18 to 22 minutes for medium (160°F). (For a gas grill, preheat grill. Reduce heat to medium. Place steaks on grill rack over heat. Cover and grill as above.)

2. Meanwhile, in a small saucepan cook and stir mushrooms, onions, and garlic in hot butter over medium heat until vegetables are tender. In a small bowl combine vegetable juice, arrowroot, and beef bouillon granules. Add to saucepan. Cook and stir until thickened (do not boil). Season with salt and pepper. Serve the sauce over steaks.

To broil: Preheat broiler. Place the meat on the unheated rack of a broiler pan. Broil 3 to 4 inches from the heat until desired doneness, turning once halfway through broiling. Allow 15 to 17 minutes for medium rare (145°F) or 20 to 22 minutes for medium (160°F).

4 beef top sirloin steaks, cut
   1 inch thick (1½ pounds)
   Salt and black pepper
1 cup sliced fresh mushrooms
½ cup sliced green onions (4)
2 cloves garlic, minced
1 tablespoon butter
⅔ cup vegetable juice
2 teaspoons arrowroot
½ teaspoon instant beef
   bouillon granules
   Salt and black pepper

4 g carbs **1** g fiber **3** g net carbs

Nutrition Facts per serving: 275 cal., 11 g total fat (4 g sat. fat), 111 mg chol., 532 mg sodium, 4 g carbo., 1 g fiber, 38 g pro.

Mediterranean Beef Kabobs

Prep: 15 minutes Marinate: 4 hours Broil: 8 minutes Makes: 6 servings

1½ pounds boneless beef top sir
   loin steak, cut 1½ inch thick

⅓ cup thinly sliced green
   onions (3)

¼ cup olive oil

3 tablespoons lemon juice

1½ teaspoons bottled minced garlic

2 teaspoons dried tarragon,
   crushed

½ teaspoon dried oregano,
   crushed

¼ teaspoon freshly ground
   black pepper

1. Trim fat from meat. Cut meat into ¼-inch strips. Place in a plastic bag set in a shallow dish.

2. In a small bowl combine green onions, oil, lemon juice, garlic, tarragon, oregano, and pepper. Pour over meat; seal bag. Marinate in the refrigerator for 4 to 24 hours, turning bag occasionally. Drain meat, discarding marinade.

3. Preheat broiler. Loosely thread meat strips accordion-style onto 6 long metal skewers. Place skewers on the unheated rack of a broiler pan. Broil 4 to 5 inches from heat for 8 to 10 minutes or until meat is slightly pink in the center, turning occasionally.

See photo, page 218.

0 g
carbs

0 g
fiber

0 g
net carbs

Nutrition Facts per serving: 165 cal., 7 g total fat (2 g sat. fat),
69 mg chol., 56 mg sodium, 0 g carbo., 0 g fiber, 24 g pro.

Grilled Five-Spice Steak

Prep: 15 minutes Marinate: 4 hours Grill: 14 minutes Makes: 6 servings

1. Trim fat from meat. Place meat in a plastic bag set in a deep bowl. In a small bowl combine soy sauce, ginger, garlic, oil, vinegar, five-spice powder, and crushed red pepper. Pour over meat; seal bag. Turn to coat. Marinate in the refrigerator for 4 to 6 hours, turning bag occasionally. Drain meat; discard marinade.

2. For a charcoal grill, grill steaks on the rack of an uncovered grill directly over medium coals (see page 107) until desired doneness, turning once halfway through grilling. Allow 14 to 18 minutes for medium rare (145°F) and 18 to 22 minutes for medium (160°F). (For a gas grill, preheat grill. Reduce heat to medium. Place steaks on grill rack over heat. Cover and grill as above.)

6 beef top sirloin steaks, cut
    1 inch thick (1½ to 2 pounds)

½ cup reduced-sodium soy sauce

2 tablespoons finely chopped
    fresh ginger

6 cloves garlic, minced

1 tablespoon cooking oil

1 tablespoon cider vinegar

2 teaspoons five-spice powder

1 teaspoon crushed red pepper

1 g carbs   0 g fiber   1 g net carbs

Nutrition Facts per serving: 151 cal., 5 g total fat (1 g sat. fat),
53 mg chol., 153 mg sodium, 1 g carbo., 0 g fiber, 25 g pro.

Citrus Grilled Sirloin Steak

Prep: 25 minutes Grill: 15 minutes Makes: 6 servings

1 teaspoon finely shredded
  lemon peel

¼ cup lemon juice

2 tablespoons olive oil

3 cloves garlic, minced

1 teaspoon cracked black
  pepper

¾ teaspoon salt

3 small yellow sweet
  peppers, quartered

3 small zucchini, sliced
  lengthwise into 3 slices

1 1¾-pound boneless beef
  sirloin steak, cut 1 to
  1¼ inches thick

1. For dressing, in a small bowl combine lemon peel, lemon juice, oil, garlic, black pepper, and salt. In a glass baking dish toss 2 tablespoons of the dressing with sweet peppers and zucchini; set aside. Reserve 2 tablespoons dressing. Brush steak with some of the remaining dressing.

2. For a charcoal grill, place steak on the rack of an uncovered grill directly over medium coals (see tip, page 107). Grill until desired doneness, turning once and brushing with dressing halfway through grilling. Allow 15 to 20 minutes for medium rare (145°F) and 18 to 26 minutes for medium (160°F).

3. Place vegetables on grill around meat for the last 10 minutes of grilling time. Grill vegetables, turning once. (For a gas grill, preheat grill. Reduce heat to medium. Place steaks, then vegetables on grill rack over heat. Cover and grill as above.)

4. With kitchen shears, cut zucchini into bite-size pieces. In a medium bowl toss vegetables with reserved 2 tablespoons dressing. Slice steak; serve with vegetables.

11g carbs   **2**g fiber   **9**g net carbs

Nutrition Facts per serving: 247 cal., 9 g total fat (2 g sat. fat),
80 mg chol., 368 mg sodium, 11 g carbo., 2 g fiber, 30 g pro.

Beef Roll-Ups

Prep: 35 minutes   Roast: 1½ hours   Oven: 350°F   Makes: 4 servings

1. Place meat between 2 pieces of plastic wrap. Pound lightly with the flat side of a meat mallet into a rectangle about ¼ inch thick. Remove plastic wrap.

2. In a medium bowl combine sweet pepper, ½ cup cilantro, the Parmesan cheese, mustard, garlic, salt, and black pepper. Mound filling at one short end of meat. Roll up the meat from the end nearest the filling, tucking in the edges as you roll. Tie roll in several places with 100%-cotton string. In a large ovenproof skillet brown meat in hot oil over medium-high heat, turning to brown evenly. Carefully add broth to skillet; bring to boiling. Cover; roast in a 350° oven for 1½ to 2 hours or until meat is tender. Remove meat from liquid. Cover and keep warm.

3. Remove 1 cup cooking liquid from skillet; skim off fat (discard fat and remaining cooking liquid). Transfer 1 cup cooking liquid to medium saucepan. Stir in tomato paste. Bring to boiling; reduce heat. Simmer for 5 minutes or until reduced to ¾ cup. Stir in tomato and 1 tablespoon cilantro; heat through. To serve, remove and discard string from meat. Cut meat roll into 4 slices. Spoon sauce over meat.

*Note: Look for single steak of this size.

1   1½- to 2-pound boneless beef
    round steak*, cut ½ inch thick
½   cup seeded and finely chopped
    yellow or red sweet pepper
½   cup snipped fresh cilantro
¼   cup finely shredded Parmesan
    cheese
1   teaspoon Dijon-style mustard
1   clove garlic, minced
¼   teaspoon salt
¼   teaspoon black pepper
1   tablespoon olive oil
1   cup reduced-sodium beef broth
2   tablespoons tomato paste
½   cup chopped tomato (1 medium)
1   tablespoon snipped fresh cilantro

7g carbs   **1**g fiber   **6**g net carbs

Nutrition Facts per serving: 417 cal., 19 g total fat (8 g sat. fat), 120 mg chol., 939 mg sodium, 7 g carbo., 1 g fiber, 53 g pro.

Peppered Beef Tenderloin with Horseradish Cream

Start to Finish: 15 minutes Makes: 2 servings

2 teaspoons cracked black
   pepper
2 beef tenderloin steaks, cut
   1 inch thick (10 ounces)
2 tablespoons butter
⅓ cup whipping cream
2 tablespoons horseradish
   mustard
   Salt and black pepper
   Whole green or pink
   peppercorns, slightly
   crushed

1. Sprinkle cracked black pepper over both sides of steaks, pressing pepper into steaks.

2. In a large skillet cook steaks in hot butter over medium heat to desired doneness, turning once. Allow 10 to 13 minutes for medium rare (145°F) to medium (160°F). (If steaks brown too quickly, reduce heat to medium-low.) Transfer steaks to 2 warm dinner plates. Cover to keep warm.

3. Meanwhile, in a medium mixing bowl beat cream with an electric mixer on medium speed until soft peaks form (tips curl). Fold in horseradish mustard. Season with salt and black pepper.

4. Serve horseradish cream with steaks. Sprinkle cream with crushed peppercorns.

See photo, page 219.

4g carbs   **1**g fiber   **3**g net carbs

Nutrition Facts per serving: 473 cal., 37 g total fat (19 g sat. fat), 174 mg chol., 593 mg sodium, 4 g carbo., 1 g fiber, 32 g pro.

Beef Steaks with Tomato-Garlic Butter

Prep: 15 minutes Grill: 8 minutes Makes: 4 servings

1. For tomato-garlic butter, in a small bowl combine the butter, tomatoes, kalamata olives, green onion, and garlic. Set aside. Trim fat from steaks. For a charcoal grill, grill steaks on the rack of an uncovered grill directly over medium coals (see tip, page 107) until desired doneness, turning once halfway through grilling. Allow 8 to 12 minutes for medium-rare (145°F) and 12 to 15 minutes for medium (160°F). (For a gas grill, preheat grill. Reduce heat to medium. Place steaks on grill rack over heat. Cover and grill as above.)

2. If desired, season steaks with salt and pepper. To serve, spread 1 tablespoon of the tomato-garlic butter over each steak. Cover and chill the remaining tomato-garlic butter mixture for another time.

½ cup butter, softened

1 tablespoon snipped oil-packed
   dried tomatoes

1 tablespoon chopped kalamata
   olives

1 tablespoon finely chopped
   green onion

1 clove garlic, minced

4 boneless beef top loin steaks,
   cut 1 inch thick (1½ pounds)
   Salt and black pepper (optional)

0g carbs   **0**g fiber   **0**g net carbs

Nutrition Facts per serving: 383 cal., 22 g total fat (11 g sat. fat), 161 mg chol., 227 mg sodium, 0 g carbo., 0 g fiber, 45 g pro.

Beef Tenderloin with Lemon-Dijon Cream

Prep: 15 minutes Grill: 4 minutes Makes: 4 to 6 servings

1 cup low-fat cottage cheese

¼ cup whipping cream

1 tablespoon lemon juice

1 tablespoon Dijon-style

    mustard

1 teaspoon snipped fresh thyme

    or oregano

1 to 1½ pounds beef tenderloin

    Salt and black pepper

    Snipped fresh watercress or

    chives (optional)

1. For lemon-dijon cream, in a food processor bowl or blender container combine cottage cheese, whipping cream, lemon juice, mustard, and thyme. Cover and process or blend until smooth. Cover and set aside until ready to serve (up to 30 minutes).

2. Trim fat and silver skin from meat. Using a very sharp knife, cut tenderloin* across the grain into ¼- to ½-inch slices. Sprinkle meat slices with salt and pepper.

3. For a charcoal grill, grill beef slices on the rack of an uncovered grill directly over hot coals (see tip, page 107) for 4 to 8 minutes or until desired doneness, turning once halfway through grilling. (For a gas grill, preheat grill. Place beef on grill rack over high heat. Cover and grill as above.) Or coat a large nonstick skillet with *nonstick cooking spray.* Heat skillet over medium-high heat. Cook beef slices for 4 to 8 minutes or until desired doneness, turning once.

4. Serve meat with a generous amount of lemon-dijon cream. If desired, garnish with watercress.

***Tip:** Partially freeze beef for easier slicing.

3 g carbs **0** g fiber **3** g net carbs

Nutrition Facts per serving: 282 cal., 15 g total fat (7 g sat. fat), 92 mg chol., 523 mg sodium, 3 g carbo., 0 g fiber, 32 g pro.

Filet Mignon with Portobello Sauce

Prep: 15 minutes   Grill: 8 minutes   Makes: 4 servings

1. Trim fat from steaks. Rub both sides of steaks with oil and pepper. For a charcoal grill, grill steaks on the rack of an uncovered grill directly over medium coals (see tip, page 107) to desired doneness, turning once halfway through grilling. Allow 8 to 12 minutes for medium rare (145°F) and 12 to 15 minutes for medium (160°F). (For a gas grill, preheat grill. Reduce heat to medium. Place steaks on grill rack over heat. Cover and grill as above.)

2. Meanwhile, for sauce, in a large skillet cook and stir mushrooms and onions in hot butter over medium heat about 5 minutes or until vegetables are tender. Stir in broth and Madeira. Bring to boiling. Remove from heat. Thinly slice steaks diagonally and serve with sauce.

4 beef tenderloin steaks, cut 1 inch
   thick (1¼ pounds)

1 teaspoon olive oil

¼ teaspoon black pepper

2 large portobello mushrooms,
   halved and sliced

8 green onions, cut into 1-inch pieces

1 tablespoon butter

⅓ cup beef broth

2 tablespoons Madeira or port wine

4g carbs   **1**g fiber   **3**g net carbs

Nutrition Facts per serving: 260 cal., 13 g total fat (4 g sat. fat),
80 mg chol., 160 mg sodium, 4 g carbo., 1 g fiber, 29 g pro.

Fennel-Lime-Crusted Beef Tenderloin

Prep: 30 minutes Chill: 30 minutes Roast: 45 minutes Stand: 10 minutes
Oven: 425°F Makes: 12 appetizer servings

8 tablespoons olive oil

¼ cup fennel seeds

¼ cup snipped fresh tarragon

¼ cup finely shredded lime

   peel (from 5 to 6 limes)

1 3-pound center-cut beef

   tenderloin

1 pound peeled onions, such as

   cipollini onions, pearl onions,

   and/or yellow onions cut into

   8 wedges each

3 cups sliced fennel bulb

½ cup dry red wine

1 pound fresh green beans,

   trimmed

1. In a small bowl combine 6 tablespoons of the oil, fennel seeds, tarragon, lime peel, 2 teaspoons *black pepper*, and ½ teaspoon *salt.* Stir well. Coat the tenderloin with seed mixture. Place meat in a glass baking dish; cover loosely with foil. Chill in the refrigerator for 30 minutes or up to 1 hour.

2. Place meat on a rack in a shallow roasting pan. Insert an oven-going meat thermometer into center of roast. In a bowl toss onions and 1 tablespoon olive oil. Place onions in half of the roasting pan alongside meat. Roast, uncovered, in a 425° oven for 30 minutes. In the same bowl toss fennel and the remaining 1 tablespoon oil. Stir onions and add fennel mixture to other half of roasting pan. Roast 15 to 20 minutes or until thermometer registers 140°F for medium rare.

3. Remove meat from oven. Transfer meat to cutting board. Cover with foil; let stand 10 minutes. Wrap roast in plastic wrap; refrigerate until ready to serve. Transfer onions and fennel to separate bowls. Cover; refrigerate until ready to serve. Place roasting pan on stove top over low heat. Add red wine, stirring constantly to dissolve browned bits. Transfer sauce to bowl. Cover; refrigerate until ready to serve.

4. To serve, cook green beans in a small amount of boiling salted water for 5 minutes; drain. Rinse with cold water; drain. Toss green beans with reserved sauce. Arrange on platter. Slice meat into thin slices and arrange on top of beans. Serve with roasted onion and fennel.

9 g carbs   **3** g fiber   **6** g net carbs

Nutrition Facts per serving : 310 cal., 18 g total fat (5 g sat. fat), 70 mg chol., 167 mg sodium, 9 g carbo., 3 g fiber, 25 g pro.

Beef with Morel-Bourbon Cream Sauce

Prep: 30 minutes Roast: 1½ hours Stand: 15 minutes
Oven: 325°F Makes: 8 servings

1. Trim fat from meat. Rub cracked black pepper onto meat.

2. Place the meat on a rack in a shallow roasting pan. Insert an oven-going meat thermometer into center of roast. Roast, uncovered, in a 325° oven for 1½ to 1¾ hours or until thermometer registers 140°F for medium rare. Cover meat with foil and let stand for 10 minutes. (The temperature of the meat will rise about 5°F while standing.)

3. In a bowl cover dried mushrooms with boiling water; let stand 20 minutes. Drain. Rinse mushrooms under warm running water; squeeze out excess moisture. Slice mushrooms. Set aside.

4. In a saucepan melt butter over medium heat. Add shallots; cook and stir 3 minutes or until tender. Add broth and wine. Bring to boiling. Simmer, uncovered, over medium–high heat for 6 to 8 minutes or until liquid is reduced to ¼ cup.

5. Stir in ginger, salt, and white pepper. Whisk in cream. Cook, whisking constantly, over medium heat about 5 minutes or until mixture thickens.

6. Stir in the reserved mushrooms and the bourbon. Cook and stir until heated through. Season with salt and pepper.

7. Thinly slice meat across the grain. Arrange on a serving platter. Pour some sauce over meat. Pass the remaining sauce.

1 2½- to 3-pound boneless beef eye round roast

1 tablespoon cracked black pepper

1 ounce dried morel mushrooms

2 tablespoons butter

2 tablespoons finely chopped shallots (1 medium)

⅓ cup beef broth

⅓ cup dry white wine or water

½ teaspoon ground ginger

¼ teaspoon salt

¼ teaspoon ground white pepper

1 cup whipping cream

1 to 2 tablespoons bourbon

Salt and ground white pepper

5g carbs   **1**g fiber   **4**g net carbs

Nutrition Facts per serving: 362 cal., 22 g total fat (11 g sat. fat), 125 mg chol., 281 mg sodium, 5 g carbo., 1 g fiber, 32 g pro.

Beef & Mushroom Kabobs

Prep: 25 minutes Marinate: 1 hour Grill: 8 minutes Makes: 6 servings

1 cup dry red wine

2 tablespoons olive oil

2 sprigs fresh thyme or
½ teaspoon dried thyme, crushed

2 cloves garlic, minced

2 tablespoons snipped fresh oregano or 2 teaspoons dried oregano, crushed

1 shallot, thinly sliced

¾ teaspoon salt

½ teaspoon black pepper

1½ pounds beef tenderloin, cut into 1- to 1½-inch cubes

8 ounces fresh mushrooms

12 cherry tomatoes

1. In a medium bowl combine wine, oil, thyme, garlic, oregano, shallot, salt, and pepper.

2. Place meat in a plastic bag set in a deep bowl. Pour marinade over meat; seal bag. Marinate in refrigerator for 1 to 3 hours, turning bag occasionally. Drain meat, discarding marinade. On 6 to 8 long metal skewers, alternately thread beef, mushrooms, and tomatoes, leaving a ¼-inch space between pieces.

3. For a charcoal grill, grill kabobs on grill rack directly over medium coals (see tip, page 107) until desired doneness, turning skewers occasionally. Allow 8 to 12 minutes for medium rare (145°F) and 12 to 15 minutes for medium (160°F). (For a gas grill, preheat grill. Reduce heat to medium. Place kabobs on grill rack over heat. Cover and grill as above.)

4 g carbs   **1** g fiber   **3** g net carbs

Nutrition Facts per serving: 238 cal., 12 g total fat (4 g sat. fat), 70 mg chol., 204 mg sodium, 4 g carbo., 1 g fiber, 25 g pro.

Prime Rib with Horseradish Cream

Prep: 15 minutes Roast: 2 hours Stand: 10 minutes
Oven: 350°F Makes: 8 to 10 servings

1. In a small bowl combine 1 teaspoon salt, the pepper, and thyme. Sprinkle onto roast; rub into meat using your fingers. Place meat, fat side up, on a rack in a shallow roasting pan. Insert an oven-going meat thermometer into center of roast. The thermometer should not touch the bone.

2. Roast, uncovered, in a 350° oven until desired doneness. Allow 2 to 2½ hours for medium rare (135°F) and 2½ to 3 hours for medium (155°F). Cover with foil and let stand for 10 minutes. (The temperature of the meat will rise about 5°F while standing.)

3. Meanwhile, for the horseradish cream, in a small bowl combine sour cream, horseradish, shallot, vinegar, and ¼ teaspoon salt. Cover and chill until ready to serve.

4. Serve horseradish cream with sliced meat.

See photo, page 220.

1 teaspoon kosher salt or salt

½ teaspoon black pepper

½ teaspoon dried thyme, crushed

1 5- to 7-pound beef rib roast

1 8-ounce container dairy sour
    cream

2 tablespoons grated fresh
    horseradish or
    prepared horseradish

1 tablespoon finely chopped
    shallot

2 teaspoons white balsamic
    vinegar or white wine vinegar

¼ teaspoon kosher salt or salt

3g carbs **0**g fiber **3**g net carbs

Nutrition Facts per serving: 318 cal., 17 g total fat (8 g sat. fat), 112 mg chol., 408 mg sodium, 3 g carbo., 0 g fiber, 35 g pro.

Beef Adobo with Lime Cream

Prep: 25 minutes Marinate: 2 hours Cook: 8 minutes Makes: 4 servings

2 dried New Mexico red chile

    peppers or 2 dried ancho

    chile peppers (see tip,

    page 59)

1½ cups boiling water

1 teaspoon cumin seeds

1 teaspoon dried oregano, crushed

2 tablespoons sherry vinegar

2 cloves garlic, quartered

4 beef tenderloin steaks, cut

    1 inch thick (about 1 pound)

¼ cup dairy sour cream

¼ cup mayonnaise

⅛ teaspoon finely shredded

    lime peel

1 tablespoon lime juice

1. Remove and discard stems from dried peppers. Cut peppers in half lengthwise; remove and discard seeds. Place peppers in a small bowl; cover with 1½ cups boiling water. Cover and let stand for 10 minutes.

2. Meanwhile, for marinade, heat a skillet over medium heat; add cumin seeds. Cook and stir for 30 seconds. Add oregano; cook and stir about 1 minute or until cumin seeds are toasted.

3. Transfer toasted seed mixture to a blender container or food processor bowl. Drain peppers, reserving 1 cup liquid. Add peppers, reserved liquid, vinegar, garlic, and ¼ teaspoon *salt* to the seed mixture. Cover; blend or process until smooth.

4. Place steaks in a plastic bag set in a dish. Pour marinade over steaks; seal bag. Marinate in the refrigerator for at least 2 hours or up to 4 hours, turning bag occasionally.

5. Drain steaks, discarding marinade. Lightly coat an unheated skillet with *nonstick cooking spray*. Heat skillet over medium-high heat. Sprinkle steaks on both sides with *salt*. Reduce heat to medium; add steaks. Cook until desired doneness, turning once. Allow 8 to 11 minutes for medium rare (145°F) and 12 to 14 minutes for medium (160°F). Meanwhile, in a small bowl combine sour cream, mayonnaise, lime juice, and lime peel. Season to taste with *garlic pepper*. Cover and chill until ready to serve. Serve with steaks.

2g carbs   **0**g fiber   **2**g net carbs

Nutrition Facts per serving: 318 cal., 23 g total fat (6 g sat. fat), 85 mg chol., 445 mg sodium, 2 g carbo., 0 g fiber, 24 g pro.

Beef Steak with Avocado Sauce

Prep: 25 minutes Chill: 30 Minutes Grill: 14 minutes Makes: 4 to 6 servings

1. Trim fat from around the edges of steaks. Place steaks in a shallow dish. In a small bowl combine chili powder, garlic salt, and black pepper. Sprinkle on both sides of the steaks. Cover dish and chill for 30 minutes.

2. Meanwhile, for sauce, in a small saucepan combine the quartered tomatillos and water. Bring to boiling; reduce heat. Simmer, covered, for 5 to 7 minutes or until soft. Add the cream cheese; stir until melted. Cool mixture slightly.

3. In a food processor bowl or blender container combine the tomatillo mixture, avocado, sliced green onions, and salt. Cover and process or blend until sauce mixture is smooth. Transfer sauce to a serving bowl.

4. For a charcoal grill, grill steaks on the rack of an uncovered grill directly over medium coals (see tip, page 107) until desired doneness, turning halfway through grilling. Allow 14 to 18 minutes for medium rare (145°F) and 18 to 22 minutes for medium (160°F). Brush the whole green onions and jalapeños lightly with *oil;* grill jalapeños about 10 minutes and green onions about 5 minutes or until soft and lightly charred, turning occasionally. (For a gas grill, preheat grill. Reduce heat to medium. Place steaks on grill rack over heat. Cover and grill as above.)

5. To serve, slice steaks. Serve with sauce, grilled jalapeños, and grilled green onions. Sprinkle with tomato.

2 beef ribeye steaks or top loin steaks, cut
   1¼ to 1½ inches thick (1½ pounds)

1 teaspoons chili powder

½ teaspoon garlic salt

½ teaspoon black pepper

6 medium fresh tomatillos, husked and
   quartered (8 ounces)

¼ cup water

2 ounces cream cheese

1 medium avocado, halved, seeded, peeled,
   and chopped

¼ cup sliced green onions (4)

½ teaspoon salt

8 to 12 green onions, trimmed to 6-inch pieces

4 to 6 jalapeño chile peppers (see tip, page 59)

⅔ cup chopped tomato (1 large)

12g carbs **5**g fiber **7**g net carbs

Nutrition Facts per serving: 413 cal., 23 g total fat (8 g sat. fat),
96 mg chol., 560 mg sodium, 12 g carbo., 5 g fiber, 41 g pro.

Ribeyes with Chipotle Butter

Prep: 20 minutes Grill: 14 minutes Makes: 4 servings

¼ cup butter, softened

1 tablespoon finely chopped shallots

2 teaspoons snipped fresh basil

1½ teaspoons lime juice

1 teaspoon finely chopped chipotle

pepper in adobo sauce

2 teaspoons ground cumin

1 teaspoon paprika

½ teaspoon ground white pepper

1 tablespoon olive oil

¼ teaspoon adobo sauce (from canned

chipotle pepper in adobo sauce)

4 beef ribeye steaks, cut 1 inch thick

(1½ to 2 pounds)

Fresh basil sprigs

Lime wedges

1. For chipotle butter, in a small bowl, combine butter, shallots, snipped basil, lime juice, and chipotle pepper; set aside.

2. In another small bowl combine cumin, paprika, ½ teaspoon *salt,* and pepper. Stir in oil and adobo sauce until a paste forms. Spread mixture over both sides of steaks.

3. For a charcoal grill, grill steaks on the rack of an uncovered grill directly over medium coals (see tip, page 107) until desired doneness, turning once halfway through grilling. Allow 14 to 18 minutes for medium rare (145°F) and 18 to 22 minutes for medium (160°F). Serve steaks with chipotle butter and garnish with basil sprigs and lime wedges.

2g carbs   **1**g fiber   **1**g net carbs

Nutrition Facts per serving: 416 cal., 27 g total fat (12 g sat. fat), 118 mg chol., 519 mg sodium, 2 g carbo., 1 g fiber, 40 g pro.

Brisket with Sour Cream Sauce

Prep: 15 minutes Bake: 3 hours Oven: 325°F Makes: 6 servings

1. Trim fat from meat. Place meat in a 13×9×2-inch baking pan. In a medium bowl combine broth, red wine, shallots, poblano pepper, and paprika. Pour over meat. Cover with foil. Bake in a 325° oven about 3 hours or until tender, turning once. Remove meat, reserving juices. Cover meat; keep warm.

2. For sauce, skim fat from pan juices. Measure $1/2$ cup pan juices; transfer to a small saucepan. Reserve remaining pan juices. Whisk sour cream into pan juices in saucepan. Cook and stir over low heat just until heated through (do not boil). Season to taste with salt and black pepper. Thinly slice meat across the grain. Drizzle meat with some of the reserved pan juices (discard remaining pan juices). Serve meat with sauce. If desired, sprinkle with cilantro.

1 2- to 2½-pound fresh beef brisket

1 14-ounce can beef broth

½ cup dry red wine

¼ cup finely chopped shallots
   (2 medium) or ¼ cup
   chopped onion

¾ cup finely chopped poblano chile
   pepper (see tip, page 59) or
   finely chopped green sweet
   pepper

1 teaspoon paprika

1 8-ounce carton dairy sour cream

   Salt and black pepper

   Snipped fresh cilantro (optional)

5 g carbs **0** g fiber **5** g net carbs

Nutrition Facts per serving: 337 cal., 19 g total fat (8 g sat. fat), 111 mg chol., 492 mg sodium, 5 g carbo., 0 g fiber, 33 g pro.

Flank Steak Spirals

Prep: 30 minutes Marinate: 4 hours Grill: 10 minutes Makes: 4 servings

1 1¼-pound beef flank steak

1 cup dry red wine

¼ cup finely chopped green
    onions (4)

1 bay leaf

1½ teaspoons Worcestershire sauce

1 clove garlic, minced

½ teaspoon salt

¼ teaspoon black pepper

6 slices bacon

¼ cup finely chopped onion

2 tablespoons snipped fresh parsley

2 cloves garlic, minced

½ teaspoon coarsely ground
    black pepper

¼ teaspoon salt

1. Score both sides of meat.

2. Place meat between 2 pieces of plastic wrap. Working from center to edges, use flat side of a meat mallet to pound steak into a 12×8-inch rectangle. Remove plastic wrap. Place meat in a plastic bag set in a shallow dish.

3. In a bowl combine wine, green onions, bay leaf, Worcestershire sauce, 1 clove minced garlic, ½ teaspoon salt, and ¼ teaspoon black pepper. Pour over meat; seal bag. Marinate in refrigerator for 4 to 24 hours, turning occasionally.

4. In a skillet cook bacon just until done but not crisp. Drain on paper towels. In a bowl combine onion, parsley, 2 cloves minced garlic, ½ teaspoon black pepper, and ¼ teaspoon salt.

5. Drain meat, reserving marinade. Sprinkle one side of steak with parsley mixture. Lay bacon strips lengthwise on steak. Roll up meat from a short side; secure with wooden toothpicks at 1-inch intervals. Cut between the toothpicks into eight 1-inch-thick slices.

6. For a charcoal grill, grill steak on rack of an uncovered grill over medium coals (see tip, page 107) until desired doneness, turning and brushing with reserved marinade halfway through grilling. Allow 10 to 12 minutes for medium (160°F). (For a gas grill, preheat grill. Reduce heat to medium. Place steak on grill rack over heat. Cover and grill as above.) Discard remaining marinade.

3 g
carbs

0 g
fiber

3 g
net carbs

Nutrition Facts per serving: 324.0 cal., 16 g total fat (6 g sat. fat), 67 mg chol., 575 mg sodium, 3 g carbo., 0 g fiber, 35 g pro.

See photo, page 217.

Flank
Steak
Spirals
p. 216

Mediterranean
Beef
Kabobs
p. 200

Peppered
Beef
Tenderloin with
Horseradish
Cream
p. 204

Prime Rib
with
Horseradish
Cream
p. 211

Rosemary
Beef with
Sweet Pepper
Relish
p. 239

Salsa
Steak
p. 241

Stuffed Veal
Chops with
Gorgonzola
p. 250

Asian
Braised
Short Ribs
p. 225

Asian Braised Short Ribs

Prep: 20 minutes Cook: 2 hours Makes: 6 servings

1. Trim fat from meat; set aside.

2. In a Dutch oven heat oil over medium heat. Add onion; cook and stir for 5 minutes. Add garlic, ginger, and five-spice powder; cook and stir for 1 minute. Add short ribs, tomato puree, broth, salt, and pepper. Bring to boiling; reduce heat. Simmer, covered, for 1½ hours.

3. If using shiitake mushrooms, remove stems and discard; cut caps in half. (If using button mushrooms, cut into quarters.) Add mushrooms to mixture in Dutch oven. Cook, covered, about 30 minutes more or until short ribs are tender.

4. Divide ribs among 6 shallow serving bowls. Skim fat from cooking liquid; spoon cooking liquid over ribs. Sprinkle with parsley.

See photo, page 224.

3 to 4 pounds beef short ribs, cut into serving-size pieces

2 tablespoons cooking oil

⅓ cup chopped onion (1 small)

2 cloves garlic, minced

1 teaspoon grated fresh ginger

½ teaspoon five-spice powder

1 15-ounce can tomato puree

1 cup beef broth

¼ teaspoon salt

⅛ teaspoon black pepper

3 ounces fresh shiitake or button mushrooms

2 tablespoons snipped fresh flat-leaf parsley

6g carbs   **1**g fiber   **5**g net carbs

Nutrition Facts per serving: 222 cal., 13 g total fat (4 g sat. fat), 43 mg chol., 335 mg sodium, 6 g carbo., 1 g fiber, 20 g pro.

Burgers with Mustard Sauce

Prep: 20 minutes Broil: 12 minutes Makes: 4 servings

¼ cup finely chopped onion

¼ cup snipped fresh parsley or

½ teaspoon dried dill

½ teaspoon salt

1 pound ground beef or lamb

¼ cup dairy sour cream

2 tablespoons mayonnaise

1 tablespoon Dijon-style

mustard

¼ teaspoon dried dill

¼ cup chopped seeded

cucumber

1. In a large bowl combine onion, parsley, and salt. Add meat; mix well. Shape into four ¾-inch-thick patties.

2. Preheat broiler. Place patties on the unheated rack of a broiler pan. Broil 3 to 4 inches from the heat for 12 to 14 minutes or until done (160°F), turning once halfway through broiling.

3. Meanwhile, for sauce, in a small bowl combine sour cream, mayonnaise, mustard, and ¼ teaspoon dill. Stir in cucumber. Spoon sauce over burgers.

3 g carbs   **0** g fiber   **3** g net carbs

Nutrition Facts per serving: 304 cal., 22 g total fat (8 g sat. fat), 82 mg chol., 491 mg sodium, 3 g carbo., 0 g fiber, 23 g pro.

Steak with Sweet Pepper Mustard

Prep: 30 minutes Grill: 14 minutes Makes: 4 servings

1. Brush sweet peppers with olive oil. For a charcoal grill, grill sweet peppers, cut side up, on the rack of an uncovered grill directly over medium-high coals (see tip, page 107) about 10 minutes or until sweet pepper skins are blistered and dark. (For a gas grill, preheat grill. Reduce heat to medium-high. Place sweet peppers, cut side up, on grill rack over heat. Cover and grill as above.)

2. Wrap sweet peppers in foil; let stand for 20 minutes. Remove and discard pepper skins. Cut 2 pepper pieces lengthwise into thin strips; set aside. In a blender container or food processor bowl combine the remaining pepper pieces, 1 tablespoon fresh thyme, Dijon mustard, and 1 clove garlic. Cover and blend or process until smooth; set aside.

3. Meanwhile, trim fat from steaks. For rub, in a small bowl combine remaining thyme, remaining garlic, salt, and pepper. Sprinkle mixture over steaks; rub into meat with your fingers. For a charcoal grill, grill steaks on the rack of an uncovered grill directly over medium coals until desired doneness, turning once halfway through grilling. Allow 14 to 18 minutes for medium rare (145°F) and 18 to 22 minutes for medium doneness (160°F). (For a gas grill, preheat grill. Place steaks on a grill rack over medium heat. Cover; grill as above.)

4. Garnish the steaks with the grilled sweet pepper strips. Serve with the mustard mixture.

2 **medium red sweet peppers,**
   quartered lengthwise
   Olive oil
2 **tablespoons snipped fresh**
   thyme or 2 teaspoons dried
   thyme, crushed
1 **tablespoon Dijon-style mustard**
3 **cloves garlic, minced**
4 **boneless beef sirloin steaks,**
   cut 1 inch thick (1½ to
   2 pounds)
¼ **teaspoon salt**
¼ **teaspoon black pepper**

5 g carbs   **1** g fiber   **4** g net carbs

Nutrition Facts per serving: 280 cal., 11 g total fat (3 g sat. fat), 103 mg chol., 321 mg sodium, 5 g carbo., 1 g fiber, 38 g pro.

Sizzling Southwest Short Ribs

Prep: 10 minutes Bake: 2 hours Oven: 450°/350°F Makes: 6 servings

2 teaspoons ground cumin

2 teaspoons ground coriander

1 to 2 teaspoons chili powder

1 teaspoon dried thyme, crushed

1 teaspoon dried oregano, crushed

½ teaspoon salt

¼ teaspoon cayenne pepper

1¾ pounds boneless beef short ribs

½ cup chopped onion (1 medium)

1½ cups bottled salsa or picante

sauce

¼ cup red wine vinegar

2 cloves garlic, minced

¼ cup snipped fresh cilantro

(optional)

1. Line a 13×9×2-inch baking pan with foil; set aside. For rub, in a small bowl combine cumin, coriander, chili powder, thyme, oregano, salt, and cayenne pepper. Cut ribs into serving-size pieces, if necessary. Rub spice mixture onto both sides of ribs. Place ribs in prepared baking pan. Cover with foil; bake in a 450° oven for 1 hour. Carefully pour off fat and juices. Sprinkle ribs with onion. In a medium bowl combine salsa, vinegar, and garlic. Spoon over ribs. Reduce oven temperature to 350°. Cover and bake for 1 hour more or until tender. Transfer ribs to serving platter. Spoon sauce from pan over ribs. If desired, sprinkle with cilantro.

8g
carbs

0g
fiber

8g
net carbs

Nutrition Facts per serving: 367 cal., 21 g total fat (8 g sat. fat), 112 mg chol., 509 mg sodium, 8 g carbo., 0 g fiber, 39 g pro.

228

Sautéed Sirloin & Mushrooms

Start to Finish: 30 minutes Makes: 4 servings

1. Cut steak into 4 serving-size pieces. Sprinkle meat with herb pepper. In a 10-inch skillet cook meat in hot butter over medium heat for 8 to 10 minutes or to desired doneness (145°F for medium rare), turning once. Remove steaks from pan; cover and keep warm.

2. For mushroom glaze, carefully add broth and soy sauce to skillet. Cook and stir until bubbly, scraping brown bits from the bottom of the pan. Add onion wedges and sliced mushrooms. Cook over medium-high heat about 8 minutes or until vegetables are tender and the glaze is reduced to 1 cup, stirring occasionally. Transfer warm steaks to dinner plates and spoon glaze over top.

1 1- to 1¼-pound boneless beef
   sirloin steak, cut ½ inch thick

¾ teaspoon herb pepper or
   ¼ teaspoon garlic pepper

1 tablespoon butter

¾ cup beef broth

1 tablespoon soy sauce or
   Worcestershire sauce

1 small onion, cut into very thin wedges

1¾ cups sliced fresh mushrooms

3g carbs **1**g fiber **2**g net carbs

Nutrition Facts per serving: 200 cal., 9 g total fat (3 g sat. fat),
77 mg chol., 477 mg sodium, 3 g carbo., 1 g fiber, 27 g pro.

French-Style Short Ribs

Prep: 20 minutes Cook: 1 hour 40 minutes Makes: 4 to 6 servings

2 pounds boneless beef short ribs

1 tablespoon cooking oil

¾ cup chicken broth

½ teaspoon black pepper

½ teaspoon dried rosemary, crushed

½ teaspoon dried thyme, crushed

¼ teaspoon salt

8 ounces fresh cremini, shiitake, or

   button mushrooms, halved

2 small zucchini, cut into 1-inch

   pieces (8 ounces)

4 medium leeks, cut in half lengthwise

   and sliced in 2-inch pieces

2 teaspoons finely shredded lemon peel

⅓ cup dairy sour cream

1. Cut meat into serving-size pieces, if necessary. In a 4-quart Dutch oven brown short ribs, half at a time, in hot oil over medium-high heat. Drain off fat. Add broth, ½ teaspoon pepper, the rosemary, thyme, and ¼ teaspoon salt. Bring to boiling; reduce heat. Simmer, covered, for 1½ hours or until meat is tender.

2. Add mushrooms, zucchini, leeks, and lemon peel. Simmer, covered, for 10 to 12 minutes more or until vegetables are tender. Using a slotted spoon, transfer meat and vegetables to serving dish. Cover and keep warm.

3. Measure ¾ cup of the cooking liquid. Whisk in sour cream. Transfer mixture to a small saucepan. Cook and stir over low heat just until heated through (do not boil). Season with *salt and pepper.* To serve, spoon sauce over meat and vegetables.

9 g carbs   **2** g fiber   **7** g net carbs

Nutrition Facts per serving: 260 cal., 16 g total fat (6 g sat. fat),
50 mg chol., 567 mg sodium, 9 g carbo., 2 g fiber, 22 g pro.

Indian Spiced Patties

Prep: 15 minutes Grill: 14 minutes Makes: 2 servings

1. For sauce, in a small bowl combine the sour cream and cucumber. Cover and chill until ready to serve.

2. In a medium bowl combine onion, jalapeño pepper, mint, cumin, garlic, and salt. Add the meat; mix well. Shape into two ¾-inch-thick patties.

3. For a charcoal grill, grill patties on the rack of an uncovered grill directly over medium coals (see tip, page 107) for 14 to 18 minutes or until meat is done (160°F), turning once halfway through grilling. (For a gas grill, preheat grill. Reduce heat to medium. Place patties on grill rack over heat. Cover and grill as above.)

4. Serve the patties topped with yogurt-cucumber sauce.

½ cup dairy sour cream

⅓ cup chopped, seeded cucumber

¼ cup finely chopped onion

1 medium jalapeño chile pepper, seeded and finely chopped (see tip, page 59), or 2 tablespoons canned diced green chile peppers

1 tablespoon snipped fresh mint or 1 teaspoon dried mint, crushed

½ teaspoon ground cumin

1 clove garlic, minced, or ⅛ teaspoon garlic powder

¼ teaspoon salt

8 ounces lean ground beef, pork, or turkey

6 g carbs   **1** g fiber   **5** g net carbs

Nutrition Facts per serving: 304 cal., 21 g total fat (10 g sat. fat), 93 mg chol., 359 mg sodium, 6 g carbo., 1 g fiber, 22 g pro.

Grilled Beef Fillet with Portobello Relish

Prep: 15 minutes Grill: 15 minutes Makes: 4 servings

4 beef tenderloin steaks, cut
1 inch thick (about 1¼ pounds)
Kosher salt*
Cracked black pepper

8 ounces fresh portobello
mushrooms, stems removed

1 medium yellow onion, cut into
½-inch slices

4 plum tomatoes, halved
lengthwise

3 tablespoons snipped fresh basil

2 tablespoons minced fresh garlic
(12 cloves)

2 tablespoons olive oil

1 teaspoon kosher salt*

1 teaspoon cracked black pepper

1. Trim fat from steaks. Season steaks with salt and pepper. For a charcoal grill, grill steaks on the rack of an uncovered grill directly over medium heat (see tip, page 107) until desired doneness, turning once halfway through grilling. Allow 11 to 15 minutes for medium rare (145°F) and 14 to 18 minutes for medium (160°F). (For a gas grill, preheat grill. Reduce heat to medium. Place meat on grill rack over heat. Cover and grill as above.)

2. Meanwhile, for relish, grill mushrooms, onion, and tomatoes directly over medium coals until tender, turning once halfway through grilling. Allow 15 minutes for onion and 10 minutes for mushrooms and tomatoes. Remove vegetables from grill.

3. Cut onion, mushrooms, and tomatoes into 1-inch pieces. In a medium bowl combine basil, garlic, olive oil, the 1 teaspoon salt, and the 1 teaspoon pepper; stir in grilled vegetables. To serve, spoon warm relish over steaks.

***Kosher salt:** Kosher salt is a coarse salt with no additives. It's preferred by many cooks because it has a light, flaky texture, clean taste, and less sodium than regular salt. It's ideal for use in salads and relishes, as in the recipe above. Look for it next to the regular salt in your supermarket.

9g carbs   **2**g fiber   **7**g net carbs

Nutrition Facts per serving: 329 cal., 18 g total fat (5 g sat. fat), 87 mg chol., 617 mg sodium, 9 g carbo., 2 g fiber, 33 g pro.

Top Sirloin with Caramelized Onion, Mixed Mushrooms & Wilted Tomatoes

Prep: 35 minutes Broil: 12 minutes Makes: 4 servings

1. Remove and discard stems from shiitake and oyster mushrooms. Coarsely chop mushroom caps. Set aside.

2. In a large skillet cook onion, covered, in 1 tablespoon of the butter over medium-low heat for 13 to 15 minutes or until tender, stirring occasionally. Uncover; cook for 3 to 5 minutes more or until onion is golden. Using a slotted spoon, remove onions from skillet; set aside.

3. Add shiitake, oyster, and button mushrooms and remaining 1 tablespoon butter to skillet. Cook and stir over medium-high heat about 8 minutes or until tender and liquid has evaporated. Stir in onion, tomatoes, vinegar, the 1/4 teaspoon salt, and 1/8 teaspoon pepper; heat through.

4. Meanwhile, preheat boiler. Place meat on the unheated rack of a broiler pan. Sprinkle with additional salt and pepper. Broil 3 to 4 inches from heat until desired doneness, turning once halfway through broiling. Allow 12 to 14 minutes for medium rare (145°F) and 15 to 18 minutes for medium (160°F). Spoon onion mixture over steaks.

*Note: If desired, substitute 5 ounces fresh button mushrooms for the 3 ounces fresh shiitake mushrooms and 2 ounces fresh oyster mushrooms.

1 cup fresh shiitake mushrooms* (3 ounces)

¾ cup fresh oyster mushrooms* (2 ounces)

1 large sweet onion (such as Vidalia or Walla Walla), halved lengthwise and thinly sliced (2 cups)

2 tablespoons butter

1¼ cups fresh button mushrooms, sliced (3 ounces)

2 tablespoons chopped dried oil-packed tomatoes

1 tablespoon balsamic vinegar

¼ teaspoon salt

⅛ teaspoon black pepper

2 beef top sirloin or 4 ribeye steaks, cut 1 inch thick (2½ to 3 pounds)

Salt and black pepper

7 g carbs   **1** g fiber   **6** g net carbs

Nutrition Facts per serving: 447 cal., 18 g total fat (7 g sat. fat), 150 mg chol., 444 mg sodium, 7 g carbo., 1 g fiber, 63 g pro.

Herb-Crusted Beef with Cognac Sauce

Prep: 30 minutes   Roast: 8 minutes   Oven: 425°F   Makes: 4 servings

3 tablespoons snipped fresh

flat-leaf parsley

2 tablespoons snipped fresh thyme

2 tablespoons snipped fresh basil

4 teaspoons bottled minced garlic

1 tablespoon whole wheat flour

½ teaspoon kosher salt

¼ teaspoon cracked black pepper

3 tablespoons olive oil

4 beef tenderloin steaks, cut

1¼ to 1½ inches thick

(1½ pounds)

1 cup whipping cream

¼ cup chicken broth

¼ cup cognac or other brandy

1. In a small bowl combine parsley, thyme, basil, garlic, flour, salt, and pepper. Stir in 1 tablespoon of the oil. Firmly press herb mixture onto 1 side of each steak. Set steaks aside.

2. In a large skillet heat remaining 2 tablespoons olive oil over medium-high heat. Add steaks, herbed side down, to hot skillet. Cook steaks about 5 minutes or until browned and herb coating is slightly crisp.

3. Transfer steaks to a shallow baking pan, herbed side up, reserving drippings in skillet. Roast in a 425° oven until desired doneness. Allow about 8 minutes for medium rare (145°F) and about 10 minutes for medium (160°F). Transfer steaks to serving platter; cover and keep warm.

4. Meanwhile, for cognac sauce, stir cream, broth, and cognac into drippings in skillet. Bring to boiling over medium-high heat; reduce heat. Simmer, uncovered, about 10 minutes or until slightly thickened and reduced to about ¾ cup.

5. To serve, drizzle some of the cognac sauce on 4 dinner plates; top with steaks. Drizzle with remaining sauce.

6 g carbs   **1** g fiber   **5** g net carbs

Nutrition Facts per serving: 625 cal., 46 g total fat (20 g sat. fat), 187 mg chol., 407 mg sodium, 6 g carbo., 1 g fiber, 38 g pro.

Steak Diane

Start to Finish: 25 minutes Oven: 350°F Makes: 4 servings

1. In a small mixing bowl whisk broth, Worcestershire sauce, mustard, and tomato paste until smooth. Set aside.

2. In a large skillet heat oil over medium-high heat just until it starts to smoke, about 3 minutes. Meanwhile, sprinkle both sides of steaks with salt and pepper. Increase heat to high; place steaks in skillet and cook until browned, about 1 1/2 minutes per side. Transfer steaks to a shallow roasting pan. Roast, uncovered, in a 350° oven for 12 to 18 minutes or until medium rare (145°F). Transfer steaks to 4 serving plates. Cover and keep warm.

3. Meanwhile, discard all but 2 teaspoons of the pan drippings in skillet. Add the shallots and cook over medium-low heat for 1 minute, stirring constantly. Remove from heat; add the cognac. Return to heat; cook over medium-high heat until cognac is almost evaporated, stirring to scrape up any browned bits from the pan. Stir in beef broth mixture and bring to boiling; reduce heat. Simmer for 1 minute. Stir in cream and cook until sauce is thickened, about 1 to 2 minutes, stirring occasionally. Pour the sauce through a fine-mesh sieve; drizzle sauce over steaks.

1/2 cup beef broth

2 teaspoons Worcestershire sauce

2 teaspoons Dijon-style mustard

2 teaspoons tomato paste

1 tablespoon olive oil

4 beef tenderloin steaks, cut 1 inch thick (about 1 1/2 pounds)

1/2 teaspoon salt

1/2 teaspoon freshly ground pepper

1 tablespoon finely chopped shallots

2 tablespoons cognac or brandy

1/4 cup whipping cream

3 g carbs   **0** g fiber   **3** g net carbs

Nutrition Facts per serving: 338 cal., 20 g total fat (8 g sat. fat), 108 mg chol., 567 mg sodium, 3 g carbo., 0 g fiber, 31 g pro.

Steak & Mushrooms

Start to Finish: 20 minutes Makes: 4 servings

4 beef tenderloin steaks, cut

   1 inch thick (about 1 pound)

1 tablespoon olive oil

3 cups sliced fresh cremini,

   shiitake, baby portobello,

   and/or button mushrooms

   (8 ounces)

¼ cup seasoned beef broth

¼ cup whipping cream

   Salt and black pepper

   (optional)

1. In a large skillet cook steaks in hot oil over medium heat to desired doneness, turning once. Allow 7 to 9 minutes for medium rare (145°) and 10 to 13 minutes for medium (160°). Transfer steaks to a serving platter; keep warm.

2. In the same skillet cook and stir mushrooms over medium heat for 4 to 5 minutes or until tender. Stir in broth and cream. Cook and stir about 2 minutes or until slightly thickened. If desired, season with salt and pepper. Spoon mushroom mixture over steaks.

2 g
carbs

0 g
fiber

2 g
net carbs

Nutrition Facts per serving: 271 cal., 18 g total fat (7 g sat. fat), 90 mg chol., 116 mg sodium, 2 g carbo., 0 g fiber, 26 g pro.

Steak with Creamy Onion Sauce

Prep: 10 minutes Broil: 17 minutes Makes: 4 servings

1. Preheat broiler. Place onion slices on the rack of an unheated broiler pan. Broil 3 to 4 inches from heat for 5 minutes; turn onions. Meanwhile, sprinkle steaks with 1 ½ teaspoons of the seasoning blend. Place steaks on the broiler pan rack with onion. Broil steaks and onions 5 minutes more or until onions are browned. Remove onions to a cutting board. Broil steaks to desired doneness, turning once halfway through broiling. Allow 12 to 14 minutes more for medium rare (145°F) and 15 to 18 minutes more for medium (160°F).

2. Meanwhile, coarsely chop cooked onion. In a small saucepan combine onion, sour cream, capers, and remaining 1 ½ teaspoons seasoning blend. Cook and stir over medium-low heat until heated through (do not boil). Transfer steaks to serving plates. Spoon some of the sauce over steaks. Pass remaining sauce.

1 medium sweet onion (such as
    Vidalia or Walla Walla),
    thinly sliced

4 6-ounce beef ribeye steaks, cut
    about 1 inch thick
    (1 ½ pounds)

1 tablespoon Mediterranean
    seasoning blend or lemon-
    pepper seasoning

1 8-ounce container dairy
    sour cream

2 tablespoons capers, drained

4 g carbs   0 g fiber   4 g net carbs

Nutrition Facts per serving: 398 cal., 22 g total fat (11 g sat. fat), 106 mg chol., 472 mg sodium, 4 g carbo., 0 g fiber, 39 g pro.

Sirloin with Mustard & Chives

Prep: 10 minutes Grill: 14 minutes Makes: 4 servings

4 boneless beef sirloin or ribeye steaks, cut about ¾ inch thick (about 1½ pounds)

2 teaspoons garlic-pepper seasoning

½ cup dairy sour cream

2 tablespoons Dijon-style mustard

1 tablespoon snipped fresh chives

1. Sprinkle both sides of steaks with 1½ teaspoons seasoning. For a charcoal grill, grill steaks on the rack of an uncovered grill directly over medium coals (see tip, page 107) to desired doneness, turning once halfway through grilling time. Allow 14 to 18 minutes for medium rare (145°F) and 18 to 22 minutes for medium (160°F). (For a gas grill, preheat grill. Reduce heat to medium. Place meat on grill rack over heat. Cover and grill as above.) Transfer steaks to a serving platter.

2. Meanwhile, in a small bowl combine sour cream, mustard, chives, and remaining ½ teaspoon seasoning. Spoon sour cream mixture over steaks.

2 g carbs   **0** g fiber   **2** g net carbs

Nutrition Facts per serving: 277 cal., 12 g total fat (5 g sat. fat), 114 mg chol., 619 mg sodium, 2 g carbo., 0 g fiber, 37 g pro.

Rosemary Beef with Sweet Pepper Relish

Prep: 25 minutes Grill: 8 minutes Makes: 4 servings

1. For relish, fold a 24×18-inch piece of heavy foil in half to make a 12×18-inch rectangle. Place onion and sweet pepper in center of foil. Drizzle vinegar and 2 teaspoons of the oil over vegetables; sprinkle with black pepper. Bring up two opposite edges of foil; seal with a double fold. Fold remaining ends to completely enclose vegetables, leaving space for steam to build. Set aside.

2. Combine remaining 1 teaspoon oil, the rosemary, and garlic. Trim fat from steaks. Rub steaks with rosemary mixture. Spread one side of the steaks with horseradish.

3. Grill steaks and relish on the rack of an uncovered grill directly over medium coals (see tip, page 107) until desired doneness, turning steaks and relish halfway through grilling. Allow 8 to 12 minutes for medium-rare (145°F) and 12 to 15 minutes for medium (160°F). To serve, spoon the relish over steaks.

See photo, page 221.

1 medium red onion, thinly sliced

1 cup red, yellow, and/or orange
   sweet pepper strips

1 tablespoon red wine vinegar

3 teaspoons olive oil

1/8 teaspoon black pepper

2 teaspoons snipped fresh
   rosemary

4 cloves garlic, minced

4 boneless beef top loin steaks,
   cut 1 inch thick
   (about 1 pound total)

1 tablespoon prepared
   horseradish

7g carbs   **1**g fiber   **6**g net carbs

Nutrition Facts per serving: 198 cal., 9 g total fat (2 g sat. fat), 65 mg chol., 92 mg sodium, 7 g carbo., 1 g fiber, 23 g pro.

Fajita-Style Flank Steak

Prep: 15 minutes Marinate: 8 hours Broil: 15 minutes Makes: 4 to 6 servings

1 1½-pound beef flank steak

¼ cup bottled low-carb Italian

   salad dressing

¼ cup bottled salsa

½ teaspoon finely shredded

   lime peel

1 tablespoon lime juice

1 tablespoon snipped fresh

   cilantro or parsley

⅛ teaspoon bottled hot

   pepper sauce

1. Trim fat from steak. Place steak in a plastic bag set in a shallow dish.

2. For marinade, in a bowl combine salad dressing, salsa, lime peel, lime juice, cilantro, and hot pepper sauce. Pour over steak; seal bag. Marinate in the refrigerator for 8 to 24 hours, turning occasionally. Drain steak, reserving marinade.

3. Preheat broiler. Place steak on the unheated rack of a broiler pan. Broil 3 to 4 inches from heat until desired doneness, turning once and brushing occasionally with marinade up to the last 5 minutes of broiling. Allow 15 to 18 minutes for medium (160°F).

4. Pour any remaining marinade into a small saucepan; bring to boiling. Boil for 1 minute. Thinly slice steak across the grain. Serve the steak with hot marinade.

1 g carbs   0 g fiber   1 g net carbs

Nutrition Facts per serving: 300 cal., 15 g total fat (5 g sat. fat),
68 mg chol., 301 mg sodium, 1 g carbo., 0 g fiber, 37 g pro.

Salsa Steak

Prep: 20 minutes Bake: 45 minutes Oven: 350°F Makes: 4 to 6 servings

1. Trim fat from meat. Sprinkle both sides of meat with salt and black pepper. Cut into 4 to 6 serving-size pieces. In a large skillet brown meat on both sides in hot oil over medium-high heat. Transfer to a 2-quart square baking dish.

2. In the same skillet, cook and stir mushrooms, sweet pepper, and onion over medium heat for 5 to 8 minutes or until tender (add more oil if necessary). Stir in tomato sauce, olives (if desired), and chili powder. Cook and stir until bubbly.

3. Pour mushroom mixture over meat in baking dish. Cover and bake in a 350° oven about 45 minutes or until meat is tender.

Tip: Another time, serve an Italian-flavored dish by substituting 1 to 1½ teaspoons dried Italian seasoning, crushed, for the chili powder.

See photo, page 222.

1 1- to 1½-pound boneless beef round steak, cut ½ inch thick
    Salt and black pepper
1 tablespoon cooking oil
1½ cups sliced fresh mushrooms (4 ounces)
¾ cup green sweet pepper strips (1 small)
1 small onion, sliced
1 8-ounce can tomato sauce
1 2¼-ounce can sliced pitted ripe olives, drained (optional)
2 to 3 teaspoons chili powder

8 g carbs   2 g fiber   6 g net carbs

Nutrition Facts per serving: 200 cal., 7 g total fat (1 g sat. fat), 49 mg chol., 512 mg sodium, 8 g carbo., 2 g fiber, 28 g pro.

Tequila New York Strip

Prep: 30 minutes Cook: 8 minutes Makes: 8 servings

1 cup chopped plum tomatoes (3 medium)

1/3 cup chopped yellow onion (1 small)

1/2 cup chopped red sweet pepper (1 small)

1 fresh Anaheim or poblano chile pepper, seeded and finely chopped (see tip, page 59)

1 small fresh jalapeño chile pepper, seeded and finely chopped (see tip, page 59)

4 tablespoons lime juice

2 tablespoons snipped fresh cilantro

1 teaspoon kosher salt or 3/4 teaspoon salt

4 boneless beef top loin steaks, cut 1 inch thick (1 1/2 to 2 pounds)

1 tablespoon cooking oil

1/3 cup tequila

1/4 cup butter, softened

1. For salsa, in a medium bowl combine tomatoes, onion, sweet pepper, Anaheim pepper, and jalapeño pepper. Stir in 1 tablespoon of the lime juice and the cilantro. Cover and chill up to 4 hours.

2. Use your fingers to rub salt on 1 side of each steak. In a heavy 12-inch skillet cook steaks, salted side down, in hot oil over medium heat until desired doneness, turning once. Allow 8 to 11 minutes for medium rare (145°F) and 12 to 15 minutes for medium (160°F). Transfer steaks to a serving platter, reserving drippings in skillet. Keep warm.

3. For sauce, add remaining 3 tablespoons lime juice and the tequila to skillet, scraping up any crusty browned bits. Remove from heat. Whisk in the butter, 1 tablespoon at a time, until melted. Serve sauce with steaks. Top with the salsa; serve immediately.

4g carbs **1**g fiber **3**g net carbs

Nutrition Facts per serving: 479 cal., 35 g total fat (15 g sat. fat), 124 mg chol., 368 mg sodium, 4 g carbo., 1 g fiber, 33 g pro.

Lemon Sirloin Steak

Prep: 20 minutes Marinate: 2 hours Grill: 20 minutes Makes: 6 to 8 servings

1. Trim fat from meat. Place meat in plastic bag set in shallow dish. For marinade, combine green onions, lemon peel, lemon juice, oil, Worcestershire sauce, mustard, salt, and pepper. Pour over meat; seal bag. Marinate in refrigerator for 2 to 6 hours in refrigerator, turning bag occasionally.

2. Drain meat, discarding marinade; pat dry. For a charcoal grill, grill on the rack of uncovered grill directly over medium coals (see tip, page 107) until desired doneness, turning halfway through grilling and brushing occasionally with marinade up to the last 5 minutes of grilling. Allow 20 to 24 minutes for medium rare (145°F) and 24 to 28 minutes for medium (160°F). To serve, thinly slice across grain.

1 2- to 2½-pound boneless beef
    sirloin steak, cut 1½ inches thick

¼ cup thinly sliced green onions (4)

1 teaspoon finely shredded
    lemon peel

⅔ cup lemon juice

⅓ cup cooking oil

1 tablespoon Worcestershire sauce

1 tablespoon yellow mustard

½ teaspoon salt

¼ teaspoon black pepper

1 g carbs   0 g fiber   1 g net carbs

Nutrition Facts per serving: 228 cal., 10 g total fat (3 g sat. fat), 92 mg chol., 138 mg sodium, 1 g carbo., 0 g fiber, 32 g pro.

243

Salsa-Topped Rosemary Ribeyes

Prep: 15 minutes Grill: 11 minutes Makes: 4 servings

1 tablespoon snipped fresh
    rosemary or 1 teaspoon dried
    rosemary

1 teaspoon snipped fresh thyme or
    ¼ teaspoon dried thyme

¼ teaspoon salt

⅛ teaspoon black pepper

2 beef ribeye steaks, cut 1 inch thick
    (1½ pounds)

½ cup chopped seeded tomato
    (1 medium)

¼ cup chopped red onion

¼ cup chopped yellow and/or green
    sweet pepper

1 clove garlic, minced

1. In a small bowl combine rosemary, thyme, salt, and black pepper. Rub mixture into steaks using your fingers. For a charcoal grill, grill steaks on the rack of an uncovered grill directly over medium coals (see tip, page 107) until desired doneness, turning once halfway through grilling. Allow 11 to 15 minutes for medium rare (145°F) and 14 to 18 minutes for medium (160°F). (For a gas grill, preheat grill. Reduce heat to medium. Place meat on grill rack over heat. Cover and grill as above.)

2. Meanwhile, for salsa, in a medium bowl combine tomato, onion, sweet pepper, and garlic. Stir in a dash each *salt, black pepper,* and *hot pepper sauce.* Serve with steaks.

3g carbs   **1**g fiber   **2**g net carbs

Nutrition Facts per serving: 309 cal., 17 g total fat (7 g sat. fat),
100 mg chol., 262 mg sodium, 3 g carbo., 1 g fiber, 34 g pro.

Grilled Beef Tenderloin with Cabernet Sauvignon Sauce

Prep: 15 minutes   Cook: 50 minutes   Grill: 1 hour   Stand: 15 minutes   Makes: 8 to 10 servings

1. For a charcoal grill, arrange medium-high coals around a drip pan. Test for medium heat (see tip, page 107) over drip pan. Lightly coat meat with 2 tablespoons of the oil and season with salt and black pepper. Insert an oven-going meat thermometer into center of roast. Place meat on the grill rack over drip pan. Cover and grill for 1 hour or until thermometer registers 145°F (medium rare). Cover and let stand for 15 minutes before slicing. (For a gas grill, preheat grill. Reduce heat to medium. Adjust for indirect grilling. Grill as above.)

2. Meanwhile, heat the remaining 2 tablespoons oil in a large saucepan over medium-high heat. Add onion, celery, sweet pepper, and garlic; cook and stir about 10 minutes or until vegetables are brown. Add wine, broth, vinegar, and bay leaves. Bring to boiling; reduce heat. Simmer, uncovered, for 10 minutes. Strain, reserving the liquid. Discard solids and continue to simmer the liquid, uncovered, for 25 to 30 minutes or until reduced to ½ cup and slightly thickened. (Watch the sauce closely during the final 5 minutes of cooking, as it will reduce at a more rapid rate.)

3. To serve, stir butter and rosemary into the sauce. Season with salt and black pepper. Thinly slice the meat. Serve immediately with the sauce.

1   2½-pound beef tenderloin

¼   cup olive oil

Salt and black pepper

1   cup chopped onion (2 medium)

1   cup chopped celery (2 stalks)

¾   cup chopped seeded red sweet
pepper (1 medium)

4   cloves garlic, thinly sliced

1½ cups Cabernet Sauvignon wine

1½ cups beef broth

½   cup red wine vinegar

2   bay leaves

1   tablespoon butter

½   teaspoon snipped fresh
rosemary

Salt and black pepper

5g carbs   **1**g fiber   **4**g net carbs

Nutrition Facts per serving: 311 cal., 18 g total fat (5 g sat. fat), 74 mg chol., 393 mg sodium, 5 g carbo., 1 g fiber, 25 g pro.

Mustard-Coated Beef Tenderloin

Prep: 25 minutes Roast: 30 minutes Stand: 10 minutes
Oven: 425°F Makes: 6 to 8 servings

3 tablespoons coarse-grain
   brown mustard

2 teaspoons olive oil

2 teaspoons cracked black
   pepper

2 teaspoons snipped fresh
   tarragon

1 teaspoon coarse salt

1 2- to 3-pound beef tenderloin

¼ cup dry red wine

8 cups mixed baby greens
   (mesclun) or torn romaine
   and radicchio

¼ cup fresh tarragon leaves

1. In a small bowl combine 1 tablespoon of the mustard, the oil, pepper, snipped tarragon, and salt. Spread mixture over top and sides of meat. Let stand for 15 minutes at room temperature or chill up to 4 hours.

2. Place meat on a rack in a shallow roasting pan. Insert an oven-going meat thermometer into center of roast. Roast, uncovered, in a 425° oven for 30 to 45 minutes or until medium rare (145°F). Remove meat from pan; cover with foil and let stand for 10 minutes before slicing.

3. While meat is standing, place roasting pan over low heat. Add wine to pan and cook, scraping up browned bits from bottom of pan. Stir in remaining 2 tablespoons mustard and any juices that have accumulated around the roast during standing. (If mixture seems thick, stir in 2 to 3 tablespoons of water to thin it to drizzling consistency.)

4. Toss together greens and tarragon leaves. Line a serving platter with greens. Drizzle greens with about three-fourths of the pan juices. Slice meat and overlap slices on the greens. Drizzle with remaining pan juices.

3 g carbs   **1** g fiber   **2** g net carbs

Nutrition Facts per serving: 281 cal., 14 g total fat (5 g sat. fat), 93 mg chol., 515 mg sodium, 3 g carbo., 1 g fiber, 33 g pro.

Beef with Rich Marsala Cream Sauce

Prep: 30 minutes Stand: 20 minutes Cook: 20 minutes
Grill: 11 minutes Makes: 8 servings

1. In a small bowl cover the dried mushrooms with hot water. Let stand for 20 minutes. Rinse under warm running water and squeeze out the excess moisture. Chop mushrooms.

2. In large skillet melt butter over medium heat. Add the mushrooms, onions, drained green peppercorns, and cracked black pepper; reduce heat. Cook, uncovered, over medium-low heat for 15 minutes, stirring frequently.

3. Add Marsala. Bring to boiling; reduce heat. Simmer, uncovered, for 8 to 10 minutes or until wine is reduced by half and mushroom mixture is slightly thickened, stirring occasionally.

4. Add whipping cream and beef broth. Heat over medium heat until tiny bubbles just form around edge; reduce heat. Cook over medium-low heat for 20 to 25 minutes or until mixture thickens to desired consistency, stirring occasionally with a wooden spoon. Season with salt; set aside.

5. Trim fat from steaks. For charcoal grill, grill steaks on the rack of an uncovered grill over medium coals (see tip, page 107) until desired doneness, turning once halfway through grilling. Allow 11 to 15 minutes for medium rare (145°F) and 14 to 18 minutes for medium (160°F). (For gas grill, preheat grill. Reduce heat to medium. Place steaks on grill rack over heat. Cover and grill as above.)

6. To serve, reheat the Marsala sauce; transfer to a serving bowl and pass with steaks.

1/3 cup dried mushrooms (morels or chanterelles) (1/4 ounce)

3 tablespoons butter

1 cup chopped red onions (2 medium)

1 tablespoon whole green peppercorns in brine, drained

2 teaspoons cracked black pepper

1 cup dry Marsala or dry red wine

2 cups whipping cream

1/2 cup condensed beef broth

Salt

8 beef tenderloin steaks, cut 1 inch thick (about 2 pounds)

5g carbs **1**g fiber **4**g net carbs

Nutrition Facts per serving: 465 cal., 36 g total fat (19 g sat. fat), 164 mg chol., 295 mg sodium, 5 g carbo., 1 g fiber, 26 g pro.

Basil-Stuffed Steak

Prep: 25 minutes Grill: 32 minutes Stand: 5 minutes Makes: 6 servings

1   2- to 2½-pound boneless beef
     sirloin steak, cut 1½ inches thick

½   teaspoon salt

¼   teaspoon black pepper

¼   teaspoon dried parsley flakes

1   cup lightly packed fresh basil
     leaves, coarsely chopped

¼   cup finely chopped onion

4   cloves garlic, minced

1½ teaspoons finely snipped fresh
     rosemary or ½ teaspoon dried
     rosemary, crushed

¼   teaspoon snipped fresh thyme
     or ⅛ teaspoon dried thyme,
     crushed

1   teaspoon olive oil

1. With sharp knife, make 5 lengthwise slits three-fourths of the way through the steak.

2. In a small bowl combine salt, pepper, and parsley flakes; rub over the steak. In the same bowl combine basil, onion, garlic, rosemary, and thyme. Press basil mixture into the slits in steak. Using 100%-cotton string, tie steak loosely at 2-inch intervals to close the slits and hold the filing in. Drizzle with oil.

3. For a charcoal grill, arrange medium-high coals around a drip pan. Test for medium heat (see tip, page 107) over drip pan. Place meat on the grill rack over drip pan. Cover and grill until desired doneness. Allow 32 to 36 minutes for medium rare (145°F) and 36 to 40 minutes for medium (160°F). (For a gas grill, preheat grill. Reduce heat to medium. Adjust for indirect grilling. Grill as above.)

4. Transfer meat to a carving board; remove strings. Cover with foil and let stand for 5 to 10 minutes. Carve into ½-inch slices.

2 g
carbs

0 g
fiber

2 g
net carbs

Nutrition Facts per serving: 216 cal., 8 g total fat (3 g sat. fat),
92 mg chol., 269 mg sodium, 2 g carbo., 0 g fiber, 32 g pro.

Ribeye Steaks with Caramelized Onions

Prep: 25 minutes Grill: 11 minutes Makes: 4 servings

1. In a small bowl combine salt, black pepper, and mustard seeds; divide mixture in half. Rub half of the mustard mixture onto one side of the steaks; set aside.

2. In a large skillet cook and stir onion in hot oil over medium heat for 5 minutes, stirring frequently. Add sweet pepper, jalapeño pepper, and garlic; cook and stir for 5 minutes more or until onion is golden brown and peppers are tender. Add balsamic vinegar, sage, and remaining half of the mustard seed mixture; cook and stir for 1 minute more. Remove from heat. Cover and keep warm.

3. Meanwhile, for a charcoal grill, grill steaks on the rack of an uncovered grill directly over medium coals (see tip, page 107) until desired doneness, turning once. Allow 11 to 15 minutes for medium rare (145°F) and 14 to 18 minutes for medium (160°F). (For a gas grill, preheat grill. Reduce heat to medium. Place steaks on rack over heat. Cover and grill as above.) Serve steaks with onion mixture.

1 teaspoon coarse salt

¾ teaspoon cracked black pepper

½ teaspoon mustard seeds, crushed

4 boneless beef ribeye steaks,
   cut 1 inch thick (2 to
   2½ pounds)

1 medium sweet onion, halved
   lengthwise and thinly sliced

1 tablespoon olive oil

¼ cup chopped red sweet pepper

1 fresh jalapeño chile pepper,
   seeded and finely chopped
   (see tip, page 59)

1 clove garlic, minced

1 tablespoon balsamic vinegar

½ teaspoon dried sage, crushed

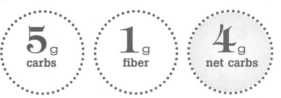

5 g carbs   **1** g fiber   **4** g net carbs

Nutrition Facts per serving: 390 cal., 18 g total fat (6 g sat. fat),
108 mg chol., 603 mg sodium, 5 g carbo., 1 g fiber, 50 g pro.

Stuffed Veal Chops with Gorgonzola

Prep: 25 minutes Grill: 30 minutes Makes: 4 servings

½ cup chopped onion
   (1 medium)

½ cup finely chopped leek
   (1 large)

2 tablespoons finely chopped
   shallot (1 medium)

2 tablespoons olive oil

1 teaspoon snipped fresh sage
   or ¼ teaspoon ground sage

¼ teaspoon salt

¼ teaspoon black pepper

4 veal loin chops, cut 1 inch
   thick (about 1¾ pounds)
   Salt and black pepper

½ cup crumbled blue cheese

1. For stuffing, in a medium skillet cook and stir onion, leek, and shallot in 1 tablespoon hot oil over medium heat just until tender. Remove from heat. Stir in sage, salt, and pepper. Set aside to cool.

2. Trim fat from chops. Make a pocket in each chop by cutting horizontally from the fat side almost to the opposite side. Spoon about 1 tablespoon of the stuffing into each pocket. If necessary, secure with wooden toothpicks. Brush chops with remaining 1 tablespoon oil; sprinkle lightly with additional salt and pepper.

3. For a charcoal grill, arrange medium-high coals around a drip pan. Test for medium heat above drip pan (see tip, page 107). Place chops on the grill rack over drip pan. Cover and grill for 30 to 40 minutes or until done (160°F), turning once halfway through grilling. (For a gas grill, preheat grill. Reduce heat to medium. Adjust for indirect cooking. Grill as above.)

4. If using toothpicks, remove them. To serve, sprinkle crumbled blue cheese over chops.

See photo, page 223.

5g carbs   **1**g fiber   **4**g net carbs

Nutrition Facts per serving: 269 cal., 15 g total fat (5 g sat. fat), 103 mg chol., 545 mg sodium, 5 g carbo., 1 g fiber, 27 g pro.

Veal Scaloppine with Marsala

Prep: 20 minutes Cook: 10 minutes Makes: 2 servings

1. In a 12-inch skillet cook and stir mushrooms and green onions in 1 tablespoon hot butter over medium heat for 4 to 5 minutes or until tender. Remove from skillet; set aside.

2. Meanwhile, cut veal into 2 serving-size pieces. Place 1 piece of veal between 2 pieces of plastic wrap. Working from center to edges, pound lightly with the flat side of a meat mallet to about ¼ inch thick. Repeat with remaining veal.

3. Sprinkle meat with salt and pepper. In the same skillet cook veal in remaining 1 tablespoon butter over medium-high heat for 4 to 6 minutes or until browned and slightly pink in center, turning once. Transfer to warm dinner plates; keep warm.

4. Add Marsala and broth to drippings in skillet. Bring to boiling; boil gently, uncovered, about 1 minute, scraping up any browned bits. Return mushroom mixture to skillet; heat through.

5. To serve, spoon the mushroom mixture over meat. Sprinkle with parsley. Serve immediately.

1½ cups quartered, halved, or sliced fresh mushrooms, such as cremini, porcini, morel, portobello, shiitake, or button

¼ cup sliced green onions (4)

2 tablespoons butter

8 ounces veal top round steak or sirloin steak or two boneless pork top loin chops, cut ½ inch thick

⅛ teaspoon salt

⅛ teaspoon black pepper

⅓ cup dry Marsala or dry sherry

¼ cup chicken broth

1 tablespoon snipped fresh parsley

6g carbs   **1**g fiber   **5**g net carbs

Nutrition Facts per serving: 310 cal., 15 g total fat (7 g sat. fat), 121 mg chol., 420 mg sodium, 6 g carbo., 1 g fiber, 27 g pro.

Veal with Fennel-Wine Sauce

Start to Finish: 25 minutes Makes: 4 servings

1 small fennel bulb

4 veal cutlets (12 ounces)

   Salt and black pepper

1 tablespoon butter

1 clove garlic, minced

½ cup dry white wine

⅓ cup chicken broth

   Salt and black pepper

1. Remove feathery tops from fennel bulb; snip enough of the tops to make 1 to 2 tablespoons. Set aside. Cut off and discard upper stalks. Remove any wilted outer layers and cut a thin slice from the fennel base. Cut fennel bulb into thin slices, removing the core; set aside.

2. Trim fat from meat; season meat with salt and pepper. In a large skillet cook meat, half at a time, in hot butter over medium-high heat for 4 to 6 minutes or until browned and slightly pink in center, turning once. Transfer meat to a serving platter. Cover and keep warm.

3. Add the sliced fennel and garlic to hot skillet; cook and stir for 1 minute. Add wine and broth. Bring to boiling; reduce heat. Simmer, uncovered, for 4 to 5 minutes or until mixture is reduced by half. Season with salt and pepper. Spoon fennel sauce over meat. Sprinkle with reserved snipped fennel tops.

5g carbs   **2**g fiber   **3**g net carbs

Nutrition Facts per serving: 165 cal., 6 g total fat (2 g sat. fat), 76 mg chol., 414 mg sodium, 5 g carbo., 2 g fiber, 18 g pro.

Pork
&
Lamb

Succulent pork and distinctive-flavored lamb graciously mingle with contrasting ingredients to create showstopping entrées. These main dishes provide plenty of protein, vitamins, and minerals while strictly limiting carbohydrates. Browse through these recipes—you'll find spectacular combinations of flavor and texture that tempt your taste buds but won't strain your dietary limits.

Dijon Vinaigrette Marinated Pork Medallions

Prep: 20 minutes Marinate: 2 hours Cook: 7 minutes Makes: 4 servings

1 16-ounce pork tenderloin

¾ cup dry white wine

2 tablespoons olive oil

2 tablespoons Dijon-style mustard

½ teaspoon dried dill

½ teaspoon salt

¼ teaspoon black pepper

1 tablespoon butter

1 9-ounce package frozen

   French-cut green beans,

   thawed

1 teaspoon dried dill

1 teaspoon lemon juice

1. Trim fat from meat. Cut meat crosswise into ¼-inch slices*. Place meat in a plastic bag set in a shallow dish. For marinade, in a small bowl combine wine, oil, mustard, ½ teaspoon dill, salt, and pepper. Pour over meat; seal bag. Marinate in refrigerator for 2 to 6 hours; turn occasionally.

2. Drain pork, discarding marinade. In a 12-inch skillet cook pork in hot butter over medium heat for 4 to 6 minutes or until no longer pink (160°F), turning once. Remove pork from skillet, reserving drippings in skillet. Keep warm.

3. Add green beans and 1 teaspoon dill to drippings in skillet. Cook and stir for 3 to 4 minutes or until beans are crisp-tender. Stir in lemon juice. Transfer beans to a serving platter. Serve pork on top of green beans.

*Note: Partially freeze meat for easier slicing.

4 g carbs   **2** g fiber   **2** g net carbs

Nutrition Facts per serving: 202 cal., 8 g total fat (3 g sat. fat), 81 mg chol., 163 mg sodium, 4 g carbo., 2 g fiber, 25 g pro.

Grilled Pork Chops with Mushroom Stuffing

Prep: 15 minutes Grill: 12 minutes Makes: 4 servings

1. For stuffing, in a large skillet heat oil over medium heat. Add green onion; cook and stir for 1 minute. Stir in mushrooms, rosemary, salt, and pepper. Cook and stir for 2 to 3 minutes more or until mushrooms are tender. Remove from heat.

2. Trim fat from chops. To cut a pocket in each chop, use a sharp knife to make a 3-inch slit in the fatty side. Work the knife inside, cutting almost to the other side. Spoon stuffing into pockets in chops. If necessary, secure with wooden toothpicks.

3. Brush chops with Worcestershire sauce. Season chops lightly with additional salt and black pepper. For a charcoal grill, grill chops on the rack of an uncovered grill directly over medium coals (see tip, page 107) for 12 to 15 minutes or until done (160°F) and juices run clear, turning once halfway through grilling. To serve, remove toothpicks.

2 teaspoons olive oil

2 tablespoons thinly sliced green

    onion (1)

1 8-ounce package fresh

    mushrooms, coarsely chopped

2 teaspoons snipped fresh

    rosemary or oregano

1/8 teaspoon salt

1/8 teaspoon black pepper

4 boneless pork loin chops, cut

    3/4 to 1 inch thick

2 teaspoons Worcestershire sauce

4g carbs   **1**g fiber   **3**g net carbs

Nutrition Facts per serving: 241 cal., 14 g total fat (4 g sat. fat), 77 mg chol., 218 mg sodium, 4 g carbo., 1 g fiber, 25 g pro.

Cumin Pork Chops with Avocado Salsa

Prep: 20 minutes   Cook: 8 minutes   Makes: 4 servings

4   boneless pork loin chops, cut

¾ inch thick (about 1 pound)

1   tablespoon cumin seeds,

slightly crushed

¼   teaspoon salt

¼   teaspoon black pepper

2   cloves garlic, minced

1   to 2 tablespoons cooking oil

Avocado Salsa (see recipe, right)

¼   cup chopped radishes

Fresh cilantro leaves

(optional)

1. Trim fat from chops. For rub, in a small bowl combine cumin seeds, salt, pepper, and garlic. Sprinkle rub over chops; rub in with your fingers.

2. In a large skillet heat oil over medium-high heat. Add chops; cook for 8 to 12 minutes or until done (160°F) and juices run clear, turning once.

3. Transfer chops to dinner plates. Top with Avocado Salsa and chopped radishes. If desired, garnish with cilantro leaves.

Avocado Salsa: In a blender container or food processor bowl combine one 4-ounce can tomatillo salsa or ½ cup salsa verde, 1 coarsely chopped green onion (including green part), and a dash salt. Cover and blend or process until smooth. Transfer to a medium bowl. Stir in 1 large ripe seeded, peeled, and chopped avocado and 1 tablespoon snipped fresh cilantro.

See photo, page 290.

7g carbs   **4**g fiber   **3**g net carbs

Nutrition Facts per serving: 302 cal., 19 g total fat (4 g sat. fat),
66 mg chol., 267 mg sodium, 7 g carbo., 4 g fiber, 26 g pro.

Spanish-Style Pork Chops

Prep: 20 minutes Cook: 18 minutes Makes: 4 servings

1. For stuffing, in a small bowl combine the cheese and ¼ cup of the chopped olives; set aside.

2. Trim fat from chops. To cut a pocket in each chop, use a sharp knife to make a 3-inch-long slit in the fatty side. Work the knife inside, cutting almost to the other side. Spoon stuffing into pockets in chops. If necessary, secure with wooden toothpicks. Sprinkle chops with pepper.

3. In a large skillet heat oil over medium-high heat. Add chops; cook for 8 to 10 minutes or until browned, turning once.

4. Carefully pour broth over chops. Bring to boiling; reduce heat. Simmer, covered, about 10 minutes or until pork is done (160°F) and juices run clear. Meanwhile, in a small bowl combine the remaining ¼ cup olives, the tomato, and parsley.

5. To serve, remove toothpicks from chops; top with tomato mixture.

See photo, page 291.

⅓ cup shredded Monterey Jack cheese

½ cup pimiento-stuffed green olives, finely chopped

4 boneless pork top loin chops, cut 1¼ inches thick

½ teaspoon black pepper

1 tablespoon olive oil

¼ cup chicken broth

¼ cup chopped tomato

1 tablespoon snipped fresh parsley

1g carbs   0g fiber   1g net carbs

Nutrition Facts per serving: 369 cal., 19 g total fat (6 g sat. fat), 118 mg chol., 614 mg sodium, 1 g carbo., 0 g fiber, 46 g pro.

Pork with Pesto Cream Sauce

Prep: 20 minutes Grill: 40 minutes Makes: 4 servings

1 12- to 16-ounce pork
   tenderloin

1 teaspoon olive oil

1½ teaspoons fines herbes or
    dried basil, crushed

¼ teaspoon salt

¼ cup dairy sour cream

3 tablespoons purchased pesto

1 tablespoon water

   Dash black pepper

1. Trim fat from pork. Brush pork with olive oil. Sprinkle pork with fines herbes and salt; rub in with your fingers.

2. For a charcoal grill, arrange hot coals around a drip pan. Test for medium-high heat above pan (see page 107). Place meat on grill rack over drip pan. Cover and grill for 40 to 50 minutes or until done (160°F) and juices run clear. (For a gas grill, preheat grill. Reduce heat to medium-high. Adjust for indirect cooking. Grill as above.)

3. Meanwhile, in a small bowl combine sour cream, pesto, water, and pepper. Set aside until ready to serve.

4. To serve, slice pork. Serve with pesto cream sauce.

3g carbs   **0**g fiber   **3**g net carbs

Nutrition Facts per serving: 237 cal., 16 g total fat (3 g sat. fat), 62 mg chol., 273 mg sodium, 3 g carbo., 0 g fiber, 20 g pro.

Curried Mustard Pork Chops

Prep: 15 minutes Marinate: 6 hours Grill: 30 minutes Makes: 4 servings

1. For marinade, in a small bowl combine mustard, wine, curry powder, oil, red pepper, green onion, and garlic.

2. Place pork in a plastic bag set in a shallow dish. Pour marinade over pork; seal bag. Marinate in the refrigerator for 6 to 24 hours, turning occasionally.

3. Drain pork, reserving marinade. For a charcoal grill, arrange medium-high coals around a drip pan. Test for medium heat above the pan (see tip, page 107). Place chops on grill rack over the drip pan. Cover and grill for 30 to 35 minutes or until done (160°F) and juices run clear, turning and brushing with marinade halfway through grilling. (For a gas grill, preheat grill. Reduce heat to medium. Adjust heat for indirect grilling. Grill as above.) Discard any remaining marinade.

½ cup spicy brown mustard

¼ cup dry white wine

1 tablespoon curry powder

1 tablespoon olive oil

¼ to ½ teaspoon crushed red

   pepper

2 tablespoons sliced green onion (1)

1 clove garlic, minced

4 boneless pork loin chops, cut

   1 inch thick

Nutrition Facts per serving: 191 cal., 12 g total fat (3 g sat. fat),
51 mg chol., 343 mg sodium, 2 g carbo., 1 g fiber, 18 g pro.

Marinated Pork Tenderloin

Prep: 10 minutes Marinate: 4 hours Grill: 40 minutes Makes: 6 servings

2 12-ounce pork tenderloins

½ cup cooking oil

⅓ cup soy sauce

2 tablespoons Worcestershire
    sauce

1 tablespoon dry mustard

¼ teaspoon black pepper

1. Place meat in a plastic bag set in a deep bowl. In a small bowl combine oil, soy sauce, Worcestershire sauce, mustard, and pepper. Pour over meat; close bag. Marinate in the refrigerator for 4 to 6 hours, turning occasionally.

2. Drain meat, reserving marinade.

3. For a charcoal grill, arrange hot coals around a drip pan. Test for medium-high heat above pan (see tip, page 107). Place meat on grill rack over drip pan. Cover and grill for 40 to 50 minutes or until done (160°F) and juices run clear, brushing with marinade twice during first half of grilling (discard remaining marinade). (For a gas grill, preheat grill. Reduce heat to medium-high. Adjust for indirect cooking. Place meat on a rack in a roasting pan, place on grill rack, and grill as above.)

2g carbs   **0**g fiber   **2**g net carbs

Nutrition Facts per serving: 264 cal., 17 g total fat (3 g sat. fat),
73 mg chol., 780 mg sodium, 2 g carbo., 0 g fiber, 24 g pro.

Peppered Pork with Chive Sauce

Prep: 10 minutes Cook: 15 minutes Makes: 4 servings

1. Trim fat from meat. Sprinkle pepper over both sides of chops; rub in with your fingers. In a large skillet heat oil over medium-high heat. Add chops; reduce heat to medium. Cook for 8 to 12 minutes or until chops are slightly pink in center and juices run clear (160°F), turning once. Remove from skillet. Cover chops; keep warm.

2. For sauce, carefully add water and sherry to skillet. Cook and stir until bubbly. Add cream cheese. Using a wire whisk, heat and whisk over medium heat until cream cheese is melted. Serve sauce over chops.

4 boneless pork loin chops, cut

   ¾ inch thick

1 teaspoon coarsely ground

   tri-colored peppercorns or

   coarsely ground black pepper

2 teaspoons cooking oil

¼ cup water

3 tablespoons dry sherry or

   chicken broth

1 3-ounce package cream cheese

   with chives, cut up

2g carbs   **0**g fiber   **2**g net carbs

Nutrition Facts per serving: 291 cal., 20 g total fat (8 g sat. fat), 92 mg chol., 117 mg sodium, 2 g carbo., 0 g fiber, 23 g pro.

Pork Medallions with Cranberry Salsa

Prep: 25 minutes Grill: 18 minutes Makes: 4 to 6 servings

12 slices bacon

½ cup frozen cranberries, thawed and coarsely chopped

½ cup seeded and chopped cucumber

⅓ cup bottled salsa

1 tablespoon snipped fresh cilantro or parsley

1½ pounds pork tenderloin

1. In a very large skillet partially cook bacon over medium heat until lightly browned but still limp. Drain on paper towels until cool enough to handle. For salsa, in a small bowl combine cranberries, cucumber, salsa, and cilantro. Toss gently to coat. Set aside.

2. Cut pork tenderloin into 12 slices, about 1 inch thick. Wrap a slice of bacon around each piece of pork. Thread wrapped meat on long metal skewers, using skewers to secure bacon.

3. For a charcoal grill, arrange medium-high coals around a drip pan. Test for medium heat above the pan (see tip, page 107). Place kabobs on grill rack over drip pan. Cover and grill for 18 to 20 minutes or until pork is done (160°F; pork may still be slightly pink in center). (For a gas grill, preheat grill. Reduce heat to medium. Adjust for indirect cooking. Grill as above.)

4. Remove meat from skewers. Serve immediately with cranberry salsa.

3 g carbs **1** g fiber **2** g net carbs

Nutrition Facts per serving: 354 cal., 18 g total fat (6 g sat. fat), 131 mg chol., 515 mg sodium, 3 g carbo., 1 g fiber, 43 g pro.

Pork Spirals with Red Pepper Sauce

Prep: 20 minutes Grill: 40 minutes Makes: 4 servings

1. Trim fat from meat. Using a sharp knife, make a lengthwise cut down center of the pork tenderloin, cutting to within ¹/₂ inch of the other side. Spread meat open. Place knife in the "v" of the first cut. Cut horizontally to cut surface and away from the first cut to within ¹/₂ inch of the other side of meat. Repeat on opposite side of "v." Spread sections open to lay meat flat. Place between 2 pieces of plastic wrap. Working from center to the edges, pound lightly with flat side of a meat mallet to form an 11×7-inch rectangle. Fold in the narrow ends as necessary to make an even rectangle. Remove plastic wrap.

2. Remove stems from spinach leaves. Stack leaves; slice into thin strips. Combine spinach, mushrooms, basil, and Parmesan. Spread mixture over pork. Begining at a long side, roll up pork. Tie with 100%-cotton string at 1¹/₂-inch intervals. Brush with 2 teaspoons oil; sprinkle with black pepper.

3. For charcoal grill, arrange hot coals around drip pan. Test for medium-high heat above pan (see tip, page 107). Place meat on grill rack over drip pan. Cover; grill for 40 to 50 minutes or until done (160°F) and juices run clear. (For gas grill, preheat grill. Reduce heat to medium high. Adjust for indirect cooking. Place meat on grill rack. Cover; grill as above.)

4. For sauce, in a food processor or blender place roasted peppers, 1 tablespoon oil, vinegar, garlic, and salt. Cover; process or blend until pureed. Transfer to saucepan. Cook over medium heat until heated through. To serve, remove strings from pork. Slice pork and serve with warm sauce.

See photo, page 294.

1   12- to 16-ounce pork tenderloin

1   cup loosely packed spinach leaves

¹/₃ cup finely chopped fresh
    mushrooms

¹/₄ cup snipped fresh basil

2   tablespoons finely shredded
    Parmesan cheese

2   teaspoons olive oil
    Coarsely ground black pepper

¹/₂ cup bottled roasted red sweet
    peppers, drained

1   tablespoon olive oil

1   teaspoon red or white wine vinegar

1   clove garlic, cut up

¹/₈ teaspoon salt

7g carbs   **2**g fiber   **5**g net carbs

Nutrition Facts per serving: 247 cal., 13 g total fat (5 g sat. fat), 67 mg chol., 398 mg sodium, 7 g carbo., 2 g fiber, 26 g pro.

263

Pork Medallions with Brandy Cream Sauce

Prep: 30 minutes Roast: 1 hour Oven: 325°F Makes: 10 servings

1 2- to 2½-pound boneless pork loin roast

   Black pepper

   Salt

½ cup chicken broth

2 tablespoons chopped shallot (1 medium) or green onion (1)

⅓ cup whipping cream

3 tablespoons brandy or cognac

¾ cup unsalted butter, cut into small pieces and softened

4 teaspoons lemon juice

¼ teaspoon ground white pepper

   Fresh chives (optional)

1. Sprinkle pork roast with black pepper; rub in with your fingers. Lightly sprinkle with salt. Place pork on a rack in a shallow roasting pan. Insert an oven-going meat thermometer into center of meat. Roast in a 325° oven for 1 to 1½ hours or until thermometer registers 155°F. Let stand, covered, for 10 minutes before slicing. (The temperature will rise about 5°F while standing.)

2. Meanwhile, for sauce, in a medium saucepan combine broth and shallot. Bring to boiling; reduce heat. Simmer, covered, for 2 minutes. Stir in cream and brandy. Simmer, uncovered, over medium heat for 12 to 14 minutes or until sauce is reduced to ½ cup. Remove from heat. Strain sauce; return to pan.

3. Add butter to sauce, one piece at a time, stirring constantly with a wire whisk. Stir in lemon juice and white pepper.

4. To serve, slice meat across the grain into thin slices. Place 2 or 3 slices on each dinner plate; spoon sauce over meat. If desired, garnish with chives.

1 g carbs   **0** g fiber   **1** g net carbs

Nutrition Facts per serving: 298 cal., 23 g total fat (13 g sat. fat), 102 mg chol., 151 mg sodium, 1 g carbo., 0 g fiber, 19 g pro.

Pork Loin Chops with Creamed Summer Squash

Prep: 10 minutes Cook: 23 minutes Makes: 2 servings

1. In a large skillet heat oil over medium heat. Season pork chops with pepper and salt. Add chops to skillet. Cook chops, uncovered, for 18 to 20 minutes or until done (160°F) and juices run clear, turning once. If necessary, cut larger squash pieces into slices or halves. Add squash to skillet during the last 5 minutes of cooking. Remove chops and squash; keep warm.

2. Drain drippings from skillet. Add half-and-half and coriander to skillet, stirring to scrape up browned bits. Bring to boiling; reduce heat. Simmer, uncovered, for 5 to 7 minutes or until sauce is slightly thickened and reduced to about ¼ cup. Spoon sauce over chops.

1 tablespoon cooking oil

2 pork loin or rib chops, cut
1¼ to 1½ inches thick

¼ teaspoon coarsely ground
black pepper

⅛ teaspoon salt

1 cup baby summer squash, such
as green or yellow pattypan
and zucchini

¾ cup half-and-half or light cream

½ teaspoon coriander seeds,
coarsely crushed

8 g carbs   2 g fiber   6 g net carbs

Nutrition Facts per serving: 758 cal., 44 g total fat (17 g sat. fat),
254 mg chol., 388 mg sodium, 8 g carbo., 2 g fiber, 76 g pro.

Roasted Pork Loin Chops with Thyme

Prep: 20 minutes   Roast: 45 minutes   Oven: 350°F   Makes: 6 servings

6   center-cut pork loin rib chops,
     cut 1½ inches thick, or
     6 pork loin rib chops, cut
     ¾ inch thick
     Salt and black pepper
2   tablespoons olive oil
1   tablespoon snipped fresh
     thyme or ½ teaspoon dried
     thyme, crushed

1. Trim fat from meat. Season chops with salt and pepper.

2. In a bowl, combine the olive oil and thyme; brush over all sides of pork chops. Place chops on a rack in a shallow roasting pan.

3. Roast 1½-inch-thick chops, uncovered, in a 350° oven for 45 to 50 minutes or until done (160°F) and juices run clear. Or roast ¾-inch-thick chops, uncovered, in a 375° oven for 25 to 30 minutes or until done (160°F) and juices run clear.

0g
carbs

0g
fiber

0g
net carbs

Nutrition Facts per serving: 431 cal., 20 g total fat (6 g sat. fat),
144 mg chol., 205 mg sodium, 0 g carbo., 0 g fiber, 58 g pro.

Cheesy Italian & Spinach Pork Spirals

Prep: 25 minutes Grill: 30 minutes Makes: 4 servings

1. Trim fat from meat. Using a sharp knife, make a lengthwise cut down the center of the pork tenderloin, cutting to within $1/2$ inch of the other side. Spread meat open. Place knife in the "v" of the first cut. Cut horizontally to the cut surface and away from the first cut to within $1/2$ inch of the other side of meat. Repeat on opposite side of "v." Spread sections open. Place between 2 pieces of plastic wrap. Working from center to edges, pound lightly with the flat side of a meat mallet to form an 11×7-inch rectangle. Fold in to make an even rectangle. Remove plastic wrap.

2. Remove stems from spinach leaves. Layer leaves on pounded side of pork, leaving a 1-inch margin along one of the long sides. Combine ricotta, 2 tablespoons of the salad dressing, the mozzarella cheese, nuts, and Parmesan. Spread mixture over spinach leaves. Roll up pork, beginning at a long side. Tie with 100%–cotton string at $1^1/2$-inch intervals. Brush meat with the olive oil; sprinkle with pepper.

3. For a charcoal grill, arrange hot coals around a drip pan. Test for medium-high heat above the pan (see tip, page 107). Place meat on the grill rack over drip pan. Cover and grill for 30 to 40 minutes or until done (160°F) and juices run clear, brushing with the remaining 1 tablespoon Italian salad dressing during last 10 minutes of grilling. (For a gas grill, preheat grill. Reduce heat to medium high. Adjust for indirect cooking. Place the meat on grill rack. Cover and grill as above.) Transfer meat to serving platter; cover with foil and let stand 10 minutes. Remove strings; slice pork.

1 12- to 16-ounce pork tenderloin

$1^1/2$ cups loosely packed
    spinach leaves

$1/3$ cup ricotta cheese

3 tablespoons bottled Italian
    salad dressing

$1/4$ cup finely shredded
    mozzarella cheese

$1/4$ cup chopped almonds, toasted

2 tablespoons finely shredded
    Parmesan cheese

1 tablespoon olive oil
    Freshly ground black pepper

5g carbs   **1**g fiber   **4**g net carbs

Nutrition Facts per serving: 333 cal., 21 g total fat (7 g sat. fat), 82 mg chol., 568 mg sodium, 5 g carbo., 1 g fiber, 30 g pro.

Coriander Pork Chops

Prep: 10 minutes Marinate: 4 hours Broil: 9 minutes Makes: 4 servings

3 tablespoons rice vinegar

2 tablespoons water

2 tablespoons reduced-sodium
   soy sauce

2 teaspoons finely shredded
   orange peel

1 teaspoon ground coriander

¼ teaspoon black pepper

1 clove garlic, minced

4 pork rib or loin chops, cut
   ¾ inch thick

1. For marinade, in a small bowl combine vinegar, water, soy sauce, orange peel, coriander, pepper, and garlic; set aside.

2. Trim fat from chops. Place chops in a plastic bag set in a deep bowl. Pour marinade over chops; seal bag. Marinate in the refrigerator for at least 4 hours or up to 6 hours, turning occasionally. Drain chops, discarding marinade.

3. Preheat broiler. Place chops on the unheated rack of a broiler pan. Broil 3 to 4 inches from heat for 9 to 12 minutes or until done (160°F) and juices run clear, turning once halfway through broiling.

0 g carbs   0 g fiber   0 g net carbs

Nutrition Facts per serving: 144 cal., 5 g total fat (2 g sat. fat),
53 mg chol., 111 mg sodium, 0 g carbo., 0 g fiber, 22 g pro.

Brats with Spicy Artichoke Relish

Start to Finish: 25 minutes Makes: 4 servings

1. Pierce bratwurst in several places with tines of fork. For a charcoal grill, arrange medium-high coals around a drip pan. Test for medium heat above the pan (see tip, page 107). Place brats on grill rack over drip pan. Cover and grill for 20 to 25 minutes or until done (160°F) and juices run clear, turning occasionally. (For a gas grill, preheat grill. Reduce heat to medium. Adjust heat for indirect grilling. Grill as above.)

2. Meanwhile, for relish, drain artichoke hearts, reserving marinade. Coarsely chop artichokes. In a small bowl combine artichokes, 2 tablespoons of the reserved marinade, the sweet pepper, zucchini, and jalapeño pepper. Serve relish with brats.

See photo, page 295.

4 uncooked bratwurst

   (about 1 pound)

1 6-ounce jar marinated

   artichoke hearts

¼ cup chopped red sweet pepper

¼ cup chopped zucchini

3 to 4 teaspoons seeded and

   finely chopped fresh jalapeño

   chile pepper (see tip,

   page 59)

8g carbs   0g fiber   8g net carbs

Nutrition Facts per serving: 316 cal., 25 g total fat (8 g sat. fat), 68 mg chol., 764 mg sodium, 8 g carbo., 0 g fiber, 17 g pro.

Five-Spice Pork & Veggie Bowl

Prep: 30 minutes   Cook: 1 hour   Makes: 6 servings

1   2- to 2½-pound boneless pork

sirloin roast

1½   cups sliced fresh mushrooms

(4 ounces)

3   cloves garlic, minced

2   teaspoons grated fresh ginger

2   14-ounce cans chicken broth

¼   cup reduced-sodium soy sauce

3   tablespoons dry sherry

1   teaspoon five-spice powder

2   tablespoons arrowroot

1   cup snow pea pods

2   cups coarsely chopped

Chinese cabbage

1   8-ounce can sliced water

chestnuts, drained

1. Trim fat from meat. Cut meat into bite–size pieces. In a 4– to 6-quart Dutch oven brown meat, half at a time, in 1 tablespoon hot *cooking oil* over medium heat. Drain fat.

2. Add mushrooms, garlic, and ginger. Stir to combine. Add chicken broth, soy sauce, sherry, and five–spice powder. Bring to boiling; reduce heat. Simmer, covered, for 45 to 60 minutes or until meat is tender. In a small bowl combine arrowroot and 2 tablespoons *water*. Stir into the pork mixture. Cook and stir until slightly thickened (do not boil). Remove from heat.

3. Meanwhile, remove strings and tips from pea pods. Add pea pods, Chinese cabbage, and water chestnuts to cooked pork mixture. Cover and let stand about 1 minute or until cabbage is wilted and pea pods are crisp–tender.

9 g carbs   **2** g fiber   **7** g net carbs

Nutrition Facts per serving: 296 cal., 11 g total fat (3 g sat. fat),
95 mg chol., 785 mg sodium, 9 g carbo., 2 g fiber, 36 g pro.

Garlic Pork Loin with Mushroom Cream Sauce

Prep: 25 minutes   Grill: 1 hour   Stand: 10 minutes   Makes: 8 servings

1. Trim fat from meat. Cut ½-inch-wide slits about 1 inch deep over surface of roast. Insert garlic slivers into slits. Sprinkle meat with salt and pepper.

2. For a charcoal grill, arrange medium coals around a drip pan. Test for medium-low heat above the pan (see tip, page 107). Place meat on grill rack over drip pan. Cover and grill for 1 to 1½ hours or until 155°F. (For a gas grill, preheat grill. Reduce heat to medium low. Adjust for indirect grilling. Place meat on grill rack. Cover and grill as above.) Remove meat from grill; cover with foil and let stand for 10 minutes. (The temperature of the meat will rise about 5°F while standing.)

3. Meanwhile, remove stems from shiitake mushrooms. Slice mushrooms. In a large skillet cook mushrooms and garlic in hot butter over medium heat for 3 to 5 minutes or until tender. Add cream and dried tarragon, if using. Bring to boiling; reduce heat. Simmer, uncovered, for 10 to 15 minutes or until liquid is thickened. Stir in sherry; heat through. Stir in fresh tarragon (if using) just before serving. Season with salt and pepper. Serve sauce with sliced meat.

1   2½- to 3-pound boneless pork
    top loin roast (single loin)

1   to 2 cloves garlic, slivered
    Salt and black pepper

8   ounces fresh shiitake or
    cremini mushrooms

2   cloves garlic, minced

2   tablespoons butter

1½ cups whipping cream

2   tablespoons snipped fresh
    tarragon or ½ teaspoon dried
    tarragon, crushed

2   teaspoons dry sherry
    Salt and black pepper

3 g carbs   **0** g fiber   **3** g net carbs

Nutrition Facts per serving: 404 cal., 28 g total fat (15 g sat. fat), 147 mg chol., 164 mg sodium, 3 g carbo., 0 g fiber, 33 g pro.

Ginger Pork Curry

Prep: 25 minutes Chill: 30 minutes Cook: 10 minutes Makes: 6 servings

1½ pounds lean boneless pork, cut into
   thin bite-size strips

2 to 3 tablespoons purchased red
   curry paste

1 tablespoon grated fresh ginger

½ cup chopped onion (1 medium)

2 cloves garlic, minced

⅔ cup unsweetened coconut milk

2 tablespoons chicken broth

½ of a medium red sweet pepper,
   seeded and cut into thin strips (½ cup)

1 small jicama, peeled and cut into
   bite-size strips (optional)

2 tablespoons chopped fresh cilantro
   Chopped peanuts and/or sliced
   green onion (optional)

1. In a medium bowl combine pork, curry paste, and ginger. Cover and refrigerate for 30 minutes.

2. In a large skillet cook and stir half of the pork mixture in 1 tablespoon hot *butter* over medium-high heat for 2 to 3 minutes or until pork is no longer pink; remove from skillet. In same skillet cook remaining pork mixture, the onion, and garlic for 2 to 3 minutes or until pork is no longer pink. Return all pork to skillet. Add coconut milk, broth, and sweet pepper. Bring to boiling; reduce heat. Simmer, uncovered, for 5 to 10 minutes or until liquid thickens slightly.

3. If desired, serve pork mixture over jicama. Top with cilantro, and, if desired, chopped peanuts and/or green onion.

5g carbs

1g fiber

4g net carbs

Nutrition Facts per serving: 272 cal., 16 g total fat (8 g sat. fat), 67 mg chol., 463 mg sodium, 5 g carbo., 1 g fiber, 26 g pro.

Greek-Stuffed Roasted Pork Loin

Prep: 25 minutes Roast: 1 hour Stand: 10 minutes Oven: 325°F Makes: 8 servings

1. To butterfly the pork roast, make a lengthwise cut down the center of the roast, cutting to within ¹/₂ inch of the opposite side, forming a "v." Spread open. Make a parallel slit on each side of the original cut. Open meat to lay flat. Place between 2 pieces of plastic wrap. Working from center to edges, pound with the flat side of a meat mallet to ¹/₂-inch thickness. Remove plastic wrap.

2. Sprinkle Greek seasoning on pounded side of pork loin. Split roasted sweet peppers, if necessary, to lay flat. Arrange sweet peppers in an even layer on top of the meat. In a small bowl combine feta cheese and garlic. Sprinkle over sweet peppers on pork loin. Roll up, starting from a short side, and tie with 100%-cotton string at 1¹/₂-inch intervals. Sprinkle with salt and black pepper.

3. Place roast on a rack in a shallow roasting pan. Insert an oven-going meat thermometer into center of roast. Roast in a 325° oven for 1 to 1¹/₂ hours or until the thermometer registers 155° F. Cover with foil and let stand for 10 minutes. (The temperature of the meat will rise about 5°F while standing.)

4. If desired, serve with steamed kale.

See photo, page 292.

1 2- to 2¹/₂-pound boneless pork
   top loin roast (single loin)
1¹/₂ teaspoons Greek seasoning
1 12-ounce jar roasted red sweet
   peppers, drained
¹/₂ cup crumbled feta cheese
2 cloves garlic, minced
   Salt and black pepper
   Steamed kale (optional)

2 g carbs **1** g fiber **1** g net carbs

Nutrition Facts per serving: 196 cal., 8 g total fat (3 g sat. fat),
68 mg chol., 171 mg sodium, 2 g carbo., 1 g fiber, 26 g pro.

Ham & Zucchini Wraps with Creamy Cranberry Spread

Start to Finish: 20 minutes Makes: 4 servings

½ of an 8-ounce package cream
   cheese, softened

3 tablespoons dairy sour cream

¼ cup finely chopped cranberries

2 tablespoons thinly sliced
   green onion (1)

1 teaspoon snipped fresh basil
   or ¼ teaspoon dried basil,
   crushed

4 8-inch low-carb whole
   wheat tortillas

12 ounces thinly sliced deli ham

1 small zucchini, cut into bite-
   size strips (1 cup)

Fresh basil leaves (optional)

1. For cranberry spread, in a medium mixing bowl beat cream cheese and sour cream on medium speed of an electric mixer until smooth. Stir in cranberries, green onion, and basil.

2. Spread cranberry spread over tortillas. Lay sliced ham over cranberry spread. Lay zucchini strips on ham along one edge. Roll up tortillas tightly. Cut in half crosswise. If desired, garnish with basil leaves.

See photo, page 293.

18g carbs   **10**g fiber   **8**g net carbs

Nutrition Facts per serving: 345 cal., 21 g total fat (10 g sat. fat), 84 mg chol., 1,441 mg sodium, 18 g carbo., 10 g fiber, 20 g pro.

Italian-Stuffed Burgers

Prep: 25 minutes Grill: 20 minutes Makes: 4 servings

1. In a small bowl combine provolone, tomato paste, basil, and garlic. Shape pork sausage into eight ¼-inch-thick patties. Divide cheese mixture on top of 4 of the patties, leaving a ½-inch border around the filling. Top with remaining patties; press edges to seal.

2. For a charcoal grill, arrange medium-high coals around a drip pan. Test for medium heat above the pan (see tip, page 107). Place the burgers on grill rack over drip pan. Cover and grill for 20 to 24 minutes or until meat is done (160°F), sprinkling Parmesan cheese over burgers the last minute of grilling. (For a gas grill, preheat grill. Reduce heat to medium. Adjust for indirect cooking. Grill as above.)

¾ cup shredded provolone or
   mozzarella cheese

3 tablespoons tomato paste

2 tablespoons snipped fresh
   basil or oregano or
   2 teaspoons dried basil
   or oregano, crushed

1 clove garlic, minced

1½ pounds bulk pork sausage

2 tablespoons finely shredded
   Parmesan cheese

4g carbs   **0**g fiber   **4**g net carbs

Nutrition Facts per serving: 673 cal., 55 g total fat (21 g sat. fat),
149 mg chol., 1,556 mg sodium, 4 g carbo., 0 g fiber, 38 g pro.

Pecan & Lime Crusted Pork

Prep: 25 minutes   Roast: 25 minutes   Oven: 425°F   Makes: 6 to 8 servings

⅔ cup very finely chopped

pecans

2 tablespoons butter, melted

1 tablespoon chili powder

1 teaspoon ground cumin

½ teaspoon salt

1 teaspoon finely shredded

lime peel

2 12- to 16-ounce pork

tenderloins

1. In a small bowl combine pecans, butter, chili powder, cumin, salt, and lime peel; set aside. Trim fat from pork. Spread pecan mixture onto meat, pressing in with fingers.

2. Place meat on rack in a shallow roasting pan. Roast in a 425° oven for 25 to 35 minutes or until thermometer registers 160°F. If necessary, cover with foil for the last 5 to 10 minutes to prevent overbrowning.

3g carbs   **2**g fiber   **1**g net carbs

Nutrition Facts per serving: 257 cal., 16 g total fat (4 g sat. fat), 84 mg chol., 281 mg sodium, 3 g carbo., 2 g fiber, 25 g pro.

Pork Roast with Tangy Blue Cheese Sauce

Prep: 20 minutes Roast: 1¼ hours Stand: 10 minutes
Oven: 325°F Makes: 6 to 8 servings

1. Place roast on rack in a shallow roasting pan. In a small bowl combine oil, thyme, salt, and pepper. Brush over roast. Insert an oven-going meat thermometer into center of roast. Roast in a 325° oven for 1¼ to 1¾ hours or until the thermometer registers 155°F.

2. Remove meat from oven. Cover meat with foil and let stand for 10 minutes. (The temperature of the meat will rise about 5°F while standing.) Slice meat and serve with Tangy Blue Cheese Sauce.

Tangy Blue Cheese Sauce: In a blender container or food processor bowl combine ½ cup dairy sour cream; ¼ cup mayonnaise; ¼ cup crumbled blue cheese; 1 teaspoon snipped fresh thyme or ¼ teaspoon dried thyme, crushed; and 1 tablespoon water. Cover and blend or process until nearly smooth. Stir in ¼ cup cranberries. Pulse until cranberries are chopped. Season with salt and black pepper.

1   2- to 3-pound boneless pork
      top loin roast (single loin)
2   tablespoons olive oil
2   teaspoons snipped fresh thyme
      or ½ teaspoon dried
      thyme, crushed
½   teaspoon salt
¼   teaspoon black pepper
    Tangy Blue Cheese Sauce
      (see recipe, left)

2g carbs   **0**g fiber   **2**g net carbs

Nutrition Facts per serving: 388 cal., 26 g total fat (8 g sat. fat),
100 mg chol., 441 mg sodium, 2 g carbo., 0 g fiber, 35 g pro.

Greek Pork Chops

Prep: 15 minutes Grill: 12 minutes Makes: 4 servings

½ cup chopped seeded tomato
   (1 medium)

1 tablespoon bottled low-carb
   balsamic vinaigrette or
   Italian salad dressing

4 boneless pork loin chops, cut
   ¾ inch thick

1 teaspoon lemon-pepper
   seasoning

¼ cup crumbled feta cheese
   with garlic and herb
   Snipped fresh oregano
   (optional)

1. In a small bowl combine tomato and salad dressing; set aside.

2. Trim fat from meat. Rub lemon-pepper seasoning on both sides of chops. For a charcoal grill, grill chops on the rack of an uncovered grill directly over medium coals (see tip, page 107) for 12 to 15 minutes or until done (160°F) and juices run clear, turning once halfway through grilling. (For a gas grill, preheat grill. Reduce heat to medium. Place chops on grill rack over heat. Cover and grill as above.)

3. Transfer chops to serving plates. Top each chop with some feta cheese and some of the tomato mixture. If desired, sprinkle with snipped oregano.

1 g carbs   0 g fiber   1 g net carbs

Nutrition Facts per serving: 227 cal., 6 g total fat (3 g sat. fat), 102 mg chol., 674 mg sodium, 1 g carbo., 0 g fiber, 40 g pro.

Sage & Bacon Meatballs

Prep: 25 minutes Bake: 25 minutes Oven: 350°F Makes: 4 servings

1. In a large skillet cook bacon until crisp; drain on paper towels. Reserve 1 tablespoon drippings in skillet. Finely chop the bacon. In a large bowl combine egg, 2 tablespoons of the whipping cream, 1/2 cup of the red onion, the pecans, 2 tablespoons fresh sage, salt, and pepper. Add pork and three-fourths of the bacon; mix well. Shape mixture into 16 meatballs.

2. Place meatballs in a 15×10×1-inch baking pan. Bake, uncovered, in a 350° oven about 25 minutes or until done (160°F).

3. Meanwhile, cook remaining 1/4 cup onion and the garlic in the reserved bacon drippings until tender. Stir in remaining cream and sage. Bring to boiling; reduce heat. Simmer, uncovered, for 5 minutes or until thickened. Stir in remaining bacon.

4. Transfer meatballs to serving dish; spoon sauce on top.

4 slices bacon

1 beaten egg

1 cup whipping cream

3/4 cup finely chopped red onion
   (1 large)

1/4 cup ground pecans or almonds,
   toasted

3 tablespoons snipped fresh
   sage or 1 1/2 teaspoons dried
   sage, crushed

1/8 teaspoon salt

1/8 teaspoon black pepper

1 pound ground pork

1 clove garlic, minced

6 g carbs   **1** g fiber   **5** g net carbs

Nutrition Facts per serving: 468 cal., 41 g total fat (20 g sat. fat), 195 mg chol., 284 mg sodium, 6 g carbo., 1 g fiber, 20 g pro.

Smoked Pork Chops with Spiced Cream

Start to Finish: 15 minutes Makes: 6 servings

6 cooked smoked boneless

   pork loin chops

1 teaspoon ground coriander

½ teaspoon ground ginger

½ teaspoon ground cinnamon

¼ teaspoon ground cumin

¼ teaspoon cayenne pepper

   Dash ground mace

1 tablespoon butter

¼ cup whipping cream

1 tablespoon dairy sour cream

1. Trim fat from meat. In a small bowl combine coriander, ginger, cinnamon, cumin, cayenne pepper, and mace. Remove ¼ teaspoon spice mixture; set aside. Rub remaining spice mixture on both sides of chops.

2. In a very large skillet cook chops in hot butter over medium heat for 8 to 10 minutes or until hot, turning once.

3. Meanwhile, in a small mixing bowl beat whipping cream with a rotary beater or wire whisk just until soft peaks form (tips curl). Fold in sour cream and reserved ¼ teaspoon spice mixture.

4. Serve chops with whipped cream mixture.

1g carbs   **0**g fiber   **1**g net carbs

Nutrition Facts per serving: 193 cal., 12 g total fat (6 g sat. fat), 80 mg chol., 1,313 mg sodium, 1 g carbo., 0 g fiber, 20 g pro.

Smoked Pork Chops with Strawberry-Balsamic Sauce

Start to Finish: 25 minutes   Makes: 4 servings

1. In a large skillet cook chops over medium heat for 8 to 10 minutes or until heated through, turning once.

2. Meanwhile, in a food processor bowl or blender container place strawberries, vinegar, water, oil, salt, and pepper. Cover and blend or process until smooth. Pour into a small saucepan; cook over low heat until heated through, stirring frequently. Spoon some sauce over chops. Pass remaining sauce.

4   cooked smoked boneless pork
    chops, cut ¾ inch thick

1   cup sliced fresh strawberries

2   tablespoons balsamic vinegar

1   tablespoon water

1   tablespoon olive oil

⅛   teaspoon salt

⅛   teaspoon black pepper

5 g carbs   **1** g fiber   **4** g net carbs

Nutrition Facts per serving: 185 cal., 9 g total fat (2 g sat. fat),
60 mg chol., 1,368 mg sodium, 5 g carbo., 1 g fiber, 20 g pro.

Southwestern Pork Wraps

Prep: 20 minutes Roast: 1¾ hours Oven: 325°F Makes: 8 servings

1 2- to 2½-pound boneless pork

   sirloin roast or pork

   shoulder blade roast

2 teaspoons ground cumin

2 teaspoons chili powder

½ teaspoon salt

½ teaspoon black pepper

1 14-ounce can beef broth

8 8-inch low-carb whole

   wheat tortillas

   Avocado Salsa (see

   recipe, right)

½ cup dairy sour cream

1. Trim fat from meat. In a small bowl combine cumin, chili powder, salt, and pepper; rub onto the meat. Place meat in a roasting pan that has a cover; add broth. Cover and roast in a 325° oven for 1¾ to 2½ hours or until very tender.

2. Using a slotted spoon, remove meat from cooking liquid. Skim fat from cooking liquid and reserve ½ cup of liquid. (Add water, if necessary, to make ½ cup.) Shred the meat using 2 forks to pull through it in opposite directions; place meat in a large bowl. Stir in the reserved cooking liquid.

3. Divide shredded meat among tortillas. Top with some of the Avocado Salsa. Roll up. Serve with remaining Avocado Salsa and the sour cream.

Avocado Salsa: In a medium bowl combine 2 medium avocados, halved, seeded, peeled, and chopped; ½ cup chopped yellow or red sweet pepper; ½ cup seeded and chopped tomato; 1 to 2 teaspoons finely chopped jalapeño chile pepper (see tip, page 59); ½ teaspoon finely shredded lime peel; and 2 tablespoons snipped fresh cilantro. In a small bowl whisk together 2 tablespoons lime juice, 1 tablespoon olive oil, ¼ teaspoon salt, and ⅛ teaspoon black pepper. Pour over avocado mixture; toss gently to coat. Season with additional salt and black pepper.

19g carbs   **12**g fiber   **7**g net carbs

Nutrition Facts per serving: 362 cal., 19 g total fat (5 g sat. fat), 77 mg chol., 713 mg sodium, 19 g carbo., 12 g fiber, 29 g pro.

Thai Pork Lettuce Wraps

Start to Finish: 30 minutes Makes: 4 servings

1. In a large skillet cook pork until brown. Drain fat. Stir in zucchini, sweet pepper, green onions, and, if desired, crushed red pepper. Cook and stir for 2 to 3 minutes or until mixture is heated through. Remove from heat; stir in half (about ⅓ cup) of the Peanut Sauce.

2. To assemble, divide pork mixture among lettuce leaves. Drizzle with remaining Peanut Sauce. Roll up.

Peanut Sauce: In a small saucepan whisk together ⅓ cup natural peanut butter; ⅓ cup water; 3 tablespoons soy sauce; 2 cloves garlic, minced; and ¼ teaspoon ground ginger. Cook over medium heat until heated through, whisking constantly. Stir in 1 tablespoon snipped fresh cilantro.

1 pound ground pork

1 medium zucchini, cut into bite-size strips

½ cup finely chopped red sweet pepper

¼ cup chopped green onions (2)

⅛ to ¼ teaspoon crushed red pepper (optional)

Peanut Sauce (see recipe, left)

8 leaves butterhead lettuce

8g carbs **2**g fiber **6**g net carbs

Nutrition Facts per serving: 297 cal., 19 g total fat (5 g sat. fat), 53 mg chol., 818 mg sodium, 8 g carbo., 2 g fiber, 22 g pro.

Moroccan Lamb Roast

Prep: 15 minutes Marinate: 2 hours Roast: 1¾ hours
Stand: 10 minutes Oven: 350°F Makes: 10 servings

1 5-pound whole leg of lamb
   (with bone)

4 to 8 cloves garlic, peeled and
   cut into slivers

2 tablespoons coriander
   seeds, crushed

2 tablespoons finely shredded
   lemon peel

1 tablespoon olive oil

1 teaspoon cumin seeds,
   crushed

½ teaspoon salt

½ teaspoon whole black
   peppercorns, crushed

1. Trim fat from meat. Cut several ½-inch-wide slits randomly into top and sides of roast. Insert garlic slivers into slits. In a small bowl combine coriander seeds, lemon peel, olive oil, cumin seeds, salt, and pepper. Rub spice mixture onto meat. Cover and marinate in the refrigerator for 2 to 24 hours.

2. Place meat, fat side up, on a rack in a shallow roasting pan. Insert an oven-going meat thermometer into center of roast. The thermometer should not touch bone. Roast in a 350° oven for 1¾ to 2¼ hours or until thermometer registers 140°F for medium rare or 155°F for medium.

3. Remove lamb from oven. Loosely cover with foil and let stand for 10 minutes. (The temperature of the meat will rise about 5°F while standing.)

1g carbs   **0**g fiber   **1**g net carbs

Nutrition Facts per serving: 235 cal., 10 g total fat (3 g sat. fat), 101 mg chol., 185 mg sodium, 1 g carbo., 0 g fiber, 32 g pro.

Pan-Seared Lamb Chops with Fresh Mint Salad

Start to Finish: 30 minutes Makes: 4 servings

1. In a small bowl combine mint, parsley, feta cheese, and pecans; set aside.

2. Trim fat from chops. Rub chops with 2 teaspoons olive oil, salt, and pepper. Heat a large heavy skillet over medium-high heat until very hot. Add chops. Cook over medium-high heat for 8 to 10 minutes or until medium rare (145°F), turning once.

3. To serve, sprinkle chops with mint mixture. If desired, drizzle with additional olive oil and/or lemon juice.

¼ cup snipped fresh mint

¼ cup snipped fresh flat-leaf parsley

¼ cup crumbled feta cheese

¼ cup chopped pecans, toasted

8 lamb rib chops or loin chops, cut 1 inch thick

2 teaspoons olive oil

¼ teaspoon salt

⅛ teaspoon black pepper

Olive oil (optional)

Lemon juice (optional)

2g carbs   **1**g fiber   **1**g net carbs

Nutrition Facts per serving: 252 cal., 17 g total fat (5 g sat. fat), 72 mg chol., 311 mg sodium, 2 g carbo., 1 g fiber, 22 g pro.

Spice-&-Herb-Rubbed Lamb Chops

Prep: 10 minutes Grill: 10 minutes Makes: 4 servings

8 lamb loin chops, cut 1 inch
   thick

1 teaspoon paprika

½ teaspoon dried thyme,
   crushed

½ teaspoon dried basil, crushed

¼ teaspoon coarsely ground
   black pepper

¼ teaspoon salt

⅛ teaspoon ground cumin

1. Trim fat from meat; set aside. For rub, in a small bowl combine paprika, thyme, basil, pepper, salt, and cumin. Rub mixture onto both sides of chops.

2. For a charcoal grill, grill chops on the rack of uncovered grill directly over medium coals (see tip, page 107) to desired doneness, turning once halfway through grilling. Allow 10 to 14 minutes for medium rare (145°F) and 14 to 16 minutes for medium (160°F). (For a gas grill, preheat grill. Reduce heat to medium. Place lamb chops on grill rack. Cover and grill as above.)

1 g carbs   **0** g fiber   **1** g net carbs

Nutrition Facts per serving: 183 cal., 9 g total fat (3 g sat. fat),
78 mg chol., 193 mg sodium, 1 g carbo., 0 g fiber, 24 g pro.

Lamb with Herb-Dijon Sauce

Prep: 20 minutes Marinate: 6 hours Grill: 1 hour Stand: 10 minutes Makes: 12 servings

1. In a small bowl combine mustard, wine, oil, garlic, rosemary, basil, oregano, thyme, and pepper.

2. Spread about ½ cup mustard mixture in bottom of a shallow dish. Place lamb in dish and spread with remaining mustard mixture over top of lamb. Cover and marinate for 6 to 24 hours in the refrigerator.

3. Drain meat, reserving the marinade. To keep the meat flat during grilling, push two 12- to 14-inch metal skewers diagonally through the meat, forming an ×.

4. For a charcoal grill, arrange medium coals around a drip pan. Test for medium–low heat above the pan (see tip, page 107). Place meat on the grill rack over drip pan. Cover and grill to desired doneness, brushing meat with reserved marinade during the first 45 minutes of grilling. Allow 1 to 1½ hours for medium-rare (140°F) and 1½ to 1¾ hours for medium (155°F). (For a gas grill, preheat grill. Reduce heat to medium-low. Adjust for indirect grilling. Place meat on grill rack. Cover and grill as above.) Remove meat from grill. Cover with foil and let stand for 10 minutes. (The temperature will rise about 5°F while standing.)

5. In a small saucepan bring remaining marinade to boiling. Boil for 1 minute, stirring constantly. Pass hot marinade with meat.

1 8-ounce jar Dijon-style mustard
   (¾ cup)
⅓ cup dry white wine
¼ cup cooking oil
2 cloves garlic, minced
1 teaspoon dried rosemary,
   crushed
1 teaspoon dried basil, crushed
½ teaspoon dried oregano,
   crushed
½ teaspoon dried thyme, crushed
¼ teaspoon black pepper
1 5- to 6-pound leg of lamb,
   boned and butterflied

4g carbs   **0**g fiber   **4**g net carbs

Nutrition Facts per serving: 226 cal., 10 g total fat (2 g sat. fat), 83 mg chol., 514 mg sodium, 4 g carbo., 0 g fiber, 31 g pro.

Roasted Ham with Cabbage

Prep: 25 minutes Bake: 1¼ hours Oven: 325°F Makes: 6 to 8 servings

1 2- to 3-pound cooked
    boneless ham

2 tablespoons Dijon-style
    mustard

1 teaspoon caraway seeds,
    crushed

¼ cup red wine vinegar

2 tablespoons olive oil

½ teaspoon caraway seeds,
    crushed

5 cups shredded red cabbage
    (1 small head)

2 tablespoons butter
    Salt and black pepper

⅓ cup coarsely chopped
    pecans, toasted

1. Score ham by making diagonal cuts in a diamond pattern. Brush ham with mustard; sprinkle with 1 teaspoon caraway seeds. Place ham on a rack in a shallow roasting pan. Insert an oven-going meat thermometer into center of ham. Bake in a 325° oven for 1¼ to 1½ hours or until thermometer registers 140°F.

2. Meanwhile, in a screw-top jar combine vinegar, oil, and ½ teaspoon caraway seeds. Cover and shake well; set aside. In a large skillet cook cabbage in hot butter over medium heat for 15 to 20 minutes or just until tender, stirring occasionally. Add dressing to cabbage in skillet; cook and stir about 2 minutes or until most of the liquid is absorbed. Remove from heat. Season with salt and pepper.

3. Serve cabbage mixture over sliced ham; sprinkle with pecans.

See photo, page 289.

11g
carbs

4g
fiber

7g
net carbs

Nutrition Facts per serving: 384 cal., 26 g total fat (7 g sat. fat), 97 mg chol., 2,180 mg sodium, 11 g carbo., 4 g fiber, 28 g pro.

Roasted
Ham with
Cabbage
p. 288

Cumin Pork
Chops with
Avocado
Salsa
p. 256

Spanish-Style Pork Chops p. 257

Greek-
Stuffed
Roasted Pork
Loin Roast
p. 273

Ham &
Zucchini Wraps
with Creamy
Cranberry
Spread
p. 274

Pork Spirals with Red Pepper Sauce p. 263

Brats with
Spicy
Artichoke
Relish
p. 269

Fragrant
Minted
Lamb Chops
p. 297

Fragrant Minted Lamb Chops

Prep: 15 minutes Marinate: 4 hours Grill: 10 minutes Makes: 4 servings

1. Trim fat from lamb chops. Place chops in a plastic bag set in a shallow dish. For marinade, in a small bowl combine ¼ cup mint, lemon juice, oil, water, ginger, garlic, paprika, cumin, salt, and cayenne pepper. Pour over chops; seal bag. Marinate in the refrigerator for 4 to 24 hours, turning bag occasionally. Drain chops, discarding marinade.

2. For a charcoal grill, grill chops on the rack of an uncovered grill directly over medium coals (see tip, page 107) until chops are desired doneness, turning once halfway through grilling. Allow 10 to 14 minutes for medium rare (145°F) or 14 to 16 minutes for medium (160°F). (For a gas grill, preheat grill. Reduce heat to medium. Place chops on the grill rack directly over heat. Cover and grill as above.)

3. Transfer lamb chops to a serving platter; sprinkle with shredded mint. If desired, garnish with snipped mint. If desired, serve with sautéed mushrooms, zucchini, and shallots.

See photo, page 296.

8	lamb rib chops, cut 1 inch thick
¼	cup snipped fresh mint
¼	cup lemon juice
2	tablespoons cooking oil
2	tablespoons water
1	tablespoon grated fresh ginger
1	large clove garlic, minced
1½	teaspoons paprika
1	teaspoon ground cumin
½	teaspoon salt
⅛	teaspoon cayenne pepper
1	to 2 tablespoons finely shredded fresh mint
	Snipped fresh mint (optional)
	Sautéed sliced mushrooms, zucchini, and shallots (optional)

1 g carbs **0** g fiber **1** g net carbs

Nutrition Facts per serving: 210 cal., 12 g total fat (4 g sat. fat), 74 mg chol., 163 mg sodium, 1 g carbo., 0 g fiber, 23 g pro.

Tandoori-Style Lamb

Prep: 15 minutes Grill: 35 minutes Stand: 10 minutes Makes: 6 to 8 servings

2   French-style lamb rib roasts,
    6 to 8 ribs each

1   tablespoon olive oil or
    cooking oil

4   cloves garlic, minced

1   tablespoon curry powder

2   teaspoons ground cumin

1   teaspoon ground ginger

½   teaspoon salt

1   8-ounce carton dairy sour
    cream

½   cup finely chopped cucumber

¼   teaspoon salt

⅛   teaspoon black pepper

1. Trim fat from meat. In a small bowl combine oil, garlic, curry powder, cumin, ginger, and ½ teaspoon salt. Wearing disposable or plastic gloves to avoid staining hands, rub spice mixture over meat.

2. For a charcoal grill, arrange medium-high coals around a drip pan. Test for medium heat above the pan (see tip, page 107). Place roasts, bone sides down, on the grill rack over the drip pan. Cover and grill to desired doneness. Allow 35 to 45 minutes for medium rare (140°F) or 45 to 60 minutes for medium (155°F). (For a gas grill, preheat grill. Reduce heat to medium. Adjust for indirect grilling. Place meat on grill rack. Cover and grill as above.) Cover meat with foil and let stand for 10 minutes. (The temperature of the meat will rise about 5°F while standing.)

3. Meanwhile, in a small bowl combine sour cream, cucumber, ¼ teaspoon salt, and the pepper. Cover and chill until ready to serve.

To roast lamb: Place roasts, bone sides down, in a foil-lined shallow roasting pan. Roast, uncovered, in a 325°F oven until desired doneness. Allow 45 to 60 minutes for medium rare (140°F) and 1 to 1¼ hours for medium (150°F). Cover meat with foil and let stand for 10 minutes. (The temperature of the meat will rise about 5°F while standing.)

4 g carbs   1 g fiber   3 g net carbs

Nutrition Facts per serving: 219 cal., 16 g total fat (7 g sat. fat), 59 mg chol., 353 mg sodium, 4 g carbo., 1 g fiber, 15 g pro.

Grilled Fennel-Cumin Lamb Chops

Prep: 10 minutes Marinate 30 minutes Grill: 12 minutes Makes: 2 servings

1. For the rub, in a bowl combine garlic, fennel seeds, cumin, coriander, salt, and pepper. Trim fat from meat. Rub mixture on both sides of lamb chops. Place lamb on a plate; cover with plastic wrap and refrigerate for at least 30 minutes or up to 24 hours.

2. For a charcoal grill, grill chops on the rack of an uncovered grill directly over medium coals (see tip, page 107) until desired doneness, turning once halfway through grilling. Allow 12 to 14 minutes for medium rare (145°F) and 15 to 17 minutes for medium (160°F). (For a gas grill, preheat grill. Reduce heat to medium. Place chops on grill rack over heat. Cover and grill as above.)

1 large clove garlic, minced

¾ teaspoon fennel seeds, crushed

¾ teaspoon ground cumin

¼ teaspoon ground coriander

¼ teaspoon salt

⅛ teaspoon cracked black pepper

4 lamb rib chops, cut about 1 inch thick

1 g carbs   **1** g fiber   **0** g net carbs

Nutrition Facts per serving: 192 cal., 7 g total fat (3 g sat. fat), 90 mg chol., 361 mg sodium, 1 g carbo., 1 g fiber, 29 g pro.

Rosemary Lamb Chops

Prep: 35 minutes Marinate: 2 hours Grill: 12 minutes Makes: 4 servings

8 lamb chops, cut about

   1 inch thick

1 cup dry red wine

3 tablespoons finely chopped

   fresh rosemary

3 cloves garlic, finely chopped

1 tablespoon balsamic vinegar

½ teaspoon coarsely ground

   black pepper

¼ teaspoon salt

1 tablespoons butter

   Salt and black pepper

   Fresh rosemary sprigs

   (optional)

1. Trim fat from chops. Place chops in a plastic bag set in a shallow dish. In a small bowl combine wine, 2 tablespoons chopped rosemary, garlic, vinegar, pepper, and salt. Pour over meat; seal bag. Marinate in the refrigerator for 2 to 48 hours, turning occasionally. Drain chops, reserving marinade.

2. For a charcoal grill, grill lamb chops on the rack of an uncovered grill directly over medium coals (see tip, page 107) until desired doneness, turning once halfway through grilling. Allow 12 to 14 minutes for medium rare (145°F) and 15 to 17 minutes for medium (160°F). (For a gas grill, preheat grill. Reduce heat to medium. Place chops on grill rack over heat. Cover and grill as above.)

3. Meanwhile, strain reserved marinade into a small saucepan; discard solids. Bring to boiling; reduce heat. Simmer, uncovered, over medium heat for 5 to 10 minutes or until reduced to ½ cup. Add butter and the remaining 1 tablespoon chopped rosemary; cook for 1 minute. Season with salt and pepper. Serve sauce with the chops. If desired, top with rosemary sprigs.

4 g carbs   0 g fiber   4 g net carbs

Nutrition Facts per serving: 280 cal., 11 g total fat (4 g sat. fat), 98 mg chol., 327 mg sodium, 4 g carbo., 0 g fiber, 29 g pro.

Lamb with Herbed Mushrooms

Start to Finish: 25 minutes Makes: 4 servings

1. Trim fat from chops. In a large nonstick skillet heat oil over medium heat. Add chops; cook for 9 to 11 minutes or until medium doneness (160°F), turning once. Transfer chops to a serving platter; keep warm.

2. Add onion to drippings in skillet; cook and stir for 2 minutes. Stir in mushrooms, balsamic vinegar, salt, pepper, and garlic. Cook and stir for 3 to 4 minutes or until mushrooms are tender. Stir in tarragon. Spoon mushroom mixture over chops on platter.

8 lamb loin chops, cut 1 inch
   thick

2 teaspoons olive oil

1 small onion, thinly sliced

2 cups sliced fresh mushrooms

1 tablespoon balsamic vinegar

¼ teaspoon salt

¼ teaspoon black pepper

2 cloves garlic, minced

1 teaspoon snipped fresh
   tarragon or basil or
   ¼ teaspoon dried tarragon
   or basil, crushed

4g carbs

1g fiber

3g net carbs

Nutrition Facts per serving: 165 cal., 9 g total fat (3 g sat. fat), 48 mg chol., 280 mg sodium, 4 g carbo., 1 g fiber, 16 g pro.

Marinated Lamb Kabobs

Prep: 20 minutes Marinate: 2 hours Broil: 6 minutes Makes: 4 to 6 servings

1 pound lean boneless lamb, cut

   1 inch thick

⅓ cup water

3 tablespoons lemon juice

2 tablespoons snipped fresh

   mint or 2 teaspoons dried

   mint, crushed

1 tablespoon Dijon-style

   mustard

1 tablespoon cooking oil

1 clove garlic, minced

2 small zucchini, halved

   lengthwise and cut into

   ½-inch slices

1 cup pearl onions, peeled

6 cherry tomatoes

1. Cut lamb into ¼-inch-thick bite-size strips*. Place meat in a plastic bag set in a deep bowl. For marinade, in a small bowl combine water, lemon juice, mint, mustard, oil, and garlic. Pour marinade over lamb; seal bag. Marinate in the refrigerator for 2 hours to 24 hours, turning occasionally. Drain lamb, reserving marinade.

2. On 6 long metal skewers, alternately thread lamb accordion-style with zucchini and onions. Preheat broiler. Place skewers on the unheated rack of a broiler pan; brush with marinade. Broil 3 to 4 inches from the heat for 6 to 8 minutes or until lamb is no longer pink, turning once and adding a cherry tomato to the end of each skewer during the last 1 minute of broiling. Discard remaining marinade.

***Note:** Partially freeze lamb for easier slicing.

10 g
carbs

2 g
fiber

8 g
net carbs

Nutrition Facts per serving: 207 cal., 8 g total fat (2 g sat. fat),
72 mg chol., 153 mg sodium, 10 g carbo., 2 g fiber, 25 g pro.

Spiced Leg of Lamb with Thyme Cream Sauce

Prep: 30 minutes Marinate: 4 hours Cook: 20 minutes Roast: 2 hours
Stand: 10 minutes Oven: 325°F Makes: 8 servings

1. For spice mixture, in a small bowl combine mustard seeds, coriander seeds, pepper, and ½ teaspoon dried thyme. Set aside.

2. On a cutting board sprinkle salt over 6 cloves minced garlic and press with the side of a knife to form a paste. Transfer to a small bowl; stir in parsley.

3. Brush lamb with oil. Rub garlic-parsley paste onto lamb. Rub spice mixture onto lamb. Place roast on a rack in a shallow roasting pan. Cover and refrigerate for 4 hours or overnight.

4. Insert an oven-going meat thermometer into center of roast. Roast in a 325° oven for 2 to 3 hours or until thermometer registers 140°F for medium rare or 155°F for medium doneness. Remove lamb from oven. Loosely cover with foil and let stand for 10 minutes. (The temperature of the meat will rise about 5°F while standing.)

5. Meanwhile, in a small saucepan cook and stir shallot and 2 cloves minced garlic in hot butter until tender. Add broth and ½ teaspoon dried thyme (if using). Bring to boiling; reduce heat. Simmer, uncovered, about 15 minutes or until mixture is reduced to ½ cup. Add cream. Return to boiling; reduce heat. Simmer, uncovered, until thickened to desired consistency. Stir in fresh thyme (if using). Serve warm sauce with sliced lamb.

1 tablespoon whole mustard seeds, crushed

1 tablespoon coriander seeds, crushed

2 teaspoons cracked black pepper

½ teaspoon dried thyme, crushed

1½ teaspoons salt

6 cloves garlic, minced

¼ cup snipped fresh flat-leaf parsley

1 5- to 6-pound boned and tied leg of lamb

1 tablespoon olive oil

1 medium shallot, thinly sliced

2 cloves garlic, minced

1 tablespoon butter

¾ cup beef broth

2 teaspoons snipped fresh thyme or

   ½ teaspoon dried thyme, crushed

½ cup whipping cream

3 g carbs   **1** g fiber   **2** g net carbs

Nutrition Facts per serving: 507 cal., 28 g total fat (11 g sat. fat), 207 mg chol., 689 mg sodium, 3 g carbo., 1 g fiber, 57 g pro.

Savory Lamb Shanks

Prep: 15 minutes Bake: 3 hours Oven: 400°/350°F Makes: 6 servings

4 lamb shanks

    (about 1 pound each)

½ teaspoon salt

⅛ teaspoon black pepper

4 cups beef broth

½ cup finely chopped onion

    (1 medium)

2 teaspoons dried

    rosemary, crushed

1 teaspoon garlic powder

1 teaspoon dry mustard

1. Place lamb shanks in an ungreased 13×9×2-inch baking pan. Sprinkle with salt and pepper. Bake, uncovered, in a 400° oven for 30 minutes.

2. Remove from oven; reduce heat to 350°. Carefully add broth to pan. Sprinkle lamb with onion, rosemary, garlic powder, and mustard. Cover with foil and bake for 2½ to 3 hours more or until very tender. Remove pan from oven. Transfer lamb shanks to a platter; cover and keep warm.

3. Skim fat from pan juices. To serve, if desired, spoon some of the pan juices over lamb.

2 g carbs **1** g fiber **1** g net carbs

Nutrition Facts per serving: 141 cal., 3 g total fat (1 g sat. fat),
76 mg chol., 874 mg sodium, 2 g carbo., 1 g fiber, 24 g pro.

Poultry

The beauty of chicken and turkey is your ability to infinitely change them. Dress poultry up for pure dining decadence like the White Wine & Italian Herb Marinated Chicken (p. 320). Or keep it simple for casual dining, such as Bistro Chicken & Garlic (p. 346). With so many ways to serve it, you can prepare poultry two or three times a week and never risk dinnertime boredom.

Caraway-Rubbed Chicken

Prep: 20 minutes Roast: 1¼ hours Stand: 10 minutes
Oven: 375°F Makes: 6 servings

2   tablespoons caraway seeds

¼   teaspoon whole

    black peppercorns

1   teaspoon finely shredded

    lemon peel

½   teaspoon kosher salt or

    regular salt

1   3- to 4-pound whole broiler-

    fryer chicken

2   tablespoons lemon juice

    Lemon slices

1. With a mortar and pestle, slightly crush caraway seeds and peppercorns. Or in a blender container combine caraway seeds with peppercorns; cover and blend on high for 30 seconds. Stir in lemon peel and salt; set aside.

2. Skewer neck skin of chicken to back; tie legs to tail. Twist wings under back. Rub caraway mixture over entire bird and under skin of breast. Place chicken, breast side up, on a rack in a shallow pan. If desired, insert a meat thermometer into center of an inside thigh muscle, not touching bone.

3. Roast, uncovered, in a 375° oven for 1¼ to 1¾ hours or until drumsticks move easily and chicken is no longer pink (180°F). Remove chicken from oven. Cover: let stand for 10 minutes. Drizzle lemon juice over chicken before carving. If desired, serve with lemon slices.

2g carbs   **0**g fiber   **2**g net carbs

Nutrition Facts per serving: 223 cal., 13 g total fat (3 g sat. fat), 79 mg chol., 251 mg sodium, 2 g carbo., 0 g fiber, 25 g pro.

Roasted Tomato & Wild Mushroom-Stuffed Chicken

Prep: 40 minutes Bake: 30 minutes Oven: 350°F Makes: 6 servings

1. In a medium skillet cook and stir mushrooms in 1 tablespoon hot olive oil for 3 to 5 minutes or until tender. Remove skillet from heat.

2. Season chicken lightly with salt and pepper. Place in a 3-quart rectangular baking dish. Spread pesto on top of breast halves. Layer mushrooms, then cheese slices over pesto. Bake, uncovered, in a 350° oven for 30 to 35 minutes or until chicken is tender and no longer pink (170°F).

3. Meanwhile, in a large skillet cook and stir shallots and garlic in the remaining 1 tablespoon hot olive oil until tender. Stir in spinach and the salt. Cook and stir for 2 minutes more or just until spinach is wilted and heated through.

4. To serve, spoon wilted spinach onto 6 dinner plates. Cut each chicken breast into 1-inch bias slices. Arrange chicken slices over spinach.

1½ cups sliced assorted fresh mushrooms, such as cremini, shiitake, porcini, and/or button (4 ounces)

2 tablespoons olive oil

6 skinless, boneless chicken breast halves (1¾ pounds)

Salt and black pepper

¾ cup purchased dried tomato pesto

6 slices fresh mozzarella cheese (6 ounces)

¼ cup finely chopped shallots (2 medium)

2 cloves garlic, minced

1 10-ounce package fresh spinach

¼ teaspoon salt

9 g carbs **3** g fiber **6** g net carbs

Nutrition Facts per serving: 378 cal., 19 g total fat (5 g sat. fat), 97 mg chol., 571 mg sodium, 9 g carbo., 3 g fiber, 41 g pro.

Sage-Scented Chicken with Wine Sauce

Prep: 20 minutes   Bake: 40 minutes   Oven: 375°F   Makes: 4 servings

4   medium chicken breast halves

(about 2½ pounds)

¼   cup finely snipped fresh sage

2   cloves garlic, minced

½   teaspoon salt

1   teaspoon finely shredded

lemon peel

2   tablespoons lemon juice

2   tablespoons olive oil

1   14-ounce can reduced-sodium

chicken broth

¾   cup dry white wine

2   tablespoons finely chopped

shallot (1 medium)

¾   cup whipping cream

1   tablespoon shredded fresh sage

1. Using your fingers, gently loosen the skin on each chicken breast half. In a small bowl combine ¼ cup sage, the garlic, and ¼ teaspoon of the salt. (Set lemon peel aside.) Rub sage mixture evenly under the skin of each chicken breast half.

2. In a small bowl combine the remaining ¼ teaspoon salt, the lemon juice, oil, and ¼ teaspoon *black pepper*; brush over chicken. Place chicken, bone side down, on a rack in a shallow roasting pan. Bake in a 375° oven for 40 to 45 minutes or until chicken is no longer pink (170°F).

3. Meanwhile, for sauce, in a large saucepan bring reserved lemon peel, the broth, wine, and shallot to boiling; reduce heat. Simmer, uncovered, about 12 minutes or until reduced to 1½ cups. (At this point, you may cover and chill the sauce for several hours; reheat before proceeding.) Stir in the whipping cream; return to boiling. Boil gently for 18 to 20 minutes or until sauce is thickened and reduced to ¾ cup. Stir in 1 tablespoon sage. Serve sauce with chicken breast halves.

5 g
carbs

0 g
fiber

5 g
net carbs

Nutrition Facts per serving: 358 cal., 25 g total fat (12 g sat. fat),
111 mg chol., 621 mg sodium, 5 g carbo., 0 g fiber, 22 g pro.

Coriander Grilled Chicken with Cilantro Sauce

Prep: 30 minutes Grill: 35 minutes Makes: 4 servings

1. In a small bowl combine coriander, salt, and cayenne pepper. Rub into chicken thighs. For a charcoal grill, grill chicken, bone side up, on the greased rack of an uncovered grill directly over medium coals (see tip, page 107) for 35 to 45 minutes or until chicken is no longer pink (180°F), turning once halfway through grilling. (For a gas grill, preheat grill. Reduce heat to medium. Place chicken on greased grill rack over heat. Cover and grill as above.) Serve thighs with avocado slices, sour cream, and Tomato Cilantro Sauce.

Tomato Cilantro Sauce: In a blender container or food processor bowl place $1/2$ cup coarsely chopped tomato; 2 tablespoons chopped red onion; 1 small clove of garlic; $1/2$ of a 7-ounce jar roasted red sweet peppers, drained; 2 tablespoons snipped fresh cilantro; $1/8$ teaspoon salt; and a dash black pepper. Cover and blend or process until smooth. Makes about $1 1/3$ cups.

1 teaspoon ground coriander

$1/2$ teaspoon salt

$1/4$ teaspoon cayenne pepper

8 chicken thighs, skinned

   (about $2 1/2$ pounds)

1 avocado, halved, seeded,

   peeled, and sliced

  Dairy sour cream

  Tomato Cilantro Sauce

   (see recipe, left)

8 g carbs **4** g fiber **4** g net carbs

Nutrition Facts per serving: 274 cal., 14 g total fat (4 g sat. fat), 120 mg chol., 472 mg sodium, 8 g carbo., 4 g fiber, 29 g pro.

Roast Sage Chicken with Pancetta & Cabbage

Prep: 30 minutes   Roast: 1½ hours   Stand: 15 minutes   Oven: 375°F   Makes: 6 servings

1   4½- to 5-pound whole
    roasting chicken

10 fresh sage leaves

¼   teaspoon salt

¼   teaspoon black pepper

¼   pound pancetta or bacon, chopped

1   cup chopped fennel bulb

½   cup chopped onion (1 medium)

6   cups thinly sliced cored green
    cabbage (1 medium head)

¼   cup chicken broth

½   teaspoon salt

⅛   teaspoon crushed red pepper

1   tablespoon white wine vinegar

½   cup chicken broth

½   teaspoon arrowroot

1. Using your fingertips, loosen skin from breast and legs of chicken. Tuck sage leaves under skin. Place chicken, breast side up, on a rack in a shallow roasting pan. Drizzle chicken with 1 tablespoon *olive oil*; sprinkle with ¼ teaspoon salt and the black pepper. If desired, insert a meat thermometer into center of an inside thigh muscle, not touching bone. Roast, uncovered, in a 375° oven for 1½ to 2 hours or until drumsticks move easily and chicken is no longer pink (180°F). If necessary, loosely cover chicken with foil during the last 20 minutes of roasting time to prevent overbrowning. Transfer to a serving platter, reserving pan drippings. Cover chicken with foil and let stand for 15 minutes before carving.

2. Meanwhile, heat skillet over medium-high heat. Add pancetta; cook until browned and crisp. Using a slotted spoon, remove pancetta from skillet; drain on paper towels. Add fennel and onion to drippings in skillet; cook for 3 to 4 minutes or until softened. Reduce heat to medium. Add cabbage, ¼ cup broth, ½ teaspoon salt, and red pepper. Cover and cook 12 to 15 minutes or until tender, stirring once. Stir in vinegar and pancetta; transfer to serving bowl. Cover and keep warm.

3. Pour reserved chicken pan drippings into a glass measure; skim fat. Measure pan drippings; add chicken broth, if necessary, to make ½ cup. In a saucepan combine ½ cup broth and arrowroot; stir in half of the pan drippings. Cook and stir over medium heat until slightly thickened (do not boil). Serve chicken with sauce and cabbage.

8g carbs   **3**g fiber   **5**g net carbs

Nutrition Facts per serving: 598 cal., 41 g total fat (12 g sat. fat), 189 mg chol., 814 mg sodium, 8 g carbo., 3 g fiber, 47 g pro.

Marinated Chicken Breasts over Greens

Prep: 15 minutes Marinate: 1 hour Grill: 12 minutes Makes: 4 servings

1. Place the chicken in a plastic bag set in a shallow dish. Pour half of the Red Wine Vinaigrette over chicken; seal bag. Marinate in refrigerator for 1 to 4 hours; turn occasionally.

2. Drain chicken, reserving marinade. For a charcoal grill, grill chicken on the rack of an uncovered grill directly over medium coals (see tip, page 107) for 12 to 15 minutes or until chicken is no longer pink (170°F), turning and brushing with marinade halfway through grilling. (For a gas grill, preheat grill. Reduce heat to medium. Place chicken on grill rack over heat. Cover and grill as above.) Discard any remaining marinade.

3. Arrange the mixed greens on 4 salad plates. Cut chicken into thin slices. Place chicken on top of greens. Serve with remaining Red Wine Vinaigrette.

Red Wine Vinaigrette: In a screw-top jar combine $\frac{1}{2}$ cup olive oil; $\frac{1}{2}$ cup red wine vinegar; 1 tablespoon snipped fresh basil; 2 teaspoons snipped fresh thyme or $\frac{1}{2}$ to 1 teaspoon dried thyme, crushed; 3 cloves garlic, minced; and $\frac{1}{4}$ teaspoon crushed red pepper. Cover and shake well. Season to taste.

To broil: Preheat broiler. Place chicken breasts on the unheated rack of a broiler pan. Broil 4 to 5 inches from heat for 12 to 15 minutes or until chicken is no longer pink (170°F), turning and brushing with marinade halfway through broiling.

See photo, page 330.

4 skinless, boneless chicken breast
   halves (1$\frac{1}{4}$ to 1$\frac{1}{2}$ pounds)
   Red Wine Vinaigrette (see recipe, left)

6 cups torn mixed salad greens

3 g carbs   **1** g fiber   **2** g net carbs

Nutrition Facts per serving: 411 cal., 29 g total fat (4 g sat. fat), 82 mg chol., 86 mg sodium, 3 g carbo., 1 g fiber, 34 g pro.

Tarragon Chicken Primavera

Start to Finish: 45 minutes Makes: 4 servings

4 ounces green beans, trimmed

1 small yellow summer squash or zucchini, cut into thin bite-size strips (1½ cups)

1 medium red sweet pepper, seeded, cut into bite-size strips (1 cup)

4 skinless, boneless chicken breast halves (1¼ to 1½ pounds)

1 tablespoon finely chopped shallots

2 tablespoons tarragon vinegar or white wine vinegar

½ cup whipping cream

¼ cup chicken broth

1 tablespoon snipped fresh tarragon or 1 teaspoon dried tarragon, crushed

1. Place a steamer basket in a large saucepan. Add water to just below the basket. Bring to boiling; reduce heat to medium. Add green beans to basket; cover and cook for 15 minutes. Add squash and sweet pepper strips; cover and cook for 3 to 5 minutes more or until vegetables are crisp-tender. Keep warm.

2. Meanwhile, place a chicken breast half between 2 pieces of plastic wrap. Using the flat side of a meat mallet, pound chicken lightly to an even ½ inch thick. Remove plastic wrap. Repeat with remaining chicken breast halves. Season chicken with *salt and black pepper*.

3. In large nonstick skillet heat 1 tablespoon *cooking oil* over medium-high heat. Add chicken and cook for 8 to 10 minutes or until no longer pink (170°F), turning once. Remove from skillet; keep warm. Add shallots to skillet; cook and stir for 30 seconds. Add vinegar and cook until almost evaporated (about 30 seconds). Add cream, chicken broth, and tarragon. Bring to boiling; reduce heat. Simmer, uncovered, for 3 to 5 minutes or until slightly thickened.

4. Return chicken to skillet and turn to coat with sauce. Serve chicken and sauce with steamed vegetables.

See photo, page 331.

6g carbs **2**g fiber **4**g net carbs

Nutrition Facts per serving: 319 cal., 17 g total fat (8 g sat. fat), 123 mg chol., 299 mg sodium, 6 g carbo., 2 g fiber, 35 g pro.

Chicken Breasts with Mexican-Style Rub

Prep: 15 minutes Broil: 12 minutes Makes: 4 servings

1. For rub, using a mortar and pestle, grind together the oregano, thyme, coriander seeds, and anise seeds. Stir in chili powder, paprika, pepper, and salt.* Set rub mixture aside.

2. Using your fingers, gently rub some of the rub mixture onto both sides of chicken breast halves.

3. Preheat broiler. Place chicken on the unheated rack of a broiler pan. Broil 4 to 5 inches from heat for 12 to 15 minutes or until chicken is no longer pink (170°F), turning once halfway through broiling.

*Note: The rub mixture makes about 7 tablespoons. Store the leftover mixture, covered, in a cool, dry place and use within 6 months.

To grill: For a charcoal grill, grill chicken on the rack of an uncovered grill directly over medium coals (see tip, page 107) for 12 to 15 minutes or until chicken is no longer pink (170°F), turning halfway through grilling. (For a gas grill, preheat grill. Reduce heat to medium. Place chicken on grill rack over heat. Cover and grill as above.)

1 tablespoon dried oregano

1 tablespoon dried thyme

1 teaspoon coriander seeds

1 teaspoon anise seeds

¼ cup chili powder

1 teaspoon paprika

½ teaspoon cracked black pepper

¼ teaspoon salt

4 skinless, boneless chicken
   breast halves (1¼ to
   1½ pounds)

0 g carbs   0 g fiber   0 g net carbs

Nutrition Facts per serving: 123 cal., 3 g total fat (1 g sat. fat), 59 mg chol., 88 mg sodium, 0 g carbo., 0 g fiber, 22 g pro.

Spring Chicken Scaloppine

Start to Finish: 30 minutes Makes: 4 servings

4 medium skinless, boneless chicken breast halves (1¼ to 1½ pounds)

2 tablespoons whole wheat flour

¼ teaspoon salt

4 tablespoons butter

½ cup dry white wine and/or chicken broth

¼ cup sliced green onions (4)

¼ cup mixed snipped fresh herbs, such as oregano, thyme, lemon-thyme, and/or mint

¼ teaspoon coarsely ground black pepper

⅛ teaspoon salt

Steamed asparagus (optional)

1. Place a chicken breast half between 2 pieces of plastic wrap. Using the flat side of a meat mallet, pound meat lightly to about ¼ inch thick, working from the center to the edges. Remove plastic wrap. In a small bowl combine whole wheat flour and salt; sprinkle over chicken to coat and press in gently.

2. In a 12-inch skillet heat 2 tablespoons of the butter over medium heat. Cook the chicken, half at a time, for 6 to 8 minutes or until chicken is tender and no longer pink, turning once. Transfer chicken to a serving platter; cover and keep warm. Add wine and green onions to the skillet. Cook and stir for 1 to 2 minutes or until reduced to ⅓ cup, scraping up any browned bits in skillet. Remove from heat. Whisk in the remaining 2 tablespoons butter until melted. Stir in 2 tablespoons of the snipped fresh herbs, the pepper, and ⅛ teaspoon salt. (If using chicken broth, omit the ⅛ teaspoon salt.)

3. Serve chicken with steamed asparagus, if desired. Drizzle wine sauce over all. Sprinkle remaining fresh herbs onto each serving.

See photo, page 332.

4g carbs

1g fiber

3g net carbs

Nutrition Facts per serving: 305 cal., 14 g total fat (7 g sat. fat), 114 mg chol., 384 mg sodium, 4 g carbo., 1 g fiber, 34 g pro.

Chicken & Tarragon-Cheese Sauce

Start to Finish: 30 minutes Makes: 4 servings

1. Season the chicken with salt and pepper. In a large skillet cook chicken in hot butter over medium heat for 12 to 15 minutes or until no longer pink (170°F). Remove chicken from skillet; cover and keep warm.

2. Add cream to the same skillet. Bring to boiling; reduce heat. Simmer, uncovered, for 1 to 2 minutes or until reduced to about ¾ cup, scraping up any browned bits in skillet. Stir in the cheese until melted. Stir in tarragon. Season with additional salt and pepper. Serve sauce over chicken.

4 skinless, boneless chicken
   breast halves (1¼ to 1½ pounds)
   Salt and black pepper
2 tablespoons butter
1 cup whipping cream
½ cup finely shredded Romano
   or Parmesan cheese
2 teaspoons snipped fresh
   tarragon

2 g carbs **0** g fiber **2** g net carbs

Nutrition Facts per serving: 471 cal., 34 g total fat (20 g sat. fat), 195 mg chol., 455 mg sodium, 2 g carbo., 0 g fiber, 39 g pro.

Rosemary Pesto Roast Chicken

Prep: 20 minutes   Roast: 1½ hours   Stand: 10 minutes   Oven: 375°F   Makes: 4 to 6 servings

1 cup lightly packed fresh
  basil leaves

½ cup pine nuts

½ cup finely shredded
  Parmesan cheese

¼ cup fresh rosemary leaves

¼ cup olive oil

1 tablespoon chopped garlic

½ teaspoon salt

¼ teaspoon black pepper

1 lemon, quartered

1 4½- to 5-pound whole
  roasting chicken

1. In a food processor bowl or blender container combine basil, pine nuts, Parmesan cheese, rosemary, olive oil, garlic, salt, and pepper. Cover and process or blend until nearly smooth, stopping and scraping sides as necessary. Set pesto aside.

2. Place lemons in chicken cavity. Tie legs to tail. Twist wing tips under back. Starting at the neck on one side of the breast, slip your fingers between skin and meat, loosening the skin as you work toward the tail end. With your entire hand under the skin, carefully free the skin around the thigh and leg area up to, but not around, the tip of the drumstick. Repeat on the other side of the breast. Rub half of the pesto mixture under skin directly on meat. Securely fasten opening with wooden toothpicks. Rub remaining pesto mixture over outside of chicken.

3. Place chicken, breast side up, on a rack in a shallow roasting pan. If desired, insert a meat thermometer into center of an inside thigh muscle, not touching bone. Roast, uncovered, in a 375° oven for 1½ to 2 hours or until drumsticks move easily and chicken is no longer pink (180°F). If necessary, loosely cover chicken with foil during the last 20 minutes of roasting time to prevent overbrowning.

4. Transfer chicken to a cutting board. Cover with foil; let stand for 10 minutes before carving.

9 g carbs   **1** g fiber   **8** g net carbs

Nutrition Facts per serving: 1,286 cal., 98 g total fat (31 g sat. fat), 314 mg chol., 1,623 mg sodium, 9 g carbo., 1 g fiber, 94 g pro.

Oven-Style Jerk Chicken

Prep: 20 minutes Marinate: 4 hours Bake: 45 minutes Oven: 375°F Makes: 4 servings

1. In a blender container combine soy sauce, rum, oil, onion, garlic, thyme, allspice, nutmeg, peppercorns, cinnamon, cloves, and salt. Cover and blend until combined. Place chicken in a plastic bag set in a shallow dish. Pour soy sauce mixture over chicken; seal bag. Marinate in refrigerator for 4 to 24 hours, turning occasionally.

2. Drain chicken, discarding marinade. Arrange chicken in a 3-quart rectangular baking dish. Bake, uncovered, in a 375° oven for 45 to 55 minutes or until chicken is no longer pink (170°F for breasts; 180°F for thighs and drumsticks).

¼ cup soy sauce

2 tablespoons rum

3 tablespoons cooking oil

½ cup chopped onion (1 medium)

2 cloves garlic

1 teaspoon dried thyme, crushed

1 teaspoon ground allspice

1 teaspoon ground nutmeg

1 teaspoon whole
   black peppercorns

½ teaspoon ground cinnamon

2 whole cloves

¼ teaspoon salt

2½ to 3 pounds meaty chicken
   pieces (breast halves, thighs,
   and drumsticks)

2 g carbs   **0** g fiber   **2** g net carbs

Nutrition Facts per serving: 390 cal., 21 g total fat (5 g sat. fat), 130 mg chol., 648 mg sodium, 2 g carbo., 0 g fiber, 43 g pro.

Grilled Fresh Herb Chicken

Prep: 25 minutes Grill: 45 minutes Stand: 10 minutes Makes: 4 servings

2   tablespoons olive oil

1   tablespoon snipped fresh
    rosemary

1   tablespoon snipped fresh
    thyme

1   tablespoon snipped fresh sage

6   cloves garlic, minced

1   teaspoon finely shredded
    lemon peel

1   teaspoon salt

½   teaspoon freshly ground
    black pepper

1   3- to 4-pound whole broiler-
    fryer chicken

1   teaspoon olive oil

1. In a bowl combine 2 tablespoons oil, rosemary, thyme, sage, garlic, lemon peel, ½ teaspoon salt, and ¼ teaspoon pepper. In another bowl combine remaining ½ teaspoon salt and ¼ teaspoon pepper; set aside.

2. Remove the neck and giblets from chicken. Place chicken, breast side down, on cutting board. Use kitchen shears to make lengthwise cut down one side of the backbone, starting from neck end. Repeat the lengthwise cut on the opposite side of backbone. Remove and discard backbone. Turn chicken cut side down. Flatten chicken as much as possible with your hands. Gently loosen skin from chicken. Spread herb mixture under skin. Brush skin side of chicken with 1 teaspoon oil. Sprinkle both sides of chicken with salt and pepper mixture.

3. For a charcoal grill, arrange medium coals around the drip pan. Test for medium heat above pan (see tip, page 107). Place chicken, cut side up, on grill rack over the drip pan. Cover; grill 45 to 50 minutes or until chicken is no longer pink (180°F in thigh muscle), turning once halfway through grilling. (For a gas grill, preheat grill. Reduce heat to medium. Adjust for indirect cooking. Grill as above.)

4. Remove chicken from grill. Cover with foil; let stand 10 minutes before carving.

2g carbs   **0**g fiber   **2**g net carbs

Nutrition Facts per serving: 564 cal., 41 g total fat (11 g sat. fat), 172 mg chol., 712 mg sodium, 2 g carbo., 0 g fiber, 43 g pro

318

Savory Chicken Kabobs

Prep: 20 minutes Marinate: 2 hours Grill: 12 minutes Makes: 4 servings

1. Cut chicken into 1-inch cubes. Place chicken in a plastic bag set in a bowl. For marinade, in a small bowl combine soy sauce, wine, lemon juice, oil, garlic, fines herbes, ginger, onion powder, and a dash pepper. Pour over chicken; seal bag. Marinate in refrigerator for at least 2 hours or up to 4 hours, turning bag occasionally.

2. Drain chicken; discarding marinade. On eight short or four long metal skewers, thread chicken, leaving ¼ inch between cubes. For a charcoal grill, place kabobs on the rack of an uncovered grill directly over medium coals (see tip, page 107) for 12 to 14 minutes or until chicken is no longer pink, turning halfway through grilling. (For a gas grill, preheat grill. Reduce heat to medium. Adjust heat for indirect cooking. Grill as above.)

1 pound boneless, skinless
    chicken breast halves

¼ cup reduced-sodium soy sauce

3 tablespoons dry white wine

2 tablespoons lemon juice

2 tablespoons cooking oil

1 clove garlic

¾ teaspoon dried fines
    herbes, crushed

½ teaspoon grated fresh ginger

¼ teaspoon onion powder

Dash black pepper

1g carbs   **0**g fiber   **1**g net carbs

Nutrition Facts per serving: 153 cal., 4 g total fat (1 g sat. fat),
66 mg chol., 240 mg sodium, 1 g carbo., 0 g fiber, 27 g pro.

White Wine & Italian Herb Marinated Chicken

Prep: 15 minutes Marinate: 8 hours Grill: 50 minutes Makes: 4 to 6 servings

4 to 6 medium chicken breast halves (2 to 3 pounds)

1½ cups dry white wine

½ cup olive oil

1 tablespoon dried Italian seasoning, crushed

4 cloves garlic, minced

1. If desired, remove skin from the chicken. Put the chicken in a plastic bag set in a shallow dish. In a small bowl combine wine, oil, Italian seasoning, and garlic. Pour over chicken; seal bag. Marinate in the refrigerator for 8 hours or overnight, turning occasionally.

2. Drain chicken, reserving marinade. For a charcoal grill, arrange medium coals around a drip pan. Test for medium heat above the pan (see tip, page 107). Place chicken, bone sides up, on grill rack over drip pan. Cover and grill for 50 to 60 minutes or until chicken is no longer pink (180°F), turning and brushing with reserved marinade halfway through grilling. (For a gas grill, preheat grill. Reduce heat to medium. Adjust heat for indirect cooking. Grill as above.) Discard the remaining marinade.

1g carbs   **0**g fiber   **1**g net carbs

Nutrition Facts per serving: 462 cal., 29 g total fat (7 g sat. fat), 135 mg chol., 108 mg sodium, 1 g carbo., 0 g fiber, 41 g pro.

Cucumber-Sour Cream Chicken

Prep: 20 minutes Cook: 12 minutes Makes: 4 servings

1. In a medium bowl combine sour cream, cucumber, radishes, mayonnaise, ¼ teaspoon salt, lemon peel, lemon juice, garlic, and hot pepper sauce. Cover and chill until ready to serve.

2. Sprinkle chicken with ½ teaspoon salt and cayenne pepper. In a 12-inch nonstick skillet heat oil over medium-high heat. Add chicken; cook 12 to 15 minutes or until chicken is no longer pink (170°F), turning once. (Reduce heat to medium if chicken browns too quickly.)

3. Serve chicken with sour cream sauce.

- ½ cup dairy sour cream
- ½ cup chopped, peeled, seeded cucumber
- ¼ cup finely chopped radishes
- 1 tablespoon mayonnaise
- ¼ teaspoon salt
- ¼ teaspoon finely shredded lemon peel
- 1 tablespoon lemon juice
- 1 clove garlic, minced
- ⅛ teaspoon bottled hot pepper sauce
- 4 skinless, boneless chicken breast halves (1¼ to 1½ pounds)
- ½ teaspoon salt
- ½ teaspoon cayenne pepper
- 1 tablespoon cooking oil

2g carbs   **0**g fiber   **2**g net carbs

Nutrition Facts per serving: 272 cal., 13 g total fat (5 g sat. fat), 95 mg chol., 551 mg sodium, 2 g carbo., 0 g fiber, 34 g pro.

Blackened Chicken with Avocado Salsa

Prep: 30 minutes Bake: 15 minutes Oven: 375°F Makes: 4 servings

2 tablespoons rice vinegar

2 tablespoons olive oil

¼ teaspoon ground cumin

⅛ teaspoon salt

1 avocado, halved, seeded, peeled

   and chopped

⅔ cup chopped papaya

   (½ of a medium)

⅓ cup finely chopped red sweet

   pepper (1 small)

¼ cup snipped fresh cilantro

4 skinless, boneless chicken breast

   halves (1¼ to 1½ pounds)

1 tablespoon blackened

   steak seasoning

1 tablespoon olive oil

1. For salsa, in a large mixing bowl whisk together vinegar, 2 tablespoons oil, the cumin, salt, and a dash of *black pepper.* Add avocado, papaya, sweet pepper, and cilantro; toss to combine. Set aside.

2. Lightly sprinkle both side of the chicken with blackened steak seasoning.

3. In a large ovenproof skillet brown the chicken in 1 tablespoon oil over medium heat, turning once. Bake in a 375° oven about 15 minutes or until the chicken is no longer pink (170°F). (Or do not brown chicken. Place chicken in a 2-quart square baking dish that has been brushed with olive oil. Bake in a 375° oven for 15 to 20 minutes or until chicken is no longer pink.)

4. To serve, spoon some of the salsa over the chicken. Pass the remaining salsa.

10g carbs   **4**g fiber   **6**g net carbs

Nutrition Facts per serving: 350 cal., 19 g total fat (3 g sat. fat), 82 mg chol., 399 mg sodium, 10 g carbo., 4 g fiber, 34 g pro.

Oregano Chicken & Vegetables

Start to Finish: 45 minutes Makes: 4 servings

1. Sprinkle chicken with ¼ teaspoon *salt* and ⅛ teaspoon *black pepper*. Lightly coat a nonstick skillet with *nonstick cooking spray*. Heat skillet over medium heat. Add chicken; cook about 15 minutes or until lightly browned, turning once. Reduce heat.

2. Place the garlic, half of the lemon slices, half of the tomato, the olives, onion, parsley, and oregano over chicken pieces in skillet. Sprinkle with cayenne pepper. Add the wine and the ¾ cup broth. Simmer, covered, for 15 minutes.

3. Add the remaining tomato and the sweet peppers. Cook, covered, for 5 to 10 minutes more or until sweet peppers are crisp-tender and chicken is tender and no longer pink (170°F for breasts; 180°F for thighs and drumsticks). Transfer the chicken and vegetables to a platter. Garnish with remaining lemon slices.

1½ to 2 pounds meaty chicken pieces
  (breast halves, thighs, and drumsticks),
  skinned

1 clove garlic, minced

1 lemon, thinly sliced

¾ cup chopped peeled tomato (1 large)

½ cup pitted ripe olives

¼ cup chopped onion

¼ cup snipped fresh parsley

1 tablespoon snipped fresh oregano or
    1 teaspoon dried oregano, crushed

⅛ teaspoon cayenne pepper

¼ cup dry white wine or chicken broth

¾ cup chicken broth

1 medium green sweet pepper, cut into strips

1 medium red sweet pepper, cut into strips

7 g carbs   **1** g fiber   **6** g net carbs

Nutrition Facts per serving: 208 cal., 9 g total fat (2 g sat. fat),
69 mg chol., 425 mg sodium, 7 g carbo., 1 g fiber, 24 g pro.

Cheese-&-Bacon-Stuffed Chicken Breasts

Prep: 25 minutes Bake: 50 minutes Oven: 350°F Makes: 4 servings

4 medium chicken breast halves

(2 to 2½ pounds)

¾ cup shredded mozzarella

cheese

½ cup crumbled feta cheese

¼ cup chopped peanuts

2 slices bacon, crisp-cooked,

drained, and crumbled, or

¼ cup cooked bacon pieces

Salt

Black pepper

1. Skin chicken, if desired. Using a sharp knife, cut about a 3-inch-deep, 5-inch-long pocket in each chicken breast along the meaty side; set aside.

2. In a medium bowl combine mozzarella cheese, feta cheese, peanuts, and bacon. Spoon filling into the pockets, packing lightly (pockets will be full). Place chicken, bone sides down, in a 3-quart rectangular baking dish. Lightly sprinkle chicken with salt and pepper.

3. Bake, uncovered, in a 350° oven for 50 to 55 minutes or until no longer pink (170°F).

3 g carbs   **1** g fiber   **2** g net carbs

Nutrition Facts per serving: 457 cal., 29 g total fat (10 g sat. fat), 136 mg chol., 587 mg sodium, 3 g carbo., 1 g fiber, 44 g pro.

Down-Home Chicken 'n' Greens

Start to Finish: 35 minutes Makes: 4 servings

1. Sprinkle chicken with ¼ teaspoon black pepper and the salt. Coat a large skillet with cooking spray; heat over medium heat. Add chicken and brown on both sides. Reduce heat. Cover and cook for 10 to 12 minutes or until chicken is tender and no longer pink (170°F).

2. Meanwhile, in a very large saucepan or Dutch oven combine broth, garlic, crushed red pepper, and ¼ teaspoon black pepper. Bring to boiling. Add greens; reduce heat. Cook, covered, for 9 to 12 minutes or just until greens are tender, stirring once or twice.

3. Remove chicken from skillet and slice. Spoon greens and their juices onto 4 dinner plates. Place chicken breast slices on top of greens. If desired, drizzle lightly with balsamic vinegar and garnish with sweet pepper slices.

4 skinless, boneless chicken breast halves (1¼ to 1½ pounds)

¼ teaspoon coarsely ground black pepper

⅛ teaspoon salt

Nonstick cooking spray

⅔ cup reduced-sodium chicken broth

6 to 8 cloves garlic, minced

¼ teaspoon crushed red pepper

¼ teaspoon coarsely ground black pepper

8 cups torn fresh greens (such as mustard, beet, kohlrabi, kale, collard, and/or turnip greens) (1 pound)

Balsamic vinegar (optional)

Red sweet pepper slices (optional)

7g carbs **4**g fiber **3**g net carbs

Nutrition Facts per serving: 197 cal., 2 g total fat (1 g sat. fat), 82 mg chol., 271 mg sodium, 7 g carbo., 4 g fiber, 36 g pro.

Lemon & Herb-Roasted Chicken

Prep: 15 minutes Roast: 1¾ hours Stand: 15 minutes Oven: 325°F Makes: 8 to 12 servings

1 medium lemon

1 tablespoon olive oil

1 5- to 6-pound whole

  roasting chicken

2 cloves garlic, finely chopped

2½ teaspoons herbes de

  Provence or Greek

  seasoning

1. Halve the lemon; squeeze 2 tablespoons lemon juice from the lemon. Reserve lemon halves. In a small bowl combine oil and lemon juice; brush over chicken. In another small bowl combine garlic and herbes de Provence; rub onto chicken. Place the squeezed lemon halves in body cavity of the chicken.

2. Skewer neck skin of chicken to back; tie legs to tail. Twist wing tips under back. Place chicken, breast side up, on a rack in a shallow roasting pan. If desired, insert an oven-going meat thermometer into the center of an inside thigh muscle, not touching bone.

3. Roast, uncovered, in a 325° oven for 1¾ to 2½ hours or until drumsticks move easily and chicken is no longer pink (180°F). Cover and let stand for 15 minutes before carving.

1 g carbs | 0 g fiber | 1 g net carbs

Nutrition Facts per serving: 447 cal., 33 g total fat (9 g sat. fat), 148 mg chol., 111 mg sodium, 1 g carbo., 0 g fiber, 35 g pro.

Tangy Chicken

Prep: 15 minutes Bake: 45 minutes Oven: 375°F Makes: 4 servings

1. Skin chicken, if desired. Trim fat from chicken. In a small bowl combine salt and pepper. Sprinkle 1 teaspoon of the mixture over both sides of chicken.

2. Brush the bottom of a shallow roasting pan with the oil; add onion, garlic, 3 tablespoons sage, and the remaining salt and pepper mixture. Arrange chicken, bone sides down, on top of onions. Sprinkle 3 tablespoons vinegar over chicken.

3. Bake, uncovered, in a 375° oven for 45 to 55 minutes, or until chicken is tender and no longer pink (180°F). Drizzle remaining 1 tablespoon vinegar over chicken. Drain onion mixture. Transfer chicken and onions to a large serving plate. Sprinkle with remaining 1 tablespoon sage.

8 chicken thighs (about
    3 pounds)
1 teaspoon salt
½ teaspoon black pepper
1 teaspoon olive oil
1 large red onion, cut into
    ½-inch slices
2 cloves garlic, thinly sliced
4 tablespoons snipped fresh sage
4 tablespoons sherry vinegar

4g carbs   **1**g fiber   **3**g net carbs

Nutrition Facts per serving: 580 cal., 40 g total fat (11 g sat. fat),
224 mg chol., 747 mg sodium, 4 g carbo., 1 g fiber, 47 g pro.

Chicken with Olives

Prep: 25 minutes Bake: 40 minutes Broil: 3 minutes Oven: 400°F Makes: 4 servings

½ cup pitted kalamata olives,
    finely chopped

½ cup pitted green olives,
    finely chopped

2 tablespoons olive oil

2 tablespoons chopped fresh
    flat-leaf parsley

1 teaspoon minced garlic

4 medium chicken breast halves
    (about 2½ pounds)

1 teaspoon lemon juice

¼ teaspoon black pepper

½ cup dry white wine

1. In a small bowl combine olives, 1 tablespoon oil, 1 tablespoon parsley, and the garlic. Using your fingers, gently loosen the skin on each chicken breast. Tuck olive mixture under the skin of each breast; gently press the skin to evenly spread the olive mixture.

2. Combine the remaining 1 tablespoon oil, the lemon juice, and pepper; brush over chicken. Set aside.

3. In a 12-inch ovenproof skillet bring wine to boiling over medium heat; reduce heat. Simmer, uncovered, for 5 to 8 minutes or until reduced by one-third. Remove from heat. Place chicken, bone sides down, in skillet. Bake, uncovered, in a 400° oven for 40 to 45 minutes or until chicken is no longer pink (170°F). Preheat broiler; broil chicken 4 to 5 inches from heat for 3 to 5 minutes or just until browned.

4. Using a slotted spoon, transfer chicken to 4 serving plates. Stir remaining 1 tablespoon parsley into drippings in skillet; spoon drippings around chicken.

See photo, page 329.

3g carbs   **1**g fiber   **2**g net carbs

Nutrition Facts per serving: 492 cal., 32 g total fat (7 g sat. fat), 135 mg chol., 702 mg sodium, 3 g carbo., 1 g fiber, 42 g pro.

Chicken
with Olives
p. 328

Marinated
Chicken
Breasts over
Greens
p. 311

Tarragon
Chicken
Primavera
p. 312

Spring
Chicken
Scaloppine
p. 314

Tuscan
Chicken
p. 344

Turkey
with Mustard
Sauce
p. 353

Turkey
Tenderloins
with Cilantro
Pesto
p. 360

Mediterranean
Chicken &
Vegetables
p. 337

Mediterranean Chicken & Vegetables

Prep: 30 minutes Cook: 20 minutes Makes: 2 servings

1. Sprinkle chicken with ⅛ teaspoon *salt* and a dash of *black pepper.* Lightly coat a large skillet with cooking spray. Heat skillet over medium heat. Add chicken pieces; cook about 10 minutes or until lightly browned, turning to brown evenly.

2. Add ¼ cup of the tomato, the olives, onion, parsley, oregano, lemon peel, garlic, and a dash of *cayenne pepper* to chicken. Add the ⅓ cup broth and wine. Bring to boiling; reduce heat. Simmer, covered, for 15 minutes.

3. Add sweet pepper and the remaining ¼ cup tomato. Simmer, covered, for 5 to 10 minutes more or until chicken is no longer pink (170°F for breasts; 180°F for thighs and drumsticks) and sweet pepper is crisp-tender.

See photo, page 336.

¾ to 1 pound meaty chicken pieces
     (breast halves, thighs, and/or
     drumsticks), skinned
     Nonstick cooking spray
½ cup chopped peeled tomato (1 medium)
¼ cup pitted ripe olives, chopped
2 tablespoons chopped onion
2 tablespoons snipped fresh parsley
2 teaspoons snipped fresh oregano
1 teaspoon finely shredded lemon peel
1 clove garlic, minced
⅓ cup chicken broth
2 tablespoons dry white wine or
     chicken broth
1 cup red and/or green sweet
     pepper strips

9 g
carbs

3 g
fiber

6 g
net carbs

Nutrition Facts per serving: 171 cal., 5 g total fat (1 g sat. fat),
59 mg chol., 494 mg sodium, 9 g carbo., 3 g fiber, 20 g pro.

Chicken with Mushroom Sauce & Italian Cheeses

Prep: 30 minutes Bake: 20 minutes Oven: 375°F Makes: 4 servings

1 pound skinless, boneless

    chicken breast halves

    Black pepper

3 tablespoons butter

1 cup sliced fresh mushrooms

¹⁄₂ cup dry Marsala wine

¹⁄₃ cup chicken broth

    Dash salt

¹⁄₃ cup shredded mozzarella or

    fontina cheese

¹⁄₃ cup finely shredded

    Parmesan cheese

¹⁄₄ cup thinly sliced green

    onions (2)

1. Cut each breast half in half lengthwise. Place each piece between 2 pieces of plastic wrap. Using the flat side of a meat mallet, pound chicken lightly to about ¹⁄₄ inch thick. Remove plastic wrap. Sprinkle chicken lightly with pepper.

2. In a 12-inch skillet melt 1 tablespoon butter over medium heat; add half of the chicken pieces. Cook for 2 minutes on each side. Transfer to a 2-quart rectangular baking dish. Repeat with another 1 tablespoon butter and the remaining chicken pieces; transfer to the dish.

3. Melt the remaining 1 tablespoon butter in the skillet. Add mushrooms. Cook and stir until tender; add wine, broth, and a dash each of *salt* and *pepper*. Bring to boiling; boil gently about 5 minutes or until mixture is reduced to ¹⁄₂ cup including mushrooms. Pour over the chicken.

4. In a small bowl combine mozzarella, Parmesan cheese, and green onions; sprinkle over the chicken. Bake, uncovered, in a 375° oven for 20 minutes or until chicken is no longer pink (170°F).

2 g carbs   **0** g fiber   **2** g net carbs

Nutrition Facts per serving: 290 cal., 15 g total fat (7 g sat. fat), 102 mg chol., 368 mg sodium, 2 g carbo., 0 g fiber, 32 g pro.

Middle-Eastern Grilled Chicken

Prep: 15 minutes Grill: 15 minutes Makes: 4 servings

1. In a medium bowl combine sour cream, onion, oregano, garlic, sesame seeds, cumin, turmeric (if desired), and a pinch of salt. Set aside. Sprinkle chicken breasts with salt and pepper. Spoon sour cream mixture over chicken breasts.

2. For a charcoal grill, arrange medium-high coals around a drip pan. Test for medium heat above the pan (see tip, page 107). Place chicken on grill rack over pan. Cover and grill for 15 to 18 minutes or until chicken is no longer pink (170°F), turning once halfway through grilling. (For a gas grill, preheat grill. Reduce heat to medium. Adjust heat for indirect cooking. Grill as above.)

½ cup dairy sour cream

3 tablespoons finely chopped onion

2 teaspoons snipped fresh oregano
   or savory or ½ teaspoon dried
   oregano or savory, crushed

2 cloves garlic, minced

½ teaspoon sesame seeds, toasted

¼ teaspoon ground cumin

⅛ teaspoon ground turmeric
   (optional)

⅛ teaspoon salt

4 medium skinless, boneless
   chicken breast halves (1¼ to
   1½ pounds)

Salt and black pepper

2 g carbs   **0** g fiber   **2** g net carbs

Nutrition Facts per serving: 221 cal., 8 g total fat (4 g sat. fat), 93 mg chol., 180 mg sodium, 2 g carbo., 0 g fiber, 34 g pro.

Chicken & Asparagus Saute

Start to Finish: 20 minutes Makes: 4 servings

12 ounces asparagus spears

4 skinless, boneless chicken

breast halves (1¼ to

1½ pounds)

2 teaspoons herbes de

Provence or Cajun

seasoning

2 teaspoons butter or olive oil

1 medium red sweet pepper,

seeded and cut into

thin strips

½ cup dry white wine or

chicken broth

1. Snap off and discard woody bases from asparagus. Bias-slice asparagus into 1-inch pieces (you should have about 1½ cups); set aside.

2. Sprinkle chicken with herbes de Provence. In a large nonstick skillet cook chicken in hot butter over medium-high heat for 3 minutes.

3. Turn chicken; add asparagus, pepper strips, and wine. Bring to boiling; reduce heat. Simmer, uncovered, about 8 minutes or until chicken is no longer pink (170°F) and vegetables are crisp-tender, stirring vegetables occasionally.

3g carbs **1**g fiber **2**g net carbs

Nutrition Facts per serving: 220 cal., 5 g total fat (2 g sat. fat), 87 mg chol., 101 mg sodium, 3 g carbo., 1 g fiber, 35 g pro.

Southwest Chicken in Cream Sauce

Prep: 30 minutes Cook: 20 minutes Makes: 4 servings

1. Sprinkle chicken with ½ teaspoon *salt* and ⅛ teaspoon *black pepper*. In a large skillet brown chicken in hot oil over medium-high heat about 8 minutes, turning to brown evenly. Remove chicken from skillet; set aside.

2. Add sweet pepper and jalapeño pepper to skillet; cook and stir for 3 minutes or until peppers are tender (add more oil if necessary). Stir in cinnamon and chili powder; cook and stir for 20 seconds.

3. Stir in broth, cream, and ¼ teaspoon salt. Simmer, uncovered, about 10 minutes or until sauce is thickened. Return chicken to skillet; simmer for 8 to 10 minutes or until chicken is no longer pink (170°F). Remove from heat; stir in lime juice and sprinkle with cilantro. If desired, serve with lime wedges.

4 skinless, boneless chicken breast halves (1¼ to 1½ pounds)

1 tablespoon olive oil

¾ cup chopped seeded red or green sweet pepper (1 medium)

2 teaspoons finely chopped fresh jalapeño chile pepper (see tip, page 59)

½ teaspoon ground cinnamon

½ teaspoon chili powder

¾ cup chicken broth

⅔ cup whipping cream

¼ teaspoon salt

1 tablespoon lime juice

2 tablespoons snipped fresh cilantro

Lime wedges (optional)

4g carbs   **1**g fiber   **3**g net carbs

Nutrition Facts per serving: 343 cal., 21 g total fat (10 g sat. fat), 138 mg chol., 717 mg sodium, 4 g carbo., 1 g fiber, 35 g pro.

Chicken Breasts with Puttanesca Sauce

Start to Finish: 35 minutes Makes: 6 servings

6   skinless, boneless chicken breast halves (1¾ to 2¼ pounds)

¼   teaspoon salt

¼   teaspoon black pepper

1   tablespoon olive oil

1   14½-ounce can diced tomatoes with basil, garlic, and oregano, undrained

¼   cup pitted kalamata or ripe olives

6   cloves garlic, minced

¼   teaspoon fennel seeds, crushed

2   tablespoons snipped fresh basil

¼   cup finely shredded Asiago or Parmesan cheese

1. Sprinkle chicken breasts with salt and pepper. In a very large skillet heat oil over medium-high heat. Add chicken; cook for 10 to 12 minutes or until no longer pink (170°F), turning once. Transfer chicken to a serving platter; keep warm.

2. Meanwhile, in a medium saucepan combine undrained tomatoes, olives, garlic, and fennel seeds. Bring to boiling; reduce heat. Simmer, covered, for 10 minutes. Stir in basil just before serving. Serve sauce over chicken. Sprinkle with cheese.

8 g carbs   **1** g fiber   **7** g net carbs

Nutrition Facts per serving: 228 cal., 6 g total fat (2 g sat. fat), 82 mg chol., 634 mg sodium, 8 g carbo., 1 g fiber, 33 g pro.

Stuffed Chicken Breasts Florentine

Prep: 30 minutes Bake: 45 minutes Oven: 375°F Makes: 4 servings

1. Wash spinach. Place in a large skillet; cover and cook spinach in water clinging to leaves over medium heat just until wilted. Drain well, squeezing out excess liquid; chop spinach. Transfer to a medium bowl.

2. In same skillet cook and stir onion in 2 tablespoons butter over medium heat about 5 minutes or until onion is tender. Add mushrooms; cook about 2 minutes more or until the mushrooms are tender, stirring occasionally. Add to spinach. Stir in Parmesan, ¼ teaspoon salt, ¼ teaspoon black pepper, nutmeg, and cayenne pepper until combined; set aside.

3. Using your fingers, gently loosen the skin on each chicken breast. Season chicken under skin with salt and black pepper. Spoon about ⅓ cup of the spinach mixture between the skin and meat of each breast.

4. Place chicken, bone sides down, in a 2-quart baking dish. Brush chicken with 1 tablespoon melted butter. Bake in a 375° oven for 45 to 55 minutes or until no longer pink (170°F).

6 cups fresh spinach leaves

½ cup chopped onion (1 medium)

2 tablespoons butter

½ cup chopped fresh mushrooms

¼ cup finely shredded
   Parmesan cheese

¼ teaspoon salt

¼ teaspoon black pepper

⅛ teaspoon ground nutmeg

   Dash cayenne pepper

4 medium chicken breast halves
   (about 2½ pounds)

   Salt and black pepper

1 tablespoon butter, melted

4g carbs   **1**g fiber   **3**g net carbs

Nutrition Facts per serving: 414 cal., 27 g total fat (10 g sat. fat),
137 mg chol., 553 mg sodium, 4 g carbo., 1 g fiber, 37 g pro.

Tuscan Chicken

Start to Finish: 50 minutes Makes: 4 servings

2 to 2½ pounds meaty chicken
   pieces (breast halves,
   thighs, and drumsticks)

2 tablespoons olive oil

1¼ teaspoons pesto seasoning

½ cup kalamata olives, pitted
   if desired

½ cup dry white wine or
   chicken broth
   Fresh arugula leaves sautéed
   in olive oil (optional)

1. In a 12-inch skillet cook the chicken pieces in hot oil over medium heat for 15 minutes, turning to brown evenly. Reduce heat. Drain off excess oil. Sprinkle the seasoning evenly over chicken. Add olives. Pour wine over all. Cover tightly and simmer for 25 minutes. Uncover and cook for 5 to 10 minutes more or until chicken is no longer pink (170°F for breasts; 180°F for thighs and drumsticks). If desired, serve chicken over sautéed arugula leaves.

See photo, page 333.

2 g carbs   **1** g fiber   **1** g net carbs

Nutrition Facts per serving: 334 cal., 18 g total fat (4 g sat. fat),
104 mg chol., 280 mg sodium, 2 g carbo., 1 g fiber, 34 g pro.

Chicken with Herb Rub

Start to Finish: 25 minutes Makes: 4 servings

1. Place a chicken breast half between 2 pieces of plastic wrap. Using the flat side of a meat mallet, pound chicken lightly to ½ inch thick. Remove plastic wrap. Repeat with remaining chicken breast halves. In a small bowl combine fennel seeds, mint, sesame seeds, thyme, salt, and pepper; rub over both sides of chicken.

2. In a very large skillet cook chicken in hot oil over medium heat for 8 to 10 minutes or until no longer pink (170°F), turning once.

4 skinless, boneless chicken breast
　　halves (1¼ to 1½ pounds)

2 to 4 teaspoons fennel seeds,
　　crushed

½ cup snipped fresh mint

2 tablespoons sesame seeds

2 teaspoons dried thyme, crushed

1 teaspoon salt

¼ teaspoon freshly ground pepper

1 tablespoon olive oil or
　　cooking oil

2 g carbs   **1** g fiber   **1** g net carbs

Nutrition Facts per serving: 228 cal., 8 g total fat (1 g sat. fat),
82 mg chol., 662 mg sodium, 2 g carbo., 1 g fiber, 34 g pro.

Bistro Chicken & Garlic

Prep: 20 minutes Bake: 12 minutes Oven: 400°F Makes: 4 servings

1 head garlic

1 tablespoon olive oil

4 medium skinless, boneless chicken breast halves (1¼ to 1½ pounds)

¼ teaspoon dried basil, crushed

¼ teaspoon dried thyme, crushed

¼ teaspoon dried rosemary, crushed

¼ teaspoon salt

⅛ teaspoon freshly ground black pepper

¼ cup dry vermouth or dry white wine

Fresh herb sprigs (optional)

1. Separate cloves of garlic, discarding small papery cloves in center. Trim off stem end of each garlic clove but do not peel.

2. Heat oil in a large ovenproof skillet over medium-high heat. Add garlic cloves and chicken. Cook 4 minutes or until chicken is lightly browned, turning chicken and stirring garlic cloves once. Sprinkle chicken with basil, thyme, rosemary, salt, and pepper; transfer skillet to 400° oven. Bake, covered, for 12 to 15 minutes or until chicken is no longer pink (170°F) and garlic is tender.

3. Using a slotted spatula, transfer chicken to a serving platter; keep warm. Reserve juices in skillet. Transfer garlic cloves to a small bowl; set aside for 1 to 2 minutes to cool slightly. Add vermouth to juices in skillet. Squeeze softened garlic from skins into skillet; discard skins. Bring to boiling; reduce heat. Simmer, uncovered, about 6 minutes or until sauce thickens slightly, stirring frequently. Pour garlic sauce over chicken. If desired, garnish with herb sprigs.

3 g carbs   **0** g fiber   **3** g net carbs

Nutrition Facts per serving: 177 cal., 7 g total fat (1 g sat. fat), 60 mg chol., 189 mg sodium, 3 g carbo., 0 g fiber, 22 g pro.

Garlic Chicken Italiano

Prep: 15 minutes Roast: 1¼ to 1½ hours Stand: 10 minutes
Oven: 375°F Makes: 4 servings

1. In a small bowl combine olive oil, salt, and pepper. Separate the garlic head into cloves and peel. Mince 4 cloves and stir into olive oil mixture. Brush chicken with the oil mixture.

2. Squeeze juice from lemon over chicken. Place lemon halves inside chicken cavity. Skewer neck skin of chicken to back; tie legs to tail. Twist wing tips under back. Place bird, breast side up, on a rack in a shallow roasting pan. Pour wine and the water into pan. Add remaining garlic cloves. If desired, insert a meat thermometer into center of an inside thigh muscle, not touching bone.

3. Roast, uncovered, in a 375° oven for 1¼ to 1½ hours or until drumsticks move easily and chicken is no longer pink (180°F). Remove chicken from oven. Cover with foil; let stand for 10 minutes before carving.

4. Using a slotted spoon remove garlic from pan. Skim fat from pan juices. Carve chicken. Pour some of the pan juices over chicken. Serve garlic cloves with chicken. Pass remaining pan juices.

2 tablespoons olive oil

¼ to ½ teaspoon coarse salt

¼ teaspoon black pepper

2 heads garlic

1 3- to 3½-pound whole broiler-
   fryer chicken

1 lemon, halved

½ cup dry white wine

2 cups water

7 g carbs   **2** g fiber   **5** g net carbs

Nutrition Facts per serving: 618 cal., 44 g total fat (12 g sat. fat), 177 mg chol., 261 mg sodium, 7 g carbo., 2 g fiber, 43 g pro.

Grilled Provençal Chicken

Prep: 15 minutes Marinate: overnight Grill: 50 minutes Makes: 4 servings

5 teaspoons snipped fresh
   rosemary or 1½ teaspoons
   dried rosemary, crushed

1 tablespoon chopped fresh
   thyme or 1 teaspoon dried
   thyme, crushed

1 tablespoon olive oil

2 teaspoon finely shredded
   orange peel

½ teaspoon salt

½ teaspoon freshly ground
   pepper

1 3½-pound whole broiler-fryer
   chicken, cut up

1. In a small bowl combine rosemary, thyme, oil, orange peel, salt, and pepper in a small bowl. Rub mixture over the chicken pieces and under the skin. Wrap and refrigerate overnight.

2. For a charcoal grill, arrange medium-high coals around a drip pan. Test for medium heat above the pan (see tip, page 107). Place chicken, bone side down, on grill rack over pan. Cover and grill for 50 to 60 minutes or until chicken is no longer pink (170°F for breasts; 180°F for thighs and drumsticks), turning occasionally. (For a gas grill, preheat grill. Reduce heat to medium. Adjust heat for indirect cooking. Grill as above.)

1 g carbs • 0 g fiber • 1 g net carbs

Nutrition Facts per serving: 450 cal., 27 g total fat (7 g sat. fat),
154 mg chol., 417 mg sodium, 1 g carbo., 0 g fiber, 48 g pro.

Roasted Chicken with Oregano & Feta

Prep: 15 minutes Roast: 1¼ hours Stand: 10 minutes
Oven: 375°F Makes: 6 servings

1. In a small bowl combine feta and oregano; set aside. Juice the lemon; measure 2 tablespoons lemon juice. Quarter squeezed lemon; set aside. In another small bowl combine lemon juice, olive oil, and pepper. Set aside.

2. Starting at the neck on one side of the breast, slip your fingers between skin and meat, loosening the skin as you work toward the tail end. With your hand under the skin, carefully free the skin around the thigh and leg area up to the tip of the drumstick. Repeat on the other side of the breast.

3. Using your hands or a tablespoon, carefully stuff the cheese mixture under skin, filling the drumstick-thigh area first, working up to the breast. Press gently to distribute the feta cheese mixture throughout the space underneath the chicken skin. Securely fasten opening with wooden toothpicks.

4. Place lemon quarters inside chicken cavity. Skewer neck skin of chicken to back; tie legs to tail. Twist wing tips under back. Rub lemon-oil mixture over bird. Place chicken, breast side up, on rack in shallow roasting pan. If desired, insert a meat thermometer into center of an inside thigh muscle, not touching bone. Do not allow thermometer to touch bone.

5. Roast, uncovered, in a 375° oven for 1¼ to 1¾ hours or until drumsticks move easily and meat is no longer pink (180°F). Remove chicken from oven. Cover; let stand for 10 minutes before carving.

1 cup crumbled feta cheese

1 tablespoon dried oregano, crushed

1 lemon

1 tablespoon olive oil

¼ teaspoon coarsely ground black pepper

1 3- to 4-pound whole broiler-fryer chicken

1 g carbs   **0** g fiber   **1** g net carbs

Nutrition Facts per serving: 192 cal., 13 g total fat (5 g sat. fat), 61 mg chol., 259 mg sodium, 1 g carbo., 0 g fiber, 16 g pro.

Chicken with Mushrooms & Ham

Start to Finish: 45 minutes Makes: 4 servings

4   skinless, boneless chicken

breast halves (1¼ to

1½ pounds)

⅛ teaspoon salt

⅛ teaspoon black pepper

½ cup butter

1   cup cubed smoked ham

(6 ounces)

½ cup chopped shallots

(4 medium)

6   ounces fresh mushrooms such

as cremini, oyster, and/or

chanterelle, quartered

1   cup Riesling wine

1   cup chicken broth

½ cup sliced green onions (4)

1. Place a chicken breast half between 2 pieces of plastic wrap. Using the flat side of a meat mallet, pound meat lightly to about ½ inch thick. Remove plastic wrap. Repeat with remaining chicken. Sprinkle chicken with salt and pepper.

2. In a very large skillet melt butter over medium heat. Add chicken and cook for 4 to 6 minutes or until brown, turning once. Stir in ham and shallots. Cook for 1 minute more. Stir in mushrooms and cook for 1 minute more. Add wine and broth. Cook for 7 to 10 minutes or until sauce is slightly thickened, stirring occasionally. Spoon sauce over chicken and sprinkle with onions.

8 g
carbs

1 g
fiber

7 g
net carbs

Nutrition Facts per serving: 520 cal., 31 g total fat (14 g sat. fat),
172 mg chol., 1,131 mg sodium, 8 g carbo., 1 g fiber, 43 g pro.

Lemon-Tarragon Chicken Fricassee

Prep: 35 minutes Cook: 40 minutes Makes: 6 servings

1. Skin chicken, if desired. Season chicken with *salt* and *black pepper*. In a 12-inch skillet cook chicken in hot oil over medium heat for 10 to 15 minutes or until browned, turning to brown evenly. Remove chicken; set aside. Remove and discard all but 2 tablespoons drippings from skillet.

2. Add celery and onion to skillet. Cook and stir for 2 minutes. Carefully add water, bouillon granules, tarragon, lemon peel, ¼ teaspoon *black pepper*, and bay leaf. Bring to boiling, scraping up browned bits. Add chicken. Reduce heat. Simmer, covered, for 35 to 40 minutes or until chicken is no longer pink (170°F for breasts; 180°F for thighs and drumsticks), turning chicken once.

3. Using a slotted spoon, transfer chicken and vegetables to a serving platter; keep warm. Discard bay leaf. Transfer pan juices to a glass measure. Skim fat from juices; discard fat. Return ¾ cup of the pan juices along with cream to the same skillet. Bring to boiling; reduce heat. Simmer, uncovered, about 5 minutes or until slightly thickened.

4. In a small mixing bowl beat egg yolks. Gradually stir in half of the thickened cream mixture. Return all to skillet. Cook and stir about 1 minute or until mixture just coats a metal spoon. Stir in parsley and lemon juice. Serve sauce with chicken.

2½ to 3 pounds meaty chicken
pieces (breast halves, thighs, and drumsticks)

2 tablespoons cooking oil

1½ cups bias-sliced celery (3 stalks)

1 cup chopped onion (2 medium)

1 cup water

2 teaspoons instant chicken bouillon granules

1 teaspoon dried tarragon, crushed

½ teaspoon finely shredded lemon peel

1 bay leaf

½ cup whipping cream

2 egg yolks

¼ cup snipped fresh parsley

1 tablespoon lemon juice

5g carbs **1**g fiber **4**g net carbs

Nutrition Facts per serving: 360 cal., 24 g total fat (9 g sat. fat), 182 mg chol., 600 mg sodium, 5 g carbo., 1 g fiber, 30 g pro.

Tuscany Stuffed Chicken Breasts

Start to Finish: 50 minutes   Makes: 4 servings

4   skinless, boneless chicken

 breast halves (1¼ pounds)

 Black pepper

2   to 3 ounces fontina cheese,

 crumbled or sliced

½   cup bottled roasted red sweet

 peppers, cut into strips

12   fresh sage leaves

1   tablespoon olive oil

2   cups dry white wine

 Fresh sage leaves (optional)

1. Place a chicken breast half between 2 pieces of plastic wrap. Using the flat side of a meat mallet, pound meat lightly to ¼ inch thick. Remove plastic wrap. Repeat with remaining chicken. Sprinkle chicken lightly with black pepper. Layer cheese, sweet pepper strips, and sage in the center of each chicken piece. Fold in the bottom and sides; roll up. Secure with wooden toothpicks.

2. In a nonstick skillet heat the oil over medium heat. Cook chicken about 5 minutes, turning to brown all sides. Remove chicken from skillet. Drain off any excess fat.

3. In the same skillet bring wine to boiling; reduce heat. Simmer, uncovered, about 4 minutes or until 1 cup liquid remains. Return chicken to skillet. Simmer, covered, for 7 to 8 minutes or until chicken is no longer pink (170°F).

4. Transfer chicken to a serving plate; remove toothpicks and cover to keep warm. Strain remaining cooking liquid; return to skillet. Bring to boiling; reduce heat. Simmer, uncovered, until mixture is reduced to ½ cup. Serve over stuffed chicken breasts. If desired, garnish with fresh sage leaves.

3 g carbs   **0** g fiber   **3** g net carbs

Nutrition Facts per serving: 332 cal., 10 g total fat (4 g sat. fat), 98 mg chol., 197 mg sodium, 3 g carbo., 0 g fiber, 37 g pro.

Turkey with Mustard Sauce

Start to Finish: 45 minutes Makes: 4 servings

1. If using turkey tenderloins, cut each in half horizontally to make 4 steaks. In a large nonstick skillet cook turkey and leeks in hot oil over medium heat about 5 minutes or until turkey is brown, turning once. Stir in wine, broth, dried tarragon (if using), and pepper. Bring to boiling; reduce heat. Simmer, covered, about 5 minutes or until turkey is tender and no longer pink (170°F).

2. Transfer turkey to a serving platter, reserving liquid in skillet; cover turkey and keep warm. Bring liquid in skillet to boiling. Boil about 5 minutes or until mixture is reduced to ½ cup.

3. In a small bowl combine sour cream and mustard; whisk into liquid in skillet. Heat through but do not boil. Stir in fresh tarragon (if using). Spoon sauce over the turkey. If desired, serve with steamed carrots or asparagus.

See photo, page 334.

2 turkey breast tenderloins or

    4 skinless, boneless chicken

    breast halves (about 1 pound)

½ cup sliced leek (1 large) or

    shallots (4)

1 tablespoon olive oil or cooking oil

½ cup dry white wine

½ cup reduced-sodium chicken broth

1 teaspoon snipped fresh tarragon

    or ¼ teaspoon dried tarragon,

    crushed

    Dash black pepper

¼ cup dairy sour cream

2 tablespoons Dijon-style mustard

1 pound baby carrots or asparagus

    spears, steamed (optional)

5g carbs   **1**g fiber   **4**g net carbs

Nutrition Facts per serving: 239 cal., 8 g total fat (3 g sat. fat), 73 mg chol., 325 mg sodium, 5 g carbo., 1 g fiber, 31 g pro.

Indian-Spiced Turkey Tenderloins

Prep: 15 minutes Grill: 12 minutes Makes: 4 servings

2 turkey breast tenderloins

(about 1 pound)

1½ teaspoons ground cumin

1½ teaspoons coriander seeds,

crushed

1 teaspoon finely shredded

lime peel

¾ teaspoon salt

¾ teaspoon ground ginger

½ teaspoon crushed red pepper

½ cup dairy sour cream

2 tablespoons lime juice

Nonstick cooking spray

1. Cut turkey tenderloins in half horizontally to make 4 steaks; set aside. In a small bowl combine cumin, coriander seeds, lime peel, salt, ginger, and crushed red pepper. Set aside ½ teaspoon of the mixture. Sprinkle remaining cumin mixture over the turkey steaks; rub in with your fingers.

2. For a charcoal grill, grill turkey on the rack of an uncovered grill directly over medium coals (see tip, page 107) for 12 to 15 minutes or until no longer pink (170°F), turning once halfway through grilling. (For a gas grill, preheat grill. Reduce heat to medium. Place turkey on grill rack over heat. Cover and grill as above.)

3. Meanwhile, in a small bowl combine sour cream, lime juice, and the reserved cumin mixture. Serve sauce with grilled turkey steaks.

To broil: Preheat broiler. Coat the unheated rack of a broiler pan with cooking spray. Place turkey on prepared rack; broil 4 to 5 inches from the heat for 8 to 10 minutes or until no longer pink (170°F), turning once.

3g
carbs

1g
fiber

2g
net carbs

Nutrition Facts per serving: 191 cal., 7 g total fat (4 g sat. fat),
78 mg chol., 505 mg sodium, 3 g carbo., 1 g fiber, 28 g pro.

Stuffed Turkey Tenderloins

Prep: 15 minutes Grill: 16 minutes Makes: 4 servings

1. Make a pocket in each tenderloin by cutting lengthwise from one side almost to, but not through, the opposite side; set aside. In a medium bowl combine the spinach, cheese, and black pepper. Spoon spinach mixture into pockets. Tie 100%-cotton string around each tenderloin in 3 or 4 places to hold in stuffing.

2. In small bowl combine oil, paprika, salt, and cayenne pepper; brush evenly over tenderloins. For a charcoal grill, grill turkey on the greased rack of an uncovered grill directly over medium coals (see tip, page 107) for 16 to 20 minutes or until no longer pink (170°F), turning once halfway through grilling. (For a gas grill, preheat grill. Reduce heat to medium. Place turkey on greased grill rack over heat. Cover and grill as above.) Remove and discard strings; slice tenderloins crosswise.

2 **turkey breast tenderloins**
   (about 1 pound)

2 **cups chopped fresh spinach**
   leaves

3 **ounces semisoft goat cheese**
   (chèvre) or ¾ cup crumbled
   feta cheese

½ **teaspoon black pepper**

1 **tablespoon olive oil**

1 **teaspoon paprika**

½ **teaspoon salt**

⅛ **to ¼ teaspoon cayenne pepper**

1g carbs   **1**g fiber   **0**g net carbs

Nutrition Facts per serving: 220 cal., 12 g total fat (4 g sat. fat),
68 mg chol., 458 mg sodium, 1 g carbo., 1 g fiber, 26 g pro.

Turkey Mushroom Marsala

Prep: 20 minutes Marinate: 30 minutes Cook: 20 minutes Makes: 4 servings

2 turkey breast tenderloins
(about 1 pound)

½ cup Marsala or dry sherry

⅓ cup water

1½ teaspoons snipped fresh
thyme or ½ teaspoon dried
thyme, crushed

1 teaspoon snipped fresh
rosemary or ¼ teaspoon
dried rosemary, crushed

⅛ teaspoon salt

⅛ teaspoon black pepper

1 cup sliced fresh shiitake or
button mushrooms

1 tablespoon olive oil or
cooking oil

1. Cut each tenderloin in half horizontally to make 4 steaks. Place turkey in a plastic bag set in a shallow dish.

2. For marinade, in a small bowl combine Marsala, water, thyme, rosemary, salt, and pepper. Pour over turkey; seal bag. Marinate in the refrigerator for 30 minutes up to 2 hours, turning occasionally.

3. Drain turkey, reserving marinade. Sprinkle turkey with additional salt and pepper. In a large skillet cook mushrooms in hot oil over medium heat for 3 to 5 minutes or until tender. Using a slotted spoon, remove mushrooms from skillet. Cook turkey in hot skillet for 8 to 10 minutes or until no longer pink (170°F), turning once (add additional oil if necessary). Remove turkey; cover and keep warm. Add reserved marinade to skillet. Bring to boiling; reduce heat. Simmer, uncovered, for 5 minutes or until reduced to about ⅓ cup and slightly thickened. Stir in mushrooms. Season with additional salt and pepper. Serve sauce over turkey.

8 g carbs

1 g fiber

7 g net carbs

Nutrition Facts per serving: 222 cal., 5 g total fat (1 g sat. fat),
68 mg chol., 129 mg sodium, 8 g carbo., 1 g fiber, 27 g pro.

Turkey Breast with Roasted Asparagus

Prep: 30 minutes Roast: 1½ hours Stand: 15 minutes
Oven: 325°F Makes: 8 to 10 servings

1. In a small bowl combine butter, mustard, tarragon, ¼ teaspoon salt, and the black pepper; set aside.

2. Remove skin from turkey; set aside. Lay one turkey breast half, boned side up, on work surface. Make 4 to 5 shallow cuts in the thickest portion of breast (do not cut through). Place turkey breast between two pieces of plastic wrap. Using the flat side of a meat mallet, lightly pound turkey breast to an even thickness (about ¾ inch). Remove plastic wrap. Repeat with remaining turkey breast. Dot breast halves with half of the butter mixture; set remaining mixture aside. Top breast halves evenly with sweet peppers and parsley. Starting with a short side, roll up each breast half. Wrap reserved skin around each roll. Tie with 100%-cotton string in 3 or 4 places to secure. Place on a rack in a shallow roasting pan.

3. Melt remaining butter mixture and brush over turkey. Insert a meat thermometer into the center of one of the turkey rolls. Roast, uncovered, in a 325° oven for 1½ to 1¾ hours or until no longer pink (170°F).

4. Meanwhile, snap off and discard woody bases from asparagus. If desired, scrape off scales. In a large bowl toss asparagus, oil, and ¼ teaspoon salt. Add asparagus to the roasting pan around the turkey the last 15 to 20 minutes of roasting time. Cover roasted turkey and asparagus; let stand for 15 minutes before slicing. Serve turkey with asparagus.

¼ cup butter, softened

2 teaspoons Dijon-style mustard

¾ teaspoon dried tarragon, crushed

¼ teaspoon salt

⅛ teaspoon black pepper

2 boneless turkey breast halves (skin on) (2½ to 3 pounds)

1 7-ounce jar roasted red sweet peppers, drained and coarsely chopped

½ cup snipped fresh parsley

1½ pounds asparagus spears

1 tablespoon olive oil

¼ teaspoon salt

2g carbs   **1**g fiber   **1**g net carbs

Nutrition Facts per serving: 212 cal., 9 g total fat (2 g sat. fat), 80 mg chol., 220 mg sodium, 2 g carbo., 1 g fiber, 28 g pro.

Grilled Turkey Piccata

Prep: 15 minutes Grill: 12 minutes Makes: 4 servings

2 lemons

4 teaspoons olive oil

2 teaspoons snipped fresh
    rosemary or ½ teaspoon
    dried rosemary, crushed

¼ teaspoon salt

¼ teaspoon freshly ground
    black pepper

2 turkey breast tenderloins
    (about 1 pound)

1 tablespoon drained capers

1 tablespoon snipped fresh
    flat-leaf parsley

1. Finely shred enough peel from one of the lemons to make 1 teaspoon; set aside. Halve and squeeze the juice from that lemon (should have about 3 tablespoons); set aside. Cut the other lemon into very thin slices; set aside.

2. For rub, in a small bowl combine the shredded lemon peel, 2 teaspoons olive oil, the rosemary, salt, and pepper. Cut each tenderloin in half horizontally to make 4 steaks. Sprinkle the mixture evenly over both sides of turkey; rub in with your fingers.

3. For a charcoal grill, grill turkey on the rack of an uncovered grill directly over medium coals (see tip, page 107) for 12 to 15 minutes or until no longer pink (170°F), turning once and arranging lemon slices on top of turkey halfway through grilling. (For a gas grill, preheat grill. Reduce heat to medium. Place turkey on grill rack over heat. Cover and grill as above.)

4. Meanwhile, in a small saucepan combine remaining 2 teaspoons olive oil, the 3 tablespoons lemon juice, and the capers. Heat through.

5. Transfer turkey steaks to a serving platter. Drizzle with the warm caper mixture. Sprinkle with parsley.

1g carbs

0g fiber

1g net carbs

Nutrition Facts per serving: 159 cal., 5 g total fat (1 g sat. fat), 71 mg chol., 269 mg sodium, 1 g carbo., 0 g fiber, 26 g pro.

Parmesan-Sesame-Crusted Turkey Breast

Prep: 15 minutes   Cook: 8 minutes   Makes: 4 servings

1. Cut each tenderloin in half horizontally to make 4 steaks; set aside. In a shallow dish or pie plate combine Parmesan cheese and sesame seeds. Place egg in another shallow dish or pie plate. Dip turkey slices into egg; coat with Parmesan cheese mixture. Sprinkle each turkey slice with salt and pepper.

2. In a large skillet cook turkey in hot oil over medium-high heat for 8 to 10 minutes or until turkey is no longer pink (170°F), turning once.

2   turkey breast tenderloins

(about 1 pound)

½   cup finely shredded

Parmesan cheese

¼   cup sesame seeds

1   egg, beaten

¼   teaspoon salt

¼   teaspoon black pepper

1   tablespoon olive oil or cooking oil

3g carbs   **1**g fiber   **2**g net carbs

Nutrition Facts per serving: 498 cal., 28 g total fat (13 g sat. fat), 171 mg chol., 1,336 mg sodium, 3 g carbo., 1 g fiber, 57 g pro.

Turkey Tenderloins with Cilantro Pesto

Prep: 15 minutes Grill: 12 minutes Makes: 8 servings

4 turkey breast tenderloins

(about 2 pounds)

1½ cups lightly packed fresh

cilantro or basil leaves

⅓ cup walnuts

3 tablespoons olive oil

3 tablespoons lime juice

2 cloves garlic, minced

¼ teaspoon salt

Salt and black pepper

Lime or lemon wedges

(optional)

1. Cut each tenderloin in half horizontally to make 4 steaks; set aside. For pesto, in a blender container or food processor bowl place cilantro, walnuts, olive oil, lime juice, garlic, and salt. Cover and blend or process until nearly smooth. Cover and store in the refrigerator for 1 to 2 days.

2. Season turkey with salt and pepper. Set aside half of the pesto to use as a brush-on during grilling. Cover and chill remaining pesto until serving time.

3. For a charcoal grill, grill turkey on the rack of an uncovered grill directly over medium coals (see tip, page 107) for 12 to 15 minutes or until no longer pink (170°F), turning once and brushing lightly with cilantro pesto halfway through grilling. Discard remainder of the pesto used as a brush-on. (For a gas grill, preheat grill. Reduce heat to medium. Place turkey on grill rack over heat. Cover and grill as above.) Serve turkey with the chilled pesto. If desired, serve with lime wedges.

See photo, page 335.

2 g
carbs

1 g
fiber

1 g
net carbs

Nutrition Facts per serving: 213 cal., 10 g total fat (2 g sat. fat), 68 mg chol., 134 mg sodium, 2 g carbo., 1 g fiber, 28 g pro.

Turkey Steaks & Vegetables

Prep: 10 minutes Grill: 12 minutes Makes: 4 servings

1. For sauce, in a small bowl gradually stir vegetable juice into mayonnaise; stir in chives, thyme, and garlic. Set sauce aside.

2. Cut each tenderloin in half horizontally to make 4 steaks. Sprinkle with salt and pepper. For a charcoal grill, grill turkey, zucchini, and tomatoes on the rack of an uncovered grill directly over medium coals (see tip, page 107) for 12 to 15 minutes or until turkey is no longer pink (170°F), zucchini is tender, and tomatoes are heated through*, turning once and brushing with sauce halfway through grilling. Discard the remainder of the sauce. (For a gas grill, preheat grill. Reduce heat to medium. Place turkey, zucchini, and tomatoes on grill rack over heat. Cover and grill as above.)

*Note: If the tomatoes are done before the turkey, remove the tomatoes from the grill and keep warm.

¼ cup vegetable juice

3 tablespoons mayonnaise

1 tablespoon snipped fresh

   chives or green onion tops

2 teaspoons snipped fresh thyme

   or ½ teaspoon dried

   thyme, crushed

½ teaspoon bottled minced garlic

2 turkey breast tenderloins

   (about 1 pound)

   Salt and black pepper

2 small zucchini, halved

   lengthwise

2 large plum tomatoes,

   halved lengthwise

6g carbs   **1**g fiber   **5**g net carbs

Nutrition Facts per serving: 209 cal., 11 g total fat (2 g sat. fat), 56 mg chol., 200 mg sodium, 6 g carbo., 1 g fiber, 22 g pro.

Turkey & Peppers

Start to Finish: 30 minutes Makes: 4 servings

2 turkey breast tenderloins
   (about 1 pound)

1 tablespoon olive oil

2 medium red, green, and/or
   yellow sweet peppers,
   seeded and cut into thin strips

1 medium onion, halved
   lengthwise and sliced

1 jalapeño chile pepper, seeded
   and thinly sliced (see tip, page 59)

¾ cup chicken broth

1 tablespoon whole wheat flour

1 tablespoon snipped fresh
   oregano or ½ teaspoon dried
   oregano, crushed

1 teaspoon paprika

1. Cut each tenderloin in half horizontally to make 4 steaks. Sprinkle turkey with *salt* and *black pepper*. In a large nonstick skillet cook turkey in hot oil over medium-high heat for 8 to 10 minutes or until turkey is no longer pink (170°), turning once. (If necessary, reduce heat to medium to prevent overbrowning.) Transfer turkey to a serving platter; cover and keep warm.

2. Add sweet peppers, onion, and jalapeño pepper to skillet. Cook, covered, for 4 to 6 minutes or until vegetables are crisp-tender, stirring occasionally.

3. In a small mixing bowl whisk together broth, flour, dried oregano (if using), paprika, and ¼ teaspoon *salt* until well combined. Add to pepper mixture. Cook and stir over medium heat until slightly thickened and bubbly. Cook and stir for 1 minute more. Stir in fresh oregano (if using). Spoon the pepper mixture over turkey.

8g carbs   **2**g fiber   **6**g net carbs

Nutrition Facts per serving: 196 cal., 5 g total fat (1 g sat. fat), 68 mg chol., 531 mg sodium, 8 g carbo., 2 g fiber, 28 g pro.

Desserts

Longing for dessert? Think you'll never eat a sweet again? This chapter serves up a dozen recipes sure to satisfy your sweet tooth, but none will load you up on carbohydrates. Check out Peanut Butter Cream (p. 364), Fudge-Cinnamon Puffs (p. 368), or Heavenly Tiramisu Cream (p. 373). All fit perfectly into a phase 2 eating plan.

Peanut Butter Cream

Start to Finish: 15 minutes Makes: 8 to 10 servings

½ of an 8-ounce package cream
  cheese, softened

½ cup natural peanut butter

⅓ cup no-calorie, heat-stable granular
  sugar substitute (Splenda)

1 teaspoon vanilla

1 cup whipping cream

2 tablespoons dry-roasted
  peanuts, chopped

1. In a large mixing bowl beat cream cheese, peanut butter, sugar substitute, and vanilla with an electric mixer on medium speed until fluffy.

2. In a chilled medium mixing bowl beat whipping cream on medium speed until soft peaks form (tips curl). Gently fold about one-third of the whipped cream into peanut butter mixture. Fold in remaining whipped cream.

3. Divide peanut butter mixture among 8 to 10 dessert dishes or martini glasses. Sprinkle with chopped peanuts. Serve immediately.

6 g
carbs

1 g
fiber

5 g
net carbs

Nutrition Facts per serving: 266 cal., 25 g total fat (12 g sat. fat),
57 mg chol., 147 mg sodium, 6 g carbo., 1 g fiber, 6 g pro.

Melon Refresher

Prep: 15 minutes Freeze: 1 hour Stand: 10 minutes Makes: 8 servings

1. Line a baking sheet with plastic wrap. Arrange melon cubes in a single layer on prepared baking sheet. Freeze about 1 hour or until firm.

2. Let melon stand at room temperature for 10 minutes. In a food processor bowl combine honeydew melon, sugar substitute, melon liqueur, and lime juice. Cover and process until smooth. Divide melon mixture among 8 martini or wine glasses.

4 cups cubed honeydew melon
   (1-inch cubes)

2 tablespoons no-calorie, heat-
   stable granular sugar
   substitute (Splenda)

1 tablespoon melon liqueur

1 tablespoon lime juice

9 g carbs   **1** g fiber   **8** g net carbs

Nutrition Facts per serving: 38 cal., 0 g total fat (0 g sat. fat),
0 mg chol., 9 mg sodium, 9 g carbo., 1 g fiber, 0 g pro.

Strawberry-Citrus Slush

Start to Finish: 10 minutes Makes: 3 servings

6 ounces frozen unsweetened
  whole strawberries
  (about 1⅓ cups)

1 12-ounce can low-calorie
  grapefruit carbonated
  beverage

1 cup ice cubes

2 teaspoons no-calorie, heat-
  stable granular sugar
  substitute (Splenda)

¼ teaspoon orange extract or
  lime extract (optional)

1. In a blender container combine strawberries, carbonated beverage, ice cubes, sugar substitute, and, if desired, orange extract. Cover and blend until smooth. Divide slush among 3 wine glasses.

6 g carbs   **1** g fiber   **5** g net carbs

Nutrition Facts per serving: 22 cal., 0 g total fat (0 g sat. fat),
0 mg chol., 24 mg sodium, 6 g carbo., 1 g fiber, 0 g pro.

Berries with Orange Cream

Start to Finish: 15 minutes Makes: 4 servings

1. Divide strawberries and blackberries among 4 small dessert dishes. Set aside.

2. In a small mixing bowl beat cream cheese with an electric mixer on medium speed until fluffy. Beat in whipping cream and sugar substitute until combined. Stir in orange peel.

3. If necessary, stir in 1 to 2 tablespoons additional whipping cream to reach desired consistency. Spoon cream cheese mixture over berries.

1 **cup sliced fresh strawberries**

⅓ **cup fresh blackberries**

½ **of an 8-ounce package cream cheese, softened**

2 **tablespoons whipping cream**

1 **tablespoon no-calorie, heat-stable granular sugar substitute (Splenda)**

1 **teaspoon finely shredded orange peel**

6 g carbs **2** g fiber **4** g net carbs

Nutrition Facts per serving: 144 cal., 13 g total fat (8 g sat. fat), 41 mg chol., 87 mg sodium, 6 g carbo., 2 g fiber, 3 g pro.

Fudge-Cinnamon Puffs

Prep: 15 minutes Bake: 8 minutes Oven: 350°F Makes: 4 servings

2 tablespoons unsweetened

cocoa powder

2 tablespoons no-calorie, heat-

stable granular sugar

substitute (Splenda)

½ teaspoon ground cinnamon

4 egg whites

1 teaspoon vanilla

Whipped cream (optional)

Unsweetened cocoa

powder (optional)

1. In a small bowl combine 2 tablespoons cocoa power, sugar substitute, and cinnamon. Set aside.

2. In a large mixing bowl beat egg whites and vanilla on high speed of an electric mixer until stiff peaks form (tips stand straight). Fold in cocoa mixture. Divide mixture among four 6-ounce custard cups. Bake in a 350° oven for 8 to 10 minutes or until a knife inserted near centers comes out clean. If desired, topped with whipped cream and additional cocoa powder. Serve immediately.

3g carbs   **0**g fiber   **3**g net carbs

Nutrition Facts per serving: 33 cal., 0 g total fat (0 g sat. fat),
0 mg chol., 56 mg sodium, 3 g carbo., 0 g fiber, 4 g pro.

Key Lime Cream

Start to Finish: 15 minutes Makes: 8 servings

1. In a small bowl combine sugar substitute, lime peel, and lime juice, stirring until sugar substitute is dissolved.

2. In a medium mixing bowl beat cream cheese with an electric mixer on medium speed until fluffy. Gradually add the lime mixture in a thin stream, beating until fluffy. Set aside.

3. In a chilled medium mixing bowl beat whipping cream on medium speed until soft peaks form (tips curl). Fold into cream cheese mixture. Divide lime mixture among 8 dessert dishes. Sprinkle with toasted coconut. Serve immediately, or cover and chill up to 24 hours.

½ cup no-calorie, heat-stable granular sugar substitute (Splenda)

1 teaspoon finely shredded key lime peel or lime peel

3 tablespoons key lime juice or lime juice

1 8-ounce package cream cheese, softened

1 cup whipping cream

2 tablespoons unsweetened coconut, toasted

4g carbs 0g fiber 4g net carbs

Nutrition Facts per serving: 209 cal., 21 g total fat (14 g sat. fat), 72 mg chol., 96 mg sodium, 4 g carbo., 0 g fiber, 3 g pro.

Mocha Panna Cotta

Prep: 35 minutes Chill: 4 hours Makes: 8 servings

¼ cup cold water

1 envelope unflavored gelatin

4 cups whipping cream

2 ounces unsweetened
  chocolate, chopped

¾ cup no-calorie, heat-stable
  granular sugar substitute
  (Splenda)

1 teaspoon instant coffee crystals

1 teaspoon vanilla

1 teaspoon unsweetened
  cocoa powder

1. Place cold water in a small bowl. Sprinkle gelatin over top; set aside to allow gelatin to soften.

2. In a 2-quart saucepan combine cream and chopped unsweetened chocolate. Cook and stir over medium-high heat just until mixture begins to bubble and chocolate is melted. Reduce heat to low; stir in softened gelatin. Cook and stir until gelatin is dissolved. Remove from heat. Stir in sugar substitute, instant coffee, and vanilla.

3. Divide mocha mixture among eight 6-ounce dessert dishes. Cover the surface with plastic wrap to prevent a skin from forming. Chill at least 4 or up to 24 hours before serving. To serve, lightly sprinkle with cocoa powder.

8 g carbs   1 g fiber   7 g net carbs

Nutrition Facts per serving: 455 cal., 48 g total fat (30 g sat. fat), 164 mg chol., 49 mg sodium, 8 g carbo., 1 g fiber, 4 g pro.

Rich Lemon Dessert

Prep: 25 minutes Chill: 2 hours Makes: 6 servings

1. In a small heavy nonreactive saucepan whisk together sugar substitute, 1 teaspoon lemon peel, and the lemon juice. Whisk in eggs. Add butter. Cook and stir over low heat until mixture thickens and just begins to bubble. Do not boil.

2. Quickly cool mixture by placing saucepan in a large bowl of ice water for 1 to 2 minutes, stirring constantly. Strain lemon mixture through a fine-mesh sieve into a bowl. Cover the surface with plastic wrap to prevent a skin from forming. Chill at least 2 hours before serving. Do not stir.

3. In chilled medium mixing bowl beat whipping cream with an electric mixer on medium speed until stiff peaks form (tips stand straight). Fold in lemon mixture.

4. Divide lemon mixture among 6 wine glasses or dessert dishes. If desired, garnish with lemon peel curls and fresh berries.

⅔ cup no-calorie, heat-stable granular sugar substitute (Splenda)

1 teaspoon finely shredded lemon peel

½ cup lemon juice

3 eggs, beaten

½ cup butter, cut up

1 cup whipping cream

Lemon peel curls (optional)

Fresh berries (optional)

6 g carbs   **0** g fiber   **6** g net carbs

Nutrition Facts per serving: 323 cal., 34 g total fat (18 g sat. fat), 204 mg chol., 166 mg sodium, 6 g carbo., 0 g fiber, 4 g pro.

Decadent Peanut Butter & Chocolate Mousse

Start to Finish: 15 minutes Makes: 6 servings

¼ cup no-calorie, heat-stable granular sugar substitute (Splenda)

1 tablespoon unsweetened cocoa powder

1 cup whipping cream

1 8-ounce package cream cheese, softened

2 tablespoons natural peanut butter

1. In a small bowl combine sugar substitute and cocoa powder. Set aside.

2. In a chilled medium mixing bowl beat whipping cream with an electric mixer on medium speed until soft peaks form (tips curl); set aside.

3. In large mixing bowl beat cream cheese with an electric mixer on medium speed for 30 seconds. Add cocoa mixture and peanut butter. Beat just until combined. Add ½ cup of the whipped cream and beat on low speed just until combined. With a rubber scraper, gently fold in the remaining whipped cream.

4. Divide chocolate among 6 dessert dishes. Serve immediately, or cover and chill up to 4 hours.

5 g carbs   **0** g fiber   **5** g net carbs

Nutrition Facts per serving: 309 cal., 31 g total fat (18 g sat. fat), 96 mg chol., 147 mg sodium, 5 g carbo., 0 g fiber, 5 g pro.

Heavenly Tiramisu Cream

Start to Finish: 15 minutes Makes: 6 servings

1. In a small mixing bowl beat mascarpone cheese, sugar substitute, sour cream, and coffee liqueur with an electric mixer on low to medium speed until fluffy. Fold in whipped topping.

2. Divide mascarpone mixture among 6 martini glasses or dessert dishes. Sprinkle with chocolate.

1 8-ounce carton mascarpone cheese

¼ cup no-calorie, heat-stable granular

    sugar substitute (Splenda)

2 tablespoons dairy sour cream

2 tablespoons coffee liqueur

1 cup frozen extra-creamy whipped

    dessert topping, thawed

½ ounce unsweetened

    chocolate, grated

8g carbs   **0**g fiber   **8**g net carbs

Nutrition Facts per serving: 237 cal., 22 g total fat (14 g sat. fat), 50 mg chol., 31 mg sodium, 8 g carbo., 0 g fiber, 8 g pro.

373

Balsamic-Pepper Strawberries

Start to Finish: 10 minutes Makes: 6 servings

3 cups sliced fresh strawberries

2 tablespoons no-calorie,
   heat-stable granular sugar
   substitute (Splenda)

4 teaspoons sherry vinegar or
   balsamic vinegar

¼ teaspoon freshly ground
   black pepper

1. In a medium bowl combine strawberries, sugar substitute, vinegar, and pepper; toss gently until coated. Divide strawberries among 6 dessert dishes.

6 g carbs

2 g fiber

4 g net carbs

Nutrition Facts per serving: 25 cal., 0 g total fat (0 g sat. fat),
0 mg chol., 1 mg sodium, 6 g carbo., 2 g fiber, 0 g pro.

Summer Berries with Almond-Sour Cream Sauce

Start to Finish: 10 minutes Makes: 6 servings

1. Divide blackberries and raspberries evenly among 6 dessert dishes. Set aside.

2. In a small bowl combine sour cream, sugar substitute, and almond extract. Spoon mixture over berries.

2 cups fresh blackberries

1 cup fresh raspberries

¾ cup dairy sour cream

1½ teaspoons no-calorie, heat-stable granular sugar substitute (Splenda)

½ to ¾ teaspoon almond extract

10g carbs **4**g fiber **6**g net carbs

Nutrition Facts per serving: 90 cal., 5 g total fat (3 g sat. fat), 11 mg chol., 13 mg sodium, 10 g carbo., 4 g fiber, 1 g pro.

Suggested Shopping List

Dry goods

Canned beef, chicken, and vegetable broths

Canned fish such as tuna, salmon, and sardines

Canned pumpkin

Canned tomato paste, tomato sauce, and
chopped tomatoes

Cocoa powder

Coffee (decaffeinated)

Dried mushrooms—porcini, shiitake

Marinated artichoke hearts

Natural peanut butter and other nut butters

Nuts—

Almonds

Hazelnuts

Pecans

Pumpkin seeds

Sunflower seeds

Walnuts

Roasted red sweet peppers in the jar

Oils—

Canola

Olive

Flaxseed

Grapeseed

Peanut

Sesame

Safflower

Walnut

Olives

Sundried tomatoes in oil or dry-pack

Sugar-free gelatin and instant pudding mix

Sugar substitute in granular form

Teas-herbal, iced (decaffeinated)

Whole wheat flour

Wild rice

Refrigerator

Eggs

Fats-

Butter

Cream

Full-fat mayonnaise

Half-and-half

Sour cream

Whipped cream

Fish-catfish, cod, flounder, mahi mahi, orange roughy,
red snapper, salmon, sea bass, sole, swordfish,
trout, tuna, whitefish

Fresh fruits-avocados, blackberries,
blueberries, cranberries, lemons, limes,
raspberries, strawberries

Full-fat cheeses

Meats—beef, lamb, pork/bacon/ham, veal

Pesto

Plain full-fat yogurt

Poultry—chicken, duck, goose, turkey

Shellfish—avoid imitation shrimp or crab

Tofu (bean curd)

Fresh vegetables

Alfalfa sprouts

Artichoke hearts

Asparagus

Bamboo shoots

Bok choy

Broccoli

Broccoli rabe

Brussels sprouts

Cauliflower

Celery

Chinese cabbage

Cucumber

Eggplant

Fennel

Green beans

Green onions

Greens, assorted

Jicama

Kohlrabi

Leeks

Mushrooms

Onions

Radishes

Rhubarb

Snow peas

Spinach

Squash

Sweet peppers

Swiss chard

Tomato

Turnips

Water chestnuts

Wax beans

Zucchini

Spice Rack

Basil

Black peppercorns

Cajun spice blend

Cayenne pepper

Chili powder

Chinese 5-spice powder

Cinnamon

Crushed red pepper

Cumin

Curry powder

Fresh herbs when available

Garlic powder

Kosher salt

Marjoram

Nutmeg

Oregano

Parsley

Rosemary

Sage

Sea salt

Tarragon

Thyme

Vanilla and other flavor extracts

Condiments

Capers

Chipotle en adobo (smoked jalapeños in
vinegar-tomato sauce)

Dijon and country-style mustards

Low-sodium soy sauce

Sugar-free barbecue sauce

Sugar-free ketchup

Tabasco sauce

Tamari sauce

Wine vinegars such as balsamic, red wine,
rice wine, tarragon, and white wine

Worcestershire sauce

Carb Counts of Dairy, Fish, Meats, and Poultry

	serving size	calories	carb (g)	net carb (g)		serving size	calories	carb (g)	net carb (g)
Dairy					**Fish and Seafood**				
Cheese					Flounder, cooked	3 oz.	99	0	0
Cheddar	1 oz.	114	0	0	Orange roughy, cooked	3 oz.	76	0	0
Cottage (2% fat)	1 cup	203	8	8	Lobster, cooked	3 oz.	83	0	0
Cottage (4% fat)	1 cup	233	6	6	Salmon, cooked	3 oz.	184	0	0
Cream (fat-free)	1 tbsp.	15	1	1	Shrimp, unbreaded, cooked	3 oz.	84	0	0
Feta	1 oz.	75	1	1	Sardines, canned	3 oz.	177	0	0
Mozzarella (part skim)	1 oz.	79	1	1	Swordfish, cooked	3 oz.	132	0	0
Muenster	1 oz.	104	0	0	Tuna, cooked	3 oz.	118	0	0
Parmesan, grated	1 tbsp.	23	0	0					
Process American	1 oz.	106	0	0	**Beef**				
Provolone	1 oz.	100	1	1	73% lean ground				
Swiss	1 oz.	107	1	1	beef, cooked	3 oz.	218	0	0
Milk and Cream					83% lean ground				
Light cream	1 tbsp.	29	1	1	beef, cooked	3 oz.	246	0	0
Nonfat milk	1 cup	86	12	12	Bottom round, cooked	3 oz.	178	0	0
Pressurized					Chuck blade, cooked	3 oz.	213	0	0
lwhipped topping	1 tbsp.	8	0	0	Eye of round, cooked	3 oz.	143	0	0
Reduced-fat milk					Loin, top loin, cooked	3 oz.	176	0	0
(2% fat)	1 cup	121	12	12	Ribs, cooked	3 oz.	195	0	0
Whipping cream	1 tbsp.	52	0	0	Sirloin, cooked	3 oz.	166	0	0
Whole milk (3.3% fat)	1 cup	150	11	11	Tenderloin, cooked	3 oz.	189	0	0
Yogurt									
Fruit-flavored	8 oz.	231	43	43					
Fruit-flavored with									
low-cal sweetener	8 oz.	98	17	17					
Plain	8 oz.	144	16	16					

	serving size	calories	carb (g)	net carb (g)
Lamb				
Arm chop, cooked	3 oz.	237	0	0
Leg, cooked	3 oz.	162	0	0
Loin chop, cooked	3 oz.	184	0	0
Rib chop, cooked	3 oz.	197	0	0
Pork				
Baby back ribs, cooked	3 oz.	315	0	0
Bacon, cooked	3 slices	109	0	0
Canadian-style				
bacon, cooked	2 oz.	86	1	1
Country-style ribs, cooked	3 oz.	252	0	0
Lean ham	3 oz.	133	0	0
Loin chop, cooked	3 oz.	172	0	0
Rib chop, cooked	3 oz.	190	0	0
Shoulder cut, cooked	3 oz.	211	0	0
Spareribs, cooked	3 oz.	337	0	0
Tenderloin, cooked	3 oz.	159	0	0

	serving size	calories	carb (g)	net carb (g)
Sausages				
Bologna	2 oz.	180	2	2
Brown and serve				
links, cooked	2 links	103	1	1
Frankfurters, cooked	1 medium	144	1	1
Pork sausage, cooked	1 patty	100	0	0
Salami	2 oz.	143	1	1
Veal				
Cutlet, cooked	3 oz.	179	0	0
Rib chop, cooked	3 oz.	194	0	0
Poultry				
Chicken				
Batter-dipped				
fried breast	½ breast	364	13	13
Batter-dipped				
fried drumstick	1 drumstick	193	6	6
Breast, cooked	½ breast	142	0	0
Drumstick, cooked	1 drumstick	76	0	0
Turkey				
Dark meat, cooked	3 oz.	159	0	0
Light meat, cooked	3 oz.	133	0	0

Carb Counts of Breads, Cereals, and Crackers

	serving size	calories	carb (g)	net carb (g)
Breads				
Bagels				
Cinnamon-raisin	One 3½-inch bagel	195	39	37
Egg	One 3½-inch bagel	197	38	36
Oat-bran	One 3½-inch bagel	181	38	35
Plain	One 3½-inch bagel	195	38	36
Banana bread	1 slice	196	33	32
Biscuits				
Baking powder from recipe	1 medium	212	27	26
Low-fat from refrigerated dough	1 medium	63	12	12
Regular from refrigerated dough	1 medium	93	13	13
Bread crumbs, plain	1 cup	427	78	75
Bread crumbs, seasoned	1 cup	440	84	79
Bun, frankfurter	1 medium	123	22	21
Bun, hamburger	1 medium	123	22	21
Cinnamon roll				
with raisins	1 medium	223	31	30
Corn bread	One 2½-inch square	173	28	26
Cracked wheat bread	1 slice	65	12	11
Croissant	1 croissant	231	26	24
Croutons, seasoned	1 cup	186	25	23
Dinner roll	1 medium	84	14	13
Egg bread	1 slice	115	19	18
French bread	1 slice	69	13	12

	serving size	calories	carb (g)	net carb (g)
French toast	1 slice	149	16	15
Hard rolls	1 medium	167	30	29
Italian bread	1 slice	54	10	10
Matzo, plain	1 medium	112	24	23
Mixed grain bread	1 slice	65	12	10
Muffins				
Blueberry	1 medium	158	27	26
Bran raisin	1 medium	106	19	16
Corn	1 medium	174	29	27
English	1 medium	134	26	24
Oat bran	1 medium	154	28	25
Oatmeal bread	1 slice	73	13	12
Pancakes, plain	One 4-inch	82	16	15
Pita bread	1 large	165	33	32
Pumpernickel bread	1 slice	80	15	13
Raisin bread, unfrosted	1 slice	71	14	13
Rye bread, reduced-calorie	1 slice	47	9	6
Rye bread, regular	1 slice	83	15	13
Stuffing, made from mix	½ cup	178	22	19
Taco shell	1 medium	62	8	7
Tortilla, corn	1 medium	58	12	11
Tortilla, flour	1 medium	104	18	17
Waffle, low-fat	One 4-inch	83	15	15
Waffle, plain	One 4-inch	87	13	12
White bread, reduced-calorie	1 slice	48	10	8
White bread, regular	1 slice	67	12	11
Whole wheat bread	1 slice	69	13	11

	serving size	calories	carb (g)	net carb (g)
Cereals				
Bite-size square corn cereal	1 cup	113	26	26
Bite-size square rice cereal	1¼ cups	117	27	27
Bite-size square wheat cereal	1 cup	104	24	21
Corn flakes	1 cup	102	24	23
Crisp rice cereal	1¼ cups	124	29	29
Crisp rice cereal, chocolate-flavored	¾ cup	120	27	27
Farina, cooked	1 cup	112	24	23
Granola, plain	½ cup	248	36	32
Granola with raisins, low-fat	¾ cup	195	40	37
Hominy grits, cooked	1 cup	145	31	30
Honey-graham cereal	¾ cup	116	26	25
Oat bran, cooked	1 cup	88	25	19
Oatmeal				
Apple and cinnamon, instant	1 pkg.	125	26	24
Maple and brown sugar, instant	1 pkg.	153	31	28
Old-fashioned, cooked	1 cup	145	25	21
Oat square cereal, sweetened	¾ cup	121	25	23
Peanut butter cereal	¾ cup	112	22	21
Puffed corn cereal	1 cup	118	28	28
Puffed rice cereal	1 cup	56	13	13
Puffed wheat cereal	1 cup	44	10	10

	serving size	calories	carb (g)	net carb (g)
Raisin bran cereal	1 cup	178	43	38
Rice and wheat flakes	1 cup	115	22	21
Shredded wheat biscuits	2 biscuits	156	38	33
Toasted oat cereal	1 cup	110	23	20
Wheat cereal, cooked	1 cup	133	28	26
Wheat flakes cereal	¾ cup	95	23	18
Pasta				
Couscous, cooked	1 cup	176	36	34
Macaroni, elbow, cooked	1 cup	197	40	38
Noodles, egg, cooked	1 cup	213	40	38
Noodles, rice, cooked	1 cup	192	44	42
Noodles, spinach, cooked	1 cup	211	39	35
Spaghetti, cooked	1 cup	197	40	38
Spaghetti, whole wheat, cooked	1 cup	174	37	31
Rice and Grains				
Barley, cooked	1 cup	193	44	38
Buckwheat groats, cooked	1 cup	155	33	28
Bulgar, cooked	1 cup	151	34	26
Millet, cooked	1 cup	207	41	39
Rice, instant, cooked	1 cup	162	35	34
Rice, long grain brown, cooked	1 cup	216	45	42
Rice, long grain white, cooked	1 cup	205	45	44
Rice, wild, cooked	1 cup	166	35	32
Wheat germ, toasted	1 tbsp.	27	3	2

Carb Counts of Fruits and Vegetables

	serving size	calories	carb (g)	net carb (g)
Fruits				
Apple juice	1 cup	117	29	29
Apples, dried	5 rings	78	21	18
Apples, unpeeled	1 small	81	21	17
Applesauce, unsweetened	1 cup	105	28	25
Apricot nectar	1 cup	141	36	34
Apricots, dried	10 halves	83	22	19
Apricots, unpeeled	1 medium	17	4	3
Bananas	1 medium	109	28	25
Blackberries	1 cup	75	18	10
Blueberries	1 cup	81	20	16
Cantaloupe, cubed	1 cup	56	13	12
Cherries, sour, canned	1 cup	88	22	19
Cherries, sweet	1 cup	91	23	20
Cranberries, dried	1/4 cup	92	24	22
Dates, whole	5 dates	116	31	28
Figs, dried	2 figs	97	25	20
Grape juice	1 cup	154	38	38
Grapefruit	½ grapefruit	37	9	8
Grapefruit juice	1 cup	96	23	23
Grapes, seedless	10 grapes	36	9	8
Honeydew melon, cubed	1 cup	60	16	15
Kiwifruit	1 medium	46	11	8
Mangoes, sliced	1 cup	107	28	25
Nectarines	1 medium	67	16	14
Orange juice	1 cup	112	26	26
Oranges	1 small	62	15	12
Papayas, cubed	1 cup	55	14	12
Peaches	1 medium	42	11	9
Peaches, canned (juice pack)	1 cup	109	29	26
Peaches, dried	3 halves	93	24	21
Pear juice	1 cup	124	32	28
Pears	1 medium	98	25	21
Pineapple, cubed	1 cup	76	19	17
Pineapple chunks, canned (juice pack)	1 cup	149	39	37
Pineapple juice, unsweetened	1 cup	140	34	34
Plums	1 medium	36	9	8
Plums, canned (juice pack)	1 cup	146	38	36
Raisins, seedless	1 cup	435	115	109
Raspberries	1 cup	60	14	6
Strawberries	1 cup	50	12	8
Tangerines	1 medium	37	9	7
Watermelon, cubed	1 cup	49	11	10
Vegetables				
Artichokes, cooked	1 cup	84	19	10
Asparagus, cooked	1 cup	43	8	5
Bamboo shoots, canned	1 cup	25	4	2
Bean sprouts, cooked	1 cup	26	5	4
Beans				
Baked, vegetarian	1 cup	236	52	39
Baked with pork and tomato sauce	1 cup	236	49	37
Black, cooked	1 cup	227	41	26
Garbanzo, cooked	1 cup	269	45	32
Great Northern, cooked	1 cup	209	37	25

	serving size	calories	carb (g)	net carb (g)
Green, cooked	1 cup	44	10	6
Pinto, cooked	1 cup	234	44	29
Red kidney, cooked	1 cup	225	40	27
Beets, cooked	1 cup	75	17	14
Black-eyed peas, cooked	1 cup	200	36	25
Broccoli, cooked	1 cup	44	8	4
Broccoli, raw	1 cup	25	5	2
Brussels sprouts, cooked	1 cup	61	14	10
Cabbage, cooked	1 cup	33	7	4
Cabbage, raw	1 cup	18	4	2
Carrots, cooked	1 cup	70	16	11
Carrots, raw	1 medium	31	7	5
Cauliflower, cooked	1 cup	29	5	2
Cauliflower, raw	1 cup	25	5	2
Celery, cooked	1 cup	27	6	4
Celery, raw	1 stalk	6	1	0
Corn, cooked	1 cup	131	32	28
Corn, cream style, cooked	1 cup	184	46	43
Cucumber, unpeeled	1 cup	14	3	2
Eggplant, cooked	I cup	28	7	4
Green onion, raw	1 medium	5	1	1
Green or red sweet				
peppers, cooked	1 cup	38	9	7
Green or red sweet				
peppers, raw	1 cup	40	10	7
Green soybeans, cooked	1 cup	254	20	12
Greens				
Beet, cooked	1 cup	39	8	4
Collard, cooked	1 cup	49	9	4
Dandelion, cooked	1 cup	35	7	4
Mustard, cooked	1 cup	21	3	0
Kale, cooked	1 cup	36	7	4
Kohlrabi, cooked	1 cup	48	11	9
Leeks, cooked	1 cup	32	8	7
Lentils, cooked	1 cup	230	40	24

	serving size	calories	carb (g)	net carb (g)
Lettuces				
Butterhead	1 cup	7	1	0
Iceberg	1 cup	6	1	0
Leaf	1 cup	10	2	1
Romaine	1 cup	8	1	0
Mushrooms, cooked	1 cup	42	8	5
Mushrooms, raw	1 cup	18	3	2
Okra, cooked	1 cup	51	12	8
Onions, cooked	1 cup	92	21	18
Onions, raw	1 cup	61	14	11
Parsnips, cooked	1 cup	126	30	24
Peas, cooked	1 cup	67	11	6
Potatoes				
Baked with skin	1 medium	220	51	46
Boiled	1 cup	134	31	28
Sweet, baked with skin	1 medium	150	35	31
Pumpkin, canned	1 cup	83	20	13
Radishes	1 medium	1	0	0
Rutabagas, cooked	1 cup	66	15	12
Sauerkraut, canned	1 cup	45	10	4
Spinach, cooked	1 cup	41	7	3
Spinach, raw	1 cup	7	1	0
Split peas, cooked	1 cup	231	41	25
Summer squash, cooked	1 cup	36	8	6
Summer squash, raw	1 cup	23	5	3
Tomatillos, raw	1 medium	11	2	1
Tomato juice	1 cup	41	10	9
Tomato paste	1 cup	215	51	40
Tomato sauce	1 cup	74	18	15
Tomatoes, canned	1 cup	46	10	8
Tomatoes, dried	1 piece	5	1	1
Tomatoes, raw	1 cup	38	8	6
Turnips, cooked	1 cup	33	8	5
Vegetable juice cocktail	1 cup	46	11	9
Water chestnuts, canned	1 cup	70	17	14

Carb Counts of Snack Foods

	serving size	calories	carb (g)	net carb (g)
Almonds, whole	1 oz.	164	6	3
Brown rice cake, plain	1 medium	35	7	7
Candy-coated chocolate pieces	10 pieces	34	5	5
Candy-coated chocolate pieces with peanuts	10 pieces	103	12	11
Caramel	1 piece	39	8	8
Caramel corn with peanuts	1 cup	168	34	32
Caramel corn without peanuts	1 cup	152	28	26
Cashews, dry-roasted	1 oz.	163	9	8
Cereal mix	1 oz.	120	18	16
Cheese crackers	10 crackers	50	6	6
Cheese puffs	1 oz.	157	15	15
Cheese-flavored popcorn	1 cup	58	6	5
Chocolate fudge, plain	1 piece	65	14	14
Chocolate fudge, with nuts	1 piece	81	14	14
Chocolate-covered peanut butter cups	1 miniature	38	4	4
Corn chips, plain	1 oz.	153	16	15
Fruit and juice bar	1 medium	63	16	16
Fruit leather pieces	1 oz.	97	22	21
Granola bar, chocolate chip	1 medium	119	20	19
Granola bar, plain	1 medium	134	18	16
Gumdrops	1 medium	16	4	4
Gummy Bears	10 pieces	85	22	22
Hard candy	1 piece	24	6	6
Hummus	1 tbsp.	23	2	1
Jelly beans	10 large	104	26	26
Macadamia nuts, dry-roasted	1 oz.	203	4	2
Melba toast	4 pieces	78	15	14
Milk chocolate bar	1.55 oz.	226	26	24
Milk chocolate bar with almonds	1.45 oz.	216	22	20
Milk chocolate bar with crisp rice cereal	1.55 oz.	230	29	28
Oyster crackers	1 cup	195	32	31
Peanut butter, chunky	1 tbsp.	94	3	2
Peanut butter, reduced fat	1 tbsp.	94	6	5
Peanut butter, smooth	1 tbsp.	95	3	2
Peanuts, dry-roasted	1 oz.	166	6	4
Popcorn, air popped	1 cup	31	6	5
Popcorn, oil popped	1 cup	55	6	5
Potato chips, barbecue flavor	1 oz.	139	15	14
Potato chips, fat-free	1 oz.	75	17	16
Potato chips, plain	1 oz.	152	15	14
Potato chips, reduced-fat	1 oz.	134	19	17
Potato chips, sour cream and onion flavor	1 oz.	151	15	14
Pretzel sticks (2¼ inches long)	10 pretzels	11	2	2
Pretzels, twisted	10 pretzels	229	48	46
Pumpkin seeds, dry-roasted	1 oz.	148	4	3
Saltine crackers	4 crackers	52	9	9
Sunflower seeds, dry-roasted	1 oz.	165	7	4
Thin square wheat crackers	4 crackers	38	5	5
Tortilla chips, nacho cheese flavor	1 oz.	141	18	16
Tortilla chips, plain	1 oz.	142	18	16
Trail mix, regular	1 cup	707	66	57
Trail mix, tropical	1 cup	570	92	81
Whole wheat crackers	4 crackers	71	11	9

Carb Counts of Desserts

	serving size	calories	carb (g)	net carb (g)
Baked				
Brownies,				
unfrosted	One 2 ¾-inch square	227	36	35
Cakes				
Angel food	One 1-oz. slice	72	16	16
Chocolate, frosted	⅛ of 18-oz. cake	235	35	33
Pineapple				
upside-down	One 2½-inch square	367	58	57
Pound, fat-free	One 1-oz. slice	80	17	17
Pound, regular	One 1-oz. slice	109	14	14
Cheesecake	⅙ of 17-oz. cake	257	20	20
Cheese-filled Danish	1 medium	266	26	25
Cookies				
Butter	1 medium	23	3	3
Chocolate chip,				
reduced-fat	1 medium	45	7	7
Chocolate chip, regular	1 medium	48	7	7
Chocolate chip, sugar-free	1 medium	108	16	16
Chocolate, fat-free	1 medium	49	12	12
Chocolate-filled sandwich	1 medium	47	7	7
Fig bar	1 medium	56	11	10
Molasses	1 medium	65	11	11
Oatmeal, soft, regular	1 medium	61	10	10
Oatmeal, sugar-free	1 medium	106	16	16
Peanut butter	1 medium	72	9	9
Shortbread, plain	1 medium	40	5	5
Shortbread, pecan	1 medium	76	8	8
Sugar	1 medium	72	10	10
Vanilla wafer	1 medium	18	3	3
Vanilla-filled sandwich	1 medium	48	7	7
Éclair, filled	1 medium	262	24	23
Gingerbread	One 2½-inch square	263	36	35
Glazed doughnut	1 medium	242	27	26
Pies				
Apple	⅛ pie	277	40	38
Blueberry	⅛ pie	271	41	40
Boston cream	⅛ pie	232	39	38
Cherry	⅛ pie	304	47	46
Chocolate cream	⅛ pie	344	38	36
Coconut custard	⅛ pie	270	31	29
Lemon meringue	⅛ pie	303	53	52
Pecan	⅛ pie	452	65	61
Pumpkin	⅛ pie	229	30	27
Shortcake, biscuit type	1 medium	225	32	31
Shortcake, sponge type	1 medium	87	18	18
Frozen				
Ice cream, chocolate	½ cup	143	19	18
Ice cream, strawberry	½ cup	127	18	17
Ice cream, vanilla	½ cup	133	16	16
Ice cream, vanilla,				
no sugar added	½ cup	99	12	11
Italian ices	½ cup	61	16	16
Sherbet, orange	½ cup	102	22	22
Others				
Gelatin dessert,				
reduced-calorie	½ cup	8	1	1
Gelatin dessert, regular	½ cup	80	19	19
Pudding, chocolate, instant	½ cup	150	28	27
Pudding, tapioca	½ cup	134	22	22
Pudding, vanilla, instant	½ cup	148	28	28

Carb Count Journal

It's easier to stick with your low-carb diet when you keep track of how you're doing. This handy journal lets you record your carb grams for each meal so you don't go overboard. You can also write down how you're feeling while on the diet. After a few days, look back at your journal and note how your energy level or hunger has changed while on phase 2 of your low-carb diet.

Week __, Day __

	Foods and Beverages	Net Carb Count
Breakfast		
Lunch		
Dinner		
Snacks		

Energy Level

(low) (medium) (high)

Hunger Level

(low) (medium) (high)

Carb Cravings

(low) (medium) (high)

Week __, Day __

	Foods and Beverages	Net Carb Count
Breakfast		
Lunch		
Dinner		
Snacks		

Energy Level

(low) (medium) (high)

Hunger Level

(low) (medium) (high)

Carb Cravings

(low) (medium) (high)

Week __, Day __

	Foods and Beverages	Net Carb Count
Breakfast		
Lunch		
Dinner		
Snacks		

Energy Level

(low) (medium) (high)

Hunger Level

(low) (medium) (high)

Carb Cravings

(low) (medium) (high)

Week __, Day __

	Foods and Beverages	Net Carb Count
Breakfast		
Lunch		
Dinner		
Snacks		

Energy Level

low   medium   high

Hunger Level

low   medium   high

Carb Cravings

low   medium   high

Week __, Day __

	Foods and Beverages	Net Carb Count
Breakfast		
Lunch		
Dinner		
Snacks		

Energy Level

(low) (medium) (high)

Hunger Level

(low) (medium) (high)

Carb Cravings

(low) (medium) (high)

Week __, Day __

	Foods and Beverages	Net Carb Count
Breakfast		
Lunch		
Dinner		
Snacks		

Energy Level

(low) (medium) (high)

Hunger Level

(low) (medium) (high)

Carb Cravings

(low) (medium) (high)

Week __, Day __

	Foods and Beverages	Net Carb Count
Breakfast		
Lunch		
Dinner		
Snacks		

Energy Level

low   medium   high

Hunger Level

low   medium   high

Carb Cravings

low   medium   high

Week __, Day __

	Foods and Beverages	Net Carb Count
Breakfast		
Lunch		
Dinner		
Snacks		

Energy Level

(low) (medium) (high)

Hunger Level

(low) (medium) (high)

Carb Cravings

(low) (medium) (high)

Week __, Day __

	Foods and Beverages	Net Carb Count
Breakfast		
Lunch		
Dinner		
Snacks		

Energy Level

(low) (medium) (high)

Hunger Level

(low) (medium) (high)

Carb Cravings

(low) (medium) (high)

Week __, Day __

	Foods and Beverages	Net Carb Count
Breakfast		
Lunch		
Dinner		
Snacks		

Energy Level

(low) (medium) (high)

Hunger Level

(low) (medium) (high)

Carb Cravings

(low) (medium) (high)

Week __, Day __

	Foods and Beverages	Net Carb Count
Breakfast		
Lunch		
Dinner		
Snacks		

Energy Level

low   medium   high

Hunger Level

low   medium   high

Carb Cravings

low   medium   high

Week __, Day __

	Foods and Beverages	Net Carb Count
Breakfast		
Lunch		
Dinner		
Snacks		

Energy Level

(low) (medium) (high)

Hunger Level

(low) (medium) (high)

Carb Cravings

(low) (medium) (high)

Week __, Day __

	Foods and Beverages	Net Carb Count
Breakfast		
Lunch		
Dinner		
Snacks		

Energy Level

low medium high

Hunger Level

low medium high

Carb Cravings

low medium high

Week __, Day __

	Foods and Beverages	Net Carb Count
Breakfast		
Lunch		
Dinner		
Snacks		

Energy Level

(low) (medium) (high)

Hunger Level

(low) (medium) (high)

Carb Cravings

(low) (medium) (high)

Week __, Day __

	Foods and Beverages	Net Carb Count
Breakfast		
Lunch		
Dinner		
Snacks		

Energy Level

(low) (medium) (high)

Hunger Level

(low) (medium) (high)

Carb Cravings

(low) (medium) (high)

Week __, Day __

	Foods and Beverages	Net Carb Count
Breakfast		
Lunch		
Dinner		
Snacks		

Energy Level

(low) (medium) (high)

Hunger Level

(low) (medium) (high)

Carb Cravings

(low) (medium) (high)

Week __, Day __

	Foods and Beverages	Net Carb Count
Breakfast		
Lunch		
Dinner		
Snacks		

Energy Level

low   medium   high

Hunger Level

low   medium   high

Carb Cravings

low   medium   high

Week __, Day __

	Foods and Beverages	Net Carb Count
Breakfast		
Lunch		
Dinner		
Snacks		

Energy Level

(low) (medium) (high)

Hunger Level

(low) (medium) (high)

Carb Cravings

(low) (medium) (high)

Week __, Day __

	Foods and Beverages	Net Carb Count
Breakfast		
Lunch		
Dinner		
Snacks		

Energy Level

low   medium   high

Hunger Level

low   medium   high

Carb Cravings

low   medium   high

Index

Metric Information

The charts on this page provide a guide for converting measurements from the U.S. customary system, which is used throughout this book, to the metric system.

Product Differences

Most of the ingredients called for in the recipes in this book are available in most countries. However, some are known by different names. Here are some common American ingredients and their possible counterparts:

- Sugar (white) is granulated, fine granulated, or castor sugar.
- Powdered sugar is icing sugar.
- All-purpose flour is enriched, bleached or unbleached white household flour. When self-rising flour is used in place of all-purpose flour in a recipe that calls for leavening, omit the leavening agent (baking soda or baking powder) and salt.
- Light-colored corn syrup is golden syrup.
- Cornstarch is cornflour.
- Baking soda is bicarbonate of soda.
- Vanilla and vanilla extract are vanilla essence.
- Green, red, or yellow sweet peppers are capsicums or bell peppers.
- Golden raisins are sultanas.

Volume and Weight

The United States traditionally uses cup measures for liquid and solid ingredients. The chart below shows the approximate imperial and metric equivalents. If you are accustomed to weighing solid ingredients, the following approximate equivalents will be helpful.

- 1 cup butter, castor sugar, or rice = 8 ounces = ½ pound = 250 grams
- 1 cup flour = 4 ounces = ¼ pound = 125 grams
- 1 cup icing sugar = 5 ounces = 150 grams
- Canadian and U.S. volume for a cup measure is 8 fluid ounces (237 ml), but the standard metric equivalent is 250 ml.
- 1 British imperial cup is 10 fluid ounces.
- In Australia, 1 tablespoon equals 20 ml, and there are 4 teaspoons in the Australian tablespoon.

Spoon measures are used for smaller amounts of ingredients. Although the size of the tablespoon varies slightly in different countries, for practical purposes and for recipes in this book, a straight substitution is all that's necessary. Measurements made using cups or spoons always should be level unless stated otherwise.

Common Weight Range Replacements

Imperial / U.S.	Metric
½ ounce	15 g
1 ounce	25 g or 30 g
4 ounces (¼ pound)	115 g or 125 g
8 ounces (½ pound)	225 g or 250 g
16 ounces (1 pound)	450 g or 500 g
1¼ pounds	625 g
1½ pounds	750 g
2 pounds or 2¼ pounds	1,000 g or 1 Kg

Oven Temperature Equivalents

Fahrenheit Setting	Celsius Setting*	Gas Setting
300°F	150°C	Gas Mark 2 (very low)
325°F	160°C	Gas Mark 3 (low)
350°F	180°C	Gas Mark 4 (moderate)
375°F	190°C	Gas Mark 5 (moderate)
400°F	200°C	Gas Mark 6 (hot)
425°F	220°C	Gas Mark 7 (hot)
450°F	230°C	Gas Mark 8 (very hot)
475°F	240°C	Gas Mark 9 (very hot)
500°F	260°C	Gas Mark 10 (extremely hot)
Broil	Broil	Grill

*Electric and gas ovens may be calibrated using celsius. However, for an electric oven, increase celsius setting 10 to 20 degrees when cooking above 160°C. For convection or forced air ovens (gas or electric) lower the temperature setting 25°F/10°C when cooking at all heat levels.

Baking Pan Sizes

Imperial / U.S.	Metric
9×1½-inch round cake pan	22- or 23×4-cm (1.5 L)
9×1½-inch pie plate	22- or 23×4-cm (1 L)
8×8×2-inch square cake pan	20×5-cm (2 L)
9×9×2-inch square cake pan	22- or 23×4.5-cm (2.5 L)
11×7×1½-inch baking pan	28×17×4-cm (2 L)
2-quart rectangular baking pan	30×19×4.5-cm (3 L)
13×9×2-inch baking pan	34×22×4.5-cm (3.5 L)
15×10×1-inch jelly roll pan	40×25×2-cm
9×5×3-inch loaf pan	23×13×8-cm (2 L)
2-quart casserole	2 L

US/Standard Metric Equivalents

⅛ teaspoon = 0.5 ml
¼ teaspoon = 1 ml
½ teaspoon = 2 ml
1 teaspoon = 5 ml
1 tablespoon = 15 ml
2 tablespoons = 25 ml
¼ cup = 2 fluid ounces = 50 ml
⅓ cup = 3 fluid ounces = 75 ml
½ cup = 4 fluid ounces = 125 ml
⅔ cup = 5 fluid ounces = 150 ml
¾ cup = 6 fluid ounces = 175 ml
1 cup = 8 fluid ounces = 250 ml
2 cups = 1 pint = 500 ml
1 quart = 1 litre